FRANCO'S CRYPT

FRANCO'S CRYPT

SPANISH CULTURE
AND MEMORY SINCE 1936

JEREMY TREGLOWN

FARRAR, STRAUS AND GIROUX / NEW YORK

Farrar, Straus and Giroux
18 West 18th Street, New York 10011

Library of Congress Cataloging-in-Publication Data
Treglown, Jeremy.
    Franco's crypt : Spanish culture and memory since 1936 / Jeremy Treglown. —
First edition.
        pages   cm
    Includes index.
    ISBN 978-0-374-10842-7 (alk. paper)
    1. Spain—Intellectual life—20th century.   2. Architecture, Spanish—20th
century.   3. Motion pictures—Spain—History—20th century.   4. Spanish
literature—20th century—History and criticism.   5. Art, Spanish—History—20th
century.   6. Collective memory—Spain.   7. Franco, Francisco, 1892–1975—
Influence.   8. Spain—History—Civil War, 1936–1939—Influence.   9. Spain—
History—1939–1975.   I. Title.

DP270 .T74 2013
946.08—dc23

2012048086

Designed by Abby Kagan

Farrar, Straus and Giroux books may be purchased for educational, business, or
promotional use. For information on bulk purchases, please contact the Macmillan
Corporate and Premium Sales Department at 1-800-221-7945, extension 5442, or write
to specialmarkets@macmillan.com.

www.fsgbooks.com
www.twitter.com/fsgbooks • www.facebook.com/fsgbooks

1   3   5   7   9   10   8   6   4   2

To Holly, 1940–2010

Contents

solving the country's economic difficulties, and by left-wing extremism of a kind that gave encouragement to its equivalent on the right. The Falange, Spain's fascist party, was founded soon after, under the leadership of the charismatic José Antonio Primo de Rivera, son of the former dictator. In July 1936, Francisco Franco, a career soldier who had come to prominence in the army's struggle to hang on to "Spanish" Morocco, took part in a kind of colonial invasion in reverse, against the home country. The military uprising—justified, it was argued, by the government's manifest inability to protect sections of its own people, especially in the Church—had the support of most of Spain's disproportionately large number of army officers and of the middle and upper classes, of almost all the still-powerful bishops, and of the mostly Catholic peasant population in Castilla la Vieja and Galicia. While Britain and France prevaricated over whether to back the Spanish government, the coup gained immediate aid, including troops and weapons, from Hitler and Mussolini. Stalin came in on the Republican side. Often called the Second World War's dress rehearsal, the Spanish Civil War may be better seen as its first act.

Franco's soldiers were a mix of hardened Spanish legionaries and North African mercenaries, quickly reinforced in the Málaga region by rebel troops based on the mainland and Fascist Italian motorized columns with light tanks. The port of Málaga was bombed from the air, shelled from the sea, then invaded by land. The extent of the casualties among fleeing civilians horrified even hardened observers, the writers Arthur Koestler and Franz Borkenau among them.[3] Afterward, the rebels undertook a long purge of suspected Republican sympathizers—just as, in other areas, the Republicans were doing with suspected Nationalists, particularly priests—which continued into the 1940s under the notorious local prosecutor Carlos Arias Navarro, "the Butcher of Málaga." Diego's turn came in March 1937, when he was picked up at home in the middle of town. His son, Ignacio's father, was seven at the time and is still unable to say much about that period without crying, but the scene was often described to the young Ignacio by his grandmother, who lived to be ninety-nine, and also by a friend's voluble grandfather, who was in the same Guardia company as Diego. It's generally said that victims were shot against the cemetery wall by the light from the chapel, but Ignacio takes a practical view: "The place is very

big. It's a long way to carry a lot of dead bodies. I think they were mostly shot inside, beside the graves."

I went to the San Rafael cemetery because I was trying to make more sense of Spain—today's Spain as well as that of 1936. I had traveled all over the country, where I live for part of every year in a remote mountain *finca* that through the centuries has seen more bad times than good. The region and its inhabitants keep their secrets. Asked about events when she was growing up in the 1930s and '40s, a normally talkative, friendly woman on the next farm closed her face and said, "*No sé*," "I don't know." This was during a *matanza*, the December butchering of a pig that has been brought up in the yard, a procedure carried out by a couple dozen family and friends, old and young, who, within a day, efficiently turn the at first cheerful, then noisily indignant, then struggling, cumbersome, terrified animal into a tidy arrangement of joints, offal, and hanging sausages. Something about this struck me as resembling what must have happened in places such as San Rafael in 1936—the orderliness of the process, its unsentimentality.

Understanding Spain, though, is less a matter of seeing that its culture has been violent and cruel—which has often been said and anyway is true of most cultures, one way or another—than of recognizing more hidden respects in which the country and its component regions, for all their absorption into and enthusiastic collaborations with "Europe," remain distinctive. These are partly a twentieth-century matter. Even if you set aside eight centuries of Islamic rule in Spain between A.D. 711 and 1492—a longer period than the one that has passed since it ended—and ignore the subsequent expulsions of Muslims and Jews and the ferocious expansion into America, Spain still feels different. Is it because, there, the wrong side won the Second World War? Was the cultural impact of the dictatorship as severe as that of Nazism? How is it remembered and what are its aftereffects?

Long after Hitler and Mussolini were dead, the regime they helped establish in Spain continued. Everyone between roughly forty and their mid-seventies today who was born in Spain was born under Franco, most of them went to school during his regime, and almost every man over sixty served in his armed forces. Buildings and infrastructure are

part of his legacy, too: the creation of the monstrous crypt in which he is buried at the head of many of his troops, with its surrounding memorial park called the Valle de los Caídos, "Valley of the Fallen," was supervised by him personally, and other grandiose public edifices and sprawling municipal apartment blocks that went up in the 1950s and '60s are due to him. So also, more obliquely, is the fact that so much of the older urban architecture survives: while parts of Spain were bombed and shelled during the civil war, neutrality in 1939–45 saved it from the urban obliterations visited on other European countries. Meanwhile, the water that irrigates the fields and comes out of the tap in your hotel is as likely as not a long-term result of the dictator's program of dam building; the electricity that lights the street, of his hydroelectric schemes. And then there is his legacy in the arts: painting, novels, films.

Told that the topic of this book was to be Franco's influence on Spanish culture, more than one inquirer joked that a postcard might cover it. Such attitudes aren't solely a matter of ignorance. An English speaker asked to name countries colonized by the Americans and British in the twentieth century would be unlikely to think of Spain, yet if you ask Anglophone people what book or film they most associate with the Spanish Civil War, the answer is usually *For Whom the Bell Tolls* or *Casablanca* or *Homage to Catalonia*. In 1980, Penguin published an anthology of *Spanish Civil War Verse* which, as was pointed out by the Mexican-born poet and editor Michael Schmidt, was written entirely in English (and for the most part not very well): "It seems rash . . . to produce a national anthology out of so essentially international a series of events."[4] International involvement has indeed been crucial to Spain's modern history, and the part played by foreigners in the civil war was substantial and often honorable. No overall account of the period would be adequate that didn't mention facts such as the death of Felicia Browne, an English painter who volunteered on the Republican side and was shot in Aragón during an attempt to blow up a Nationalist munitions train; or the support given to the Nationalists by the South African poet and war correspondent Roy Campbell. Yet La Guerra de España, or La Guerra Civil Española, was, as its Spanish names asserts, Spain's own war, and in recent years the country has begun to "reclaim" its modern history. How it is doing so, and particularly the complex

role played in the process by ideas about "historical memory," are among the subjects of this book. Novels such as Javier Cercas's *Soldiers of Salamis* and Almudena Grandes's *The Frozen Heart* have in different ways reminded their international audience that while English speakers may use *Spanish Civil War* as a compound adjective, *war* is a noun, what it refers to is a fact, and in this instance the facts, however hard to understand and interpret, had most of their effects in Spain and on Spanish people. The conservative Nobel Prize–winning writer Camilo José Cela made this point forcibly when he dedicated one of his books "To the conscripts of 1937, all of whom lost something: their life, their freedom, their dreams, their hope, their decency. And not to the adventurers from abroad, Fascists and Marxists, who had their fill of killing Spaniards like rabbits and whom no one had invited to take part in our funeral."[5]

The novel those words introduce is one of many great works produced in Spain during as well as after the dictatorship that explore and embody what the civil war and the long dictatorship that followed were like. Yet these works were largely ignored abroad. People in other countries had concerns of their own, especially during and immediately after 1939–45, but a kind of political censoriousness was involved, too, not easy to distinguish in practice from censorship. Many Spanish intellectuals who were in danger from, or simply hated the idea of, the Franco regime moved out, especially to Latin America and France. Their own work, like that of the Soviet and East European dissidents who soon followed them, attracted foreign attention (though it wasn't much noticed that the two groups were escaping mutually opposed ideologies). In this situation, anything produced by people who had stayed behind in Spain was thought suspect, and relatively little of it found its way abroad. Until Franco's death there was, after all, a Spanish Republican government in exile, based in Mexico and widely recognized as the legitimate government of Spain. Mario Vargas Llosa has confessed that as a young man in Peru in the 1950s he read nothing by contemporary Spanish writers living in the Iberian Peninsula "because of a prejudice as widespread in the Latin America of those years as it was unjust: everything published *over there* reeked of fustiness, [the] sacristy, and Francoism."[6]

This book describes some of what was ignored as a result of the fas-

tidiousness Vargas Llosa speaks of: not least a whole library of books and films written and made under Franco that provide intimate, often subversive revelations about the war and what came after. The book also shows how some Spanish officials and patrons, though conservative in politics, actively helped good artists of all kinds continue to work as they wanted to. All this was part of the foundations of "cultural memory," but memory in this sense of the word has become distorted over the past half century—roughly the period since Pierre Nora published the results of a group project conducted in France under the title *Les lieux de mémoire*, "Sites of Memory." Fertile though the idea has proven, the problems with it, especially in its more diluted forms, are manyfold. They include sentimental politicization, escapism, complacency, and ignorance, and even after these are discounted, you're left with questions: Doesn't forgetting have cultural value, just as it does psychological value? Surely memory is notoriously unreliable? What about the mutations involved in generational change? (I remember some of what my parents and grandparents told me about the Second World War, but in passing it on to my children and grandchildren, I have to speak to their knowledge and preoccupations, and out of my own. What matters to us has changed and keeps changing.) In trying to identify what's special about Spain, I soon found that much of it is related to a politically manipulated, culturally amnesiac obsession with "memory."

So Spanish culture and memory are a diverse and continually evolving set of phenomena. Some novels written during the regime and about it, like some films, didn't appear until after the dictator's death in 1975, an event that in turn led to yet more recountings, each with its own new emphasis. In the last decade of the twentieth century and the first of our own, a generation that had grown used to the globalization of high culture and to national democracy began excavations that included the literal digging up of mass graves, a project related to similar ones in many other parts of the world. All this overlapped with another global phenomenon: mass tourism. It's eerie to consider that the *fosas comunes* and other physical relics of the war and the dictatorship—among them Franco's crypt in the mountains north of Madrid—were passed over by some of the first tourists speeding to the southern coast—tourists who brought money to the impoverished

Francoist regime, whose expectations increasingly shaped and helped soften its policies, and on whom the country still depends for its economic survival.

Going to the cemetery at San Rafael was part of a series of inquisitive wanderings on my part, and while some were geographical, others were mental: reading Spanish novels and histories, watching Spanish films, looking at Spanish works of art, and pondering what they seemed to say. Human productions reveal things their makers don't intend, Franco himself among them in his self-fantasizing novel *Raza* and the film based on it, and in the aggressive-defensive architecture of the Valley of the Fallen. Political systems, too, bad or good, contain the elements of their own destruction and replacement. Spain today, despite economic and social difficulties of kinds that it shares with most of its still-privileged region, is ruled by a reasonably secure, responsive parliamentary democracy. It feels, in other words, like other parts of western Europe; and yet it doesn't. Its particular system emerged in the 1970s and '80s from a determination that things should be unlike they had been for the previous three and a half decades. The dictatorship itself had been a reaction against prior arrangements and had some positive consequences. Opinion polls in Spain consistently suggest a significant, though decreasing, level of approval for the Franco regime.[7] This is found more in the old than the young—though the anecdotes of some parents of teenagers suggest that José Antonio Primo de Rivera may be gaining a new kind of appeal among the young—but democracy must involve a respect for people's views regardless of their age, and the dismissive argument that the older generation was educated under Franco, while true, is counterbalanced by the fact that the young were educated after his death in 1975, a turning point whose implications their parents and grandparents, too, have had almost forty years to get used to.

The extent to which studies of twentieth-century Spanish history and culture are polarized has so often been commented on that it's important to be clear that there are exceptions, some of which I discuss. Still, the general point made by Eric Hobsbawm and others remains true, that "in creating the world's memory of the Spanish civil war, the

pen, the brush and the camera wielded on behalf of the defeated have proved mightier than the sword and the power of those who won."[8] To take just one example, a recent collection of essays about the cultural consequences of Francoism, published by a university press, begins with an admission—or is it a boast?—by the two editors that they are not interested in hearing anything favorable about the regime, that, as they put it, as far as the anti-Nationalist orthodoxy is concerned, their work "departs from a decidedly critical stance."[9] It's not only just but satisfying to condemn past evils from the safety of the present, but given some of what has been and is still being done in the name of Western democracy, there's a touch of hypocrisy in the process, and we learn more from trying sympathetically to understand the past, however bad it was, than from simply putting what we think we know of it under our own moral template. Very many people have reason to remember bad things about the civil war and the dictatorship: to them, Franco is a bad memory, like a bad dream. But "bad memory" also means forgetfulness and falsification. When Spain's campaigners for historical memory accuse their opponents and critics of *olvido*, amnesia, they have themselves often forgotten, or overlooked, or are simply ignorant of, the rich historical deposits in their own culture that are my subject.

PART ONE

SITES AND SIGHTS

2

Whose Graves?

Salud Alberto Zarzuela, Catalina Alcaraz, Cristina Carrillo Franco, Teresa Castro Ramírez, Ana Fernández Ramírez; Isabel Gómez, her sister Josefa Gómez and their niece Lolita Gómez; Teresa Menacho, María Nogales Castro, Antonia Pérez Vega; María Rincón Barea and her sister Jerónima Rincón Barea; Isabel Román Montes, Natividad Vilchez.

These are the names of fifteen women in their twenties whose remains—along with those of a teenaged boy who, it's said locally, was forced to dig the grave—were found in 2008 among the cork oak plantations of Grazalema, a much-visited beauty spot in the mountains west of Ronda. They hadn't been involved in politics, unless you count the possibility that one of them may have been engaged to a Republican. Four were pregnant. How they died hasn't been established. No bullets were found. If stories about other atrocities in the region are anything to go by, the women were probably raped, tortured, and then buried alive—those, that is, who survived that long. In many such cases, reprisals were the main motive: men loyal to the Republican government waged a particularly effective guerrilla campaign against rebel forces in the area. Another common purpose of capturing women was to use them as hostages, in the hope of inducing Republicans who had gone into hiding to surrender. Whether or not this worked, other impulses often took over. At the time, local rebel commanders included some

notorious sadists. But "nationalism" was intrinsically brutal, closely linked as it was to fascism, founded on decades of imperial skirmishing in Morocco and, before that, on notions of racial and ideological purification (*limpieza*) that went back via the Inquisition to Spain's earliest expulsions of Muslims and Jews.

Spanish historians have recently shown that some supporters of Franco regarded socialism as a hereditary form of degeneracy, albeit cultural rather than genetic.[1] On this basis, some have argued that the rebels' avowed aim to exterminate the enemy, including women and children, was tantamount to genocide. Generals tend, of course, to threaten to wipe out the other side—it's a good way of persuading people to surrender—but you don't have to accept the genocide theory to be able to imagine the effect of the nightly radio broadcasts put out by the main rebel propagandist, General Gonzalo Queipo de Llano, on impressionable, armed young men. Queipo's threats against his enemy gave substance to the nihilistic gibberish of the Spanish Foreign Legion, with its war cry "*¡Viva la muerte!*"—"Long live death!" "Even if they're already dead, I shall kill them again," Queipo famously roared, and, in a phrase that to some survivors gives an unwelcome, if fortuitous, coloring to the exhumation campaign, "Even if they hide beneath the earth, I shall dig them out." Queipo urged his troops to rape Republican women and added to the stimulus by telling stories of sadosexual feats already performed by their fellows in arms. "Your Women Will Give Birth to Fascists" was a common piece of graffiti in recently conquered Republican towns and villages.

There are places where the executioners' work appears to have been more calmly organized. In the graves I watched being excavated in Málaga, most of the skeletons lie straight, close together, side by side or head to toe, many with their hands tied. In this particular spot there were, one of the diggers cheerfully explained to me, "*tres plantas*," "three stories." We were standing on the top floor, but pushing up from the level below was the dome of a forehead, a knee. You had to tread carefully. Even here, though, the neat rows were occasionally interrupted by signs of anger, exasperation, revenge: bodies at an angle, arms thrown above the head; a pelvis with a bullet lodged in the groin. Elsewhere, the way people died often involved the worst they could have feared. Federico García Lorca, the dramatist and poet, is such a case.

Exuberant, handsome, spoiled, uncontrollable, extravagantly gifted, Lorca always feared death. He used his feelings about it, and about sex—his homosexuality, his mix of fascination with and horror of female sexuality—in his work. Like the filmmaker Pedro Almodóvar today, he was as well known abroad as he was in Spain, with the result that the hostility of Spaniards who disliked his art, or just the idea of it, was compounded by a sense that they themselves were being impugned by it, that he gave Spain a bad name. But to think in these international terms runs the risk of forgetting the civil war's intensely local quality. In regions such as Lorca's native Granada, participants often had relatives on both sides; they had gone to church and to school together, had friends and enemies in common, knew one another's secrets, fantasies, and jealousies. When Lorca became famous outside Granada, some in his neighborhood were possessively, competitively proud, while others were envious. He was personally close to Salvador Dalí, to Luis Buñuel, names with highly charged associations of their own.

Among the most vocal supporters of the recent wave of exhumations has been Lorca's biographer Ian Gibson, whose first book, published when Franco was still in power, is an account of the poet's murder.[2] Irish by birth, Gibson has taken Spanish nationality and lives in Madrid, where people in the street and in bars come up to shake his hand. His measured description of the poet's last days relates the intricacies of regional politics in the Granada of July and August 1936, especially in the Falange and the military garrison; the publicity given in local papers to the poet's return to what he hoped was the safety of his parents' home; the petty but genuine anger he had recently caused with a published attack on the middle class; the family's mounting apprehension when their house was searched; its first wartime bereavement, when Lorca's brother-in-law, the socialist mayor of Granada, was shot; Lorca's sheer panic; the shelter bravely given him by family friends who belonged to the Falange. Crucial in all this is a psychological drama in which the main protagonist, other than Lorca himself, was an ambitious, pompous, and, of late, much derided and humiliated conservative, Ramón Ruiz Alonso, who had been in and out of the Spanish parliament as a representative of Granada. The military rebellion

brought him the first real power he knew how to use, and he nursed a personal hatred of "the poet with the big fat head" and of everything Lorca represented. On the afternoon of August 16, 1936, Ruiz and two other extremely unpleasant men came to get him.

Accounts of what happened next differ, and it is the mixture of uncertainty and of the raw facts we have that makes the story so powerful. We know that Lorca was imprisoned for at least two days and that he was unable to conceal his terror. We can guess that this in itself gave encouragement as well as scope to his tormentors. We know that, handcuffed to a Republican schoolmaster, Dióscoro Galindo González, he was taken to Víznar, in the hills behind Granada, a place of execution where, night after night, consignments of prisoners were handed over to the "Black Squad," men who had volunteered for this work because they enjoyed it. Lorca and Galindo were killed and buried with two other prisoners. The following morning, one of the party that had arrested the poet, a landowning playboy friend of Ruiz Alonso, was heard boasting that he had just helped to shoot Lorca and had fired "two bullets into his arse for being queer."

So much for what's known. What isn't known for certain is where the bodies were buried. Today there are two monuments to Lorca. One is in a shallow dip in a wooded park above Víznar, close to a footpath that runs around the hillside to the next village, Alfacar, past what you would never know is a vast mass grave—the trees were originally planted to help conceal it. The other is at the end of this path, behind a padlocked gate. It was inevitable that there would be pressure to investigate at least one of these sites, though for many years the poet's sister Isabel (who died in 2002) and his nephews and nieces were united, at least in public, in arguing that the best way to remain true to Spain's history was to leave the dead where they lay. As the campaign in favor of exhumations gained momentum, descendants of the men with whom Lorca was buried decided that they would like them to be exhumed, and this persuaded Lorca's family to reconsider. Even archaeologists can't excavate a *fosa común* selectively. Eventually, after a great deal of legal and journalistic negotiation, work began in the autumn of 2009. On October 7, it was announced in the conservative daily *ABC* that "the eyes of science had penetrated like roots into the sorrow guarded by the earth" at the exact spot where Lorca's remains were said to be;

or, less poetically, that a geo-radar device had found what seemed to be a multiple grave.[3] Heavily protected excavations began in November 2009, but nothing was found.

Practicalities apart, the case helped bring into focus some wider complications in Spain's debates about memory. In the first place, Spanish attitudes to the dead have always included a paradoxical-seeming mix of reverence and casualness. Graves are visited with a degree of ceremony on the Feast of All Souls, every November—the opening sequence of Almodóvar's *Volver*, in which Penélope Cruz and her friends squeakily polish rows of tombstones, is funny because it satirizes a recognizable fact of life. But because of the rockiness of much southern European ground, many graves here are not holes in the ground but concrete storage blocks full of human-size pigeonholes: slots in a wall into which each coffin slides neatly, followed by a slab of stone, cemented in. Tombs of this kind are leased, not owned. The initial payment lasts for a fixed period, but if no more rent is forthcoming, the corpse is evicted to a charnel house in the cemetery's corner. Visitors carrying their respectful bunches of flowers or plastic wreaths can be all too aware of a disheveled pile of bones and rotting hair close by. The relics of saints, whether religious or secular, involve similar contradictions. Few people among the crush of pilgrims at Santiago de Compostela can be unaware that the widely distributed bones attributed to the patron saint are far too many to have come from one skeleton. As for Christopher Columbus, it's thought that his son Diego's remains may at some point have been mistaken for his in the course of a series of moves in which father or son or both were successively interred, dug up, and reburied in Spain, Hispaniola, Cuba, and then back in Seville.

In this context, the fact that so many civil war graves were left unmarked itself raises questions. While it was dangerous to pay open attention to a Republican grave during the civil war and the repressive years after it, there must have been opportunities to leave a few stones as indicators. Could it be that some of those immediately concerned (especially the more rationalist, secular Republicans) didn't think the exact whereabouts of the dead all that important? The novelist Javier Marías feels so.[4] One of his uncles was killed in Madrid, together with a group of fellow students. According to Marías, his mother and her

siblings were too busy surviving to go in search of his body and, later, the family simply assumed that his remains, wherever they were, were best left with those of his friends.

There are also arguments about the way that, as in many other parts of the world, "memory" in Spain has become a tool of party politics and personal advancement. Among the most discussed examples are interventions by a former national magistrate, Baltasar Garzón, known in the Anglophone world for his 1998 attempt, making unprecedented use of "universal jurisdiction," to get General Pinochet of Chile extradited to Spain on a charge of crimes against humanity.[5] That move helped awaken attention to past atrocities in Garzón's home country, akin to those for which Pinochet was arraigned. In the summer of 2008, Garzón threw his weight behind the exhumations campaign by reminding various laggardly authorities of their obligations under the 2007 Law of Historical Memory, which, among other things, requires them to assist excavations and archival searches and, except in cases of special architectural or historical merit, to remove memorials to Franco's dictatorship. Some of Garzón's demands seemed quixotic. Acting on behalf of a number of families, he announced, for example, that he needed complete lists of the names of civil war casualties within two weeks. While historians of the twentieth century were delighted to see archivists being put under pressure to make documentary records more readily available, they also pointed out that the quantity of material is vast. A comparable investigation of records of the Nazi concentration camp at Mauthausen, where thousands of Spanish Republicans who had fled north were imprisoned and died, took eight years to establish the identities of four thousand prisoners and is still far from complete. It isn't difficult to calculate the time that would be involved in supplying a reasonably accurate list of, say, the twenty thousand or so people murdered in Spain just in the summer of 1936. A full census of civil war dead would involve seven or eight times that number.

Legal opponents of Garzón successfully argued that the 2007 memory law leaves responsibility with local rather than central authorities—democratic Spain is highly devolved administratively—and that he had been exceeding his powers. Never one to hold back from the big gesture, he persisted. Among his arguments was that any surviving

participant in the Franco regime should be prosecuted for crimes against humanity. Reminded of the amnesty passed by the elected Spanish government in 1977, he replied that no amnesty can trump human rights. Meanwhile, he continued to press for action on the findings of historians who have shown both that Francoist military psychologists experimented on Republican prisoners in the hope of identifying "red genes" and that thousands of young children of Republican women, including ones born in prison, were handed over to Francoist couples or to religious orders and given new identities.[6] Many of these forced adoptees are still alive, and some have recently found out who their real parents were.

Law is a blunter instrument than history. Garzón's advocacy, which included among its causes the opening of Lorca's grave, has often seemed shrill by comparison with the patient work he draws on. As one of Lorca's nephews complained, "We don't need a judge to come and tell us Franco was a murderer."[7] While in his late thirties Garzón was closely associated with the left-of-center PSOE and was briefly in charge of its antidrug campaign. After returning to power in 2004, the PSOE under José Luis Rodríguez Zapatero immediately began pushing through its Law of Historical Memory, with the probably intentional effect of inducing key members of the conservative Partido Popular to oppose it. By walking into this trap, the leader of the PP, Mariano Rajoy, allowed his party to be seen as not only the defender but the natural heir of Francoism—and the PSOE, by contrast, as an idealized version of the Republican movement made new. (Zapatero himself spoke often about one of his grandfathers, who was killed by the Francoists, but not about the other, who was on their side.[8]) Few people at first accused Baltasar Garzón of crude partisanship; he had been an implacable rooter-out of corruption in the PSOE, as in other quarters. But opposition grew to the campaign with which he had become associated, and was reinforced by the PP's return to power at the end of 2011. Already, in a number of municipalities where the PSOE had ruled but had been superseded by the PP, recent memorials to the Republic had been officially rededicated. In Elche, for example, in the southeast, a late 1990s public park named after the Republican heroine Dolores Ibárruri, "La Pasionaria," was officially redesignated as Republic of Argentina Garden, and the unappealing-sounding Avenida del Ferrocarril ("Railway

Avenue") was provocatively renamed after one of the town's last Francoist mayors, Vicente Quiles, who had been responsible for creating a new underground line for the railway. Garzón himself, meanwhile, whatever the legitimacy of his efforts in relation to the memory law, was judged to have gone too far in another case, where he had instructed police to make secret recordings of discussions between court witnesses and their lawyers, and was sacked.

Among the sources of disagreement over historical memory, perhaps the most emotionally powerful is the generation gap. To be sure, some of the first proponents of the exhumations were survivors of the civil war. In Málaga, I met the locally revered Francisco Espinosa, born in 1931, whose father, one of the Falange's victims, was buried in the San Rafael cemetery. Espinosa began an association "*contra el olvido,*" "against forgetting," in Málaga as early as 1977. Several other people who remember the dictatorship, though, expressed doubts to me about the excavations, doubts that often seemed to contain an element of injured pride. The peaceful transition to democracy, in their eyes, was a triumph. All those over fifty had lived through it and played their part. To be told now, by people the same ages as their own children or grandchildren, that they had shown insufficient respect to the past was hard to take. The pragmatic *pacto de olvido* (agreement to forget or overlook) of the early post-Franco period may be derided today but it served a crucial purpose.

So far as it existed, that is. The novelist and columnist Antonio Muñoz Molina, though far from being an apologist for Francoism, is among the critics of people he describes as flattering themselves that they are helping to rectify a major historical injustice without having to make much effort or put themselves in any danger. "The result of this sentimentalization and officialization of memory," he wrote, "is itself a form of amnesia . . . Anyone who claims that only now is it possible to publish novels or history books which tell the truth about the civil war and the dictatorship would do better to say that he or she has not read the ones that were written earlier, or can't be bothered to read them because they are unfashionable."[9] When I first met the writer, he dilated on his theme with good-humored exasperation. "You see pictures in the newspapers and on television of people too young to have any memory

of the civil war, in tears because some skeletons have their hands tied. *Of course* their hands were tied!"

All these criticisms have good sense behind them. To a detached outsider there *is* something futile about going in search of bodies buried seventy-odd years ago. It *is* a pity that sentiment about a distant war is being exploited for current political ends. The older generation *does*, by and large, have a juster, more complex understanding of the mid-twentieth century than do younger people. As I was told by a newly retired bystander at one attempted exhumation, "There are more than two sides to these questions." He pointed out that no one seems bothered about the remaining mass graves of Nationalists. And there are still other arguments to be heard, particularly that the memory vogue has been exaggerated by the media, that it is in danger of opening old wounds, and that it distracts attention from more urgent problems such as the environment and the economy. People were saying this before the world economic crisis broke. When Spain passed its memory law, it was already faced with Europe's steepest increase in unemployment. Today more than ever, digging up the past can seem like a new version of burying your head in the sand.

Lorca, as many have pointed out, survives in his works; finding his bones will make no difference.[10] Most of the dead, though, have no special claim on historical memory, and it may be the very fact that survivors of the civil war are fast dying off that has made a younger generation so eager to learn about their families' experiences of that time and to commemorate those who were killed. The humbler they were, and the more meaningless their deaths, the stronger this impulse can be.

Marina Gómez Pastor lived with her parents and sister in Valde-caballeros, a small town remote even by the standards of its region, Extremadura, in Spain's southwest. She is the eldest granddaughter of Benilde Ruiz Fernández, a widow who was a permanent presence in her life as she was growing up in the 1980s and '90s. This was the period Spaniards call "the Transition," the initially precarious shift to democracy after Franco's death in 1975. By general though far from

unanimous consent it seemed best, at the time, not to talk too much about the past, or at least not publicly. Who knew how long the new regime would last? A constitution took three years to draft and ratify. During that time, Spain was at first ruled by governments appointed by the young and as-yet-untested king Juan Carlos—the first of them led by none other than the former Butcher of Málaga, Carlos Arias Navarro. Most of the structures Franco had set up remained in place, and the army was loyal to his memory. Organized democratic political parties and trade unions were slow to gain strength, the Basque separatist organization, ETA,[11] was very active, and when a general election was eventually held in 1977, it brought to power Adolfo Suárez, a prime minister who proved to be an adroit liberal centrist but who, again, had begun his political career under Franco. Four years later there was a serious attempt at another military coup (see p. 146).

During the dictatorship, with its censors, its propaganda, its high-handed policing, its mysterious disappearances, people almost forgot what it meant to talk openly about anything that mattered. Conversation was less restricted, though, *en casa*, at home, and as time went by and the new freedoms began to seem increasingly real, Benilde told her grandchildren stories about the past—particularly about a day in April 1939, when she was seventeen.

She was the eldest of three sisters. Every day in their childhood, their father, Waldo (short for Ubaldo) Ruiz Belmonte, went to work in the fields between Valdecaballeros and the next village, Castilblanco. They lived through desperate times. In 1923, soon after Benilde was born, the new military dictatorship reinforced feudalism, nowhere more strongly than in impoverished Extremadura. Foreign travelers in the region earlier in the century had described how, if your meal included meat, you would be surrounded by sightseers while you ate it.[12] In the winter of 1931/32, farmworkers in Castilblanco went on strike—this was when Buñuel made his film about Extremadura, *Tierra sin pan* ("Land Without Bread")—and by the spring, they were starving. In April, during a demonstration, a member of the Guardia shot one of the strikers. Villagers turned on the police with knives and stones, killing four of them. The event caused national outrage and was a hint of what was to come.

During much of the civil war, a portion of the front line passed be-

tween the two villages. Valdecaballeros, to the south, was taken by the Nationalists, and a number of families, the Ruizes among them, fled two hundred kilometers eastward to Daimiel, an important agricultural area held by the Republicans. One of the main sources of food supplies for the Loyalists, it was also in essence a trade union fiefdom.

According to Benilde, the family was too busy staying alive to take any interest in politics. When, at the end of March 1939, Franco declared victory, they assumed the war was over and, together with their displaced neighbors, packed up such belongings as they possessed and set off for home. As the procession began to descend the mountains toward Valdecaballeros, it bumped into a group of soldiers. Waldo and some of the other men were seized and taken to a prison set up in their village by the Falange, where they were kept incommunicado for three days. Their ordeal ended in another journey, along the road toward Castilblanco and up a hill to what had been a Republican trench, where they were shot and dumped.

For Waldo's widow, it was the end of everything. Exhausted not only by the war but now also by obsessive speculations about why Waldo had been killed—he had once denounced a woman in Castilblanco who had stolen two of his mules; could that have had something to do with it?—she, too, soon died. It was left to Benilde to look after her sisters, find a husband for herself, and then bring up their children. In the 1940s, life in Spain was even poorer than in the 1920s and '30s, and for anyone connected to those who had fallen afoul of the conquerors, it was also terrifying. Franco combined triumphalism with vindictiveness. While many of those on his side who had been killed were now exhumed and ceremonially reburied, those associated with republicanism had to keep their heads down and their mouths shut. When Benilde finally began to tell her stories at home, though, she had a fascinated audience in Marina. The girl identified strongly with her grandmother. At school, where her teachers had been educated under Franco, the civil war was hardly mentioned, and this made her still more curious.

Like Marina, others in the new, European Spain were beginning to feel that their history had been getting no attention or, rather, attention of the wrong kind. Monuments to the dictatorship were still to be seen everywhere: streets with the names of Nationalist generals, Queipo de

Llano among them; town squares dominated by equestrian statues of Franco; church porches memorializing those who had died "for God and Spain"—as if anyone who had fought on the other side, or on none, was inevitably both an atheist and antipatriotic. This, indeed, was what Francoism taught, especially in church. In the cathedral at Jaén, not far from where Lorca died, each of the four pillars at the transept carries a monument to clergy of the diocese killed in the civil war. One hundred and thirty-five are named, ranging from a bishop and other cathedral dignitaries to a nun and two men studying for ordination. Most were parish priests. The murders were more than matched in other parts of Spain: about 6,800 clergy, monks, and nuns are thought to have been killed in all, more than in the French Revolution. Their deaths were an indictment of some factions of the Republican movement and made a profound impact in communities where religion still mattered. But the Jaén monument tells two lies. One is that the clergy died in "the Marxist Revolution of 1936–39"—rather than as a result of a military coup supported by the Church hierarchy. The other is a falsehood by omission. There is no monument in the cathedral to the Republican dead—to the democrats whose overthrow was called for by most of the bishops and, once accomplished, hailed by Pope Pius XII, in a public message to Franco, "with immense joy."[13]

By the 1980s and '90s, democracy was no longer on the losing side, and there was increasing pressure for monuments to some of the more flagrant evildoers to be removed. More constructively, voluntary local associations had begun to look for ways to assist people who had suffered under the dictatorship and to make such public amends as could be agreed upon. In particular, those who had been killed by the self-described representatives of "God and Spain" were at last being commemorated. One of the first public signs of the change in mood came in the early 1980s, when local families supported by trade unionists put up memorials in a field close to where the Valencia–Zaragoza road passes Caudé, in the east-central province of Teruel. There was once an immense well here, 84 meters deep. During the civil war, it was gradually filled with the bodies of hundreds of people executed without trial, most of them members of the Sociedad Obrera Agrícola (Agricultural Workers Union).

Partly under the influence of similar moves in parts of Latin Amer-

ica, families began to dig up communal graves and to give the remains a proper burial. One such exhumation made a far-reaching impression, including on the family of Waldo Ruiz. It took place at the beginning of the new millennium, in El Bierzo, a region of León province famous for having harbored members of the post–civil war resistance movement against Franco. The *fosa común* in question contained the remains of "the Priaranza Thirteen," a group of militant leftists executed by members of the Falange in October 1936. The exhumation was planned by a journalist in his early thirties named Emilio Silva. At the age of ten, Emilio's father had gone from being a cheerful schoolboy to having to take responsibility for his entire family. The reason for this change of fortune was that Emilio's grandfather, an intelligent, outspoken Republican who had emigrated to America but returned to Spain in 1925 to marry and start a shop in El Bierzo, was captured by the Falange and, along with the Priaranza Thirteen, shot and buried in a ditch. Like Marina and so many others born toward the end of, or soon after, Franco's lifetime, the young Emilio had grown up pondering what it must have meant for a child suddenly to become head of a Spanish family in the late 1930s.

Emilio Silva is named after his grandfather. In *Las fosas de Franco*—the title of the book he wrote with Santiago Macías is difficult to translate because *fosa* means "grave" but also "ditch"; a proper grave is normally given a more dignified name such as *tumba* or *sepultura*—he has written about his family, about his grandfather's journey in the back of a truck to the remote place where the men were to be shot, about the experience of waiting their turn and their last pleas for mercy:

> I have often thought about what must have been my grandfather's terror during those hours, about the terror of each of those men being driven to the *matadero* [place of slaughter]: fear for his own life, fear for the family he had left behind, about whether punishments would go on being inflicted on any of them. More than once I've closed my eyes and tried to put myself in my grandfather's place, to feel the same agony, the same powerlessness, the same panic.[14]

Emilio describes his search for the grave, prompted in part by these imaginings, in part by a wish to succeed where earlier efforts by his

grandmother to identify her husband's whereabouts were officially rebuffed. The narrative is particularly vivid when he writes about what he has since learned is a common experience: that while initially survivors often seem sure where a site is, when taken there, even the gravedigger may be confounded by changes in cultivation, by new buildings and roads. Trained as a sociologist at one of Spain's top universities, Emilio became increasingly absorbed not only in his own inquiries but in those of others with a similar emotional stake in the past. He was particularly influenced by the professionalism of two people who responded to an article he wrote in a local newspaper, *La Crónica de León*. They were Julio Vidal, an archaeologist whose mother came from Priaranza, and his wife, María Encina, a forensic anthropologist.

The couple had been following work in "contemporary archaeology" that had been going on elsewhere, both in Europe, including on First World War sites in France, and in places where war crimes had been committed—in Argentina, Rwanda, Croatia . . . "So many places," they lament. They were familiar with the protocols that had grown up around such investigations and with the use of DNA in identifying problematic remains, and they had been looking for an opportunity to extend these methods to similar activities taking place in a more haphazard way in Spain. Both had been shocked by an exhumation in Arganza, where a couple of years earlier the assorted bones of half a dozen men had simply been lifted in the jaw of a mechanical digger and tipped into a cemetery. Emilio was quick to enlist the couple's help and that of various other volunteers, among them a younger historian of the civil war, Santiago Macías. All those working at Priaranza del Bierzo were passionately committed to uncovering what they saw as the truth about the civil war. In Emilio's words, "We were beginning to make an island of historical justice in the sea of amnesia about those who, with their ideas and with their political work, built Spain's first democracy."[15]

The exhumations took time. Identification of some of the remains involved lengthy archival searches as well as DNA testing. The professionalism of all this attracted attention from the media and from local politicians, and soon local authorities in the area unanimously voted to give financial support to future projects of the kind in their jurisdictions. Emilio and Santiago, meanwhile, were deluged with inquiries

and realized that although many regional associations were pursuing related investigations of various sorts, including searches in archives that were still for the most part inaccessible and poorly catalogued, there was no national forum for such work. Together they founded what quickly became one of Spain's most powerful grassroots organizations, the Asociación para la Recuperación de la Memoria Histórica (ARMH, Association for the Recovery of Historical Memory).

From its reputation, you might expect the ARMH to be housed in a *palacio* somewhere near the Prado. Its activities are closely followed by the Spanish media, and it has an extremely efficient, informative, and much-visited website[16] and thousands of registered members. Emilio and Santiago have been invited to speak at international meetings of related bodies, among them the UN Office of the High Commissioner for Human Rights, and the association's work was to provide the Law of Historical Memory with much of its impetus. Its premises, though, when I visited them, consisted of Emilio's small flat in a suburb of Madrid, Santiago's home in western Spain, and a van. Both men spent much of their day talking into handfuls of mobile phones. Emilio's office was a Sargasso Sea of laptops, DVDs, books, pamphlets, and clippings; Santiago was usually to be found at one site or another.

On a bright, cold Wednesday afternoon in Valdecaballeros early in December 2008, Santiago had come from a new project north of Cáceres that didn't seem to be going well. He was interested in a report of a *fosa* in a small town near Guadalupe. Valdecaballeros is between the two places, and Marina had recently been in touch with the association. The seventieth anniversary of Waldo's death would fall the following April. For his daughter Benilde's sake, the family hoped to mark the occasion by finding his remains and giving them a Christian burial.

We were joined by a two-man team of ground surveyors who had come from Madrid in an SUV, bringing geo-radar equipment and a metal detector. Over lunch, I asked about the expenses involved in their work. For the current set of projects there was a state subvention, but the owner of the surveying business, a voluble man called Luis Aval—later to be involved in the abortive attempt to locate Lorca's remains—said that it didn't remotely cover his costs. He grew indignant. "If a plane crashes, there are fire engines all over the place, ambulances, Guardia. But because the civil war dead are under the ground,

nada. Besides, do you know what it costs to build one kilometer of motorway? Six million euros." I pondered these analogies while we drove to meet a small convoy at a traffic circle on the edge of the town: an elderly man in a Mercedes; Marina and her mother; Marina's sister and her boyfriend, Manuel. Grandmother Benilde was staying with relatives in Madrid.

Our route was the one along which Waldo is thought to have been taken for his last ride. We parked beside the main road, and as we walked behind the surveyors' jeep up a hillside scattered with holm oaks, Waldo's great-granddaughters looked increasingly preoccupied. Here, closer to Castilblanco than Valdecaballeros, the moorland slopes regularly and the trees are evenly spread. Other than a flat hilltop to the north—with its commanding views, a strategic point during the civil war—and a Franco-era reservoir to the south, there are few distinguishing features: one patch of thistles is very like another. Halfway up, the man with the Mercedes, who turned out to be a former mayor of Valdecaballeros, said he thought the graves were on the western side of the lightly trodden path we were following. This was where the Republicans had entrenched and where Waldo and the others, he believed, were buried.

Young Manuel, a civil war aficionado, thought differently. On the path's eastern side, about a hundred meters from where the ex-mayor was standing, the surveyors unpacked their metal detector and a device built on what resembled a state-of-the-art baby buggy: a triangular frame on three wheels with pneumatic tires; a plastic box slung below, containing the ground-penetrating radar machine; and on the handlebars, a monitor. Now began a slow procession over the bumpy, thorny ground, sometimes pushing the buggy, sometimes sweeping the metal detector from side to side, sometimes both. Unconvinced by this sporadic activity, the ex-mayor went home. He had told me he was doubtful about the whole procedure. Twenty years ago, there were people alive who knew everything. Now it would be very hard to find anyone with reliable information. Besides, relatives of his had been killed on both sides. The same was true for many people around here.

Santiago talked on his mobile. The women stood in a huddle, talking. Manuel and I took turns looking over Luis's shoulder into the monitor at oscillations that showed variations in the subsoil. He had

found what he thought might be the line of the trench, which corresponded to the orientation, though not the location, the ex-mayor had indicated. At one point an irregular, wider, roughly triangular patch seemed to indicate a pit. Santiago marked its center with a rock while a few traffic cones were placed at intervals along the line.

Luis now took a turn with the metal detector, and near the higher, western end of the newly marked line it began to bleep. He slid the plate above and around the spot, took out a trowel, and dug. A few centimeters under the surface was a tarnished, slender bullet casing, unmistakably different from the big cartridge cases that lie everywhere in this hunting territory of deer and wild boar. He scraped off the dirt, stood the case on end, called Santiago over, and carried on sweeping while the rest of us squatted, gazing at the little exhibit. Not far off, still on the same line, Luis soon found another like it.

This was a high point of the afternoon. Another came when Santiago, now confident of success, began to ask about mechanical diggers. Catching his mood, Marina told him happily that Manuel's family had two *máquinas*. Plans for the next day were discussed—Santiago still had to go back to the dig near Cáceres—and the women left. Luis, though, was dissatisfied. "It doesn't surprise me to find bullets where there was a military trench. I'd be happier if there were more of them." During what remained of the sunlight, Santiago encouraged the men to work over other parts of the land, but nothing materialized. Having agreed on a time to make contact later that night, we packed up, shook hands, and left, Luis and his colleague to Madrid, Santiago to Cáceres, I to my nearby *hostal*.

In Andalucía at the beginning of the winter olive harvest, I had learned that Spanish laborers of the kind who, forty years ago, abandoned agricultural work in favor of construction are beginning to return to the land, with the result that charities are obliged to house and feed itinerant laborers from Africa who find themselves jobless. Painful cultural memories of a different kind are involved, here: memories of the harsh, hungry Spain known all too well by Waldo Ruiz. I tried to imagine that time as I waited beside the Valdecaballeros–Castilblanco road the morning after the survey, while Manuel chugged up on his yellow digger through a dense, cold mist. He was followed by Santiago in a Volkswagen minivan and by another car bringing six volunteers,

mostly in their twenties or early thirties, university educated, some of them trained as archaeologists. In the back of the VW was a sackful of picks and trowels and also a large portable canopy, in case privacy should be needed.

At about 10:30, the machine made its first, cautious, half-meter-deep incision where Santiago had left his stone. Everyone stretched to stare at the pile of earth it removed, then into the hole it left. The soil was tipped gently to one side. A young woman who worked full-time on ARMH digs raked through it. Nothing. Directed by an older regular member of the team, Manuel slowly repeated the process along the line marked the day before, until he had made a shallow trench about six meters long. He was then asked to go back and dig down another half meter. This is the level at which remains are often found, and once again the mood was expectant. Several times, one or another of the team signaled to Manuel to stop, climbed into the trench, and scratched around in an area where the earth looked softer or had a different color. When the excavation was almost two meters deep, a new one was begun, parallel to it and about a meter distant.

Any quest takes on a life of its own, becomes its own justification. Although the mood was now relaxed and jokey, everyone was bent on finding something. The team had been disappointed yesterday. Some of them had other jobs and could join digs for only a few days at a time. We were all cold and damp. Santiago was clamped to his mobile when Marina and her mother and sister returned. I talked to them for some time. I wanted to hear Waldo's story from them but realized that I was also trying to occupy them as the digger went in and out and the volunteers raked carefully through one heap of earth, then the next.

Santiago spread some cushions on thorny ground a few yards from the excavations and produced bags of chips and nuts. In pairs and one by one, his team broke off. A weak sun had begun to disperse the mist. Cars passing below slowed while their drivers tried to work out what was going on. Manuel filled in his two unproductive trenches and began another, then another, parallel to the first but higher up. The digger's bites were greedier now, less tentative, and were watched by fewer people.

Later that afternoon, after lunch, Santiago had time to talk to me. Born in El Bierzo in 1973, he had been so gripped as a boy by the stories told him by older people that he began to record them. A particu-

lar episode, involving the lives of anti-Francoist guerrillas in a mountain hideout, was to become the subject of a book by him, *Los Corrales, 1942*. He had also written the accounts of almost twenty digs that make up the second part of *Las fosas de Franco*. Valdecaballeros would reveal something, he said—today, tomorrow, he couldn't be sure when. The process often involved false leads, temporary disappointments. So much depended on evidence that only old people could provide. It was a pity that Benilde was still in Madrid. He had heard of a woman in the village who might know something and who he hoped would come to the site. The *máquina* dipped, pushed back against its haunches, scraped, pulled, and reached gracefully across toward the volunteers' rakes. Everyone cursorily examined the rubber sole of a sandal, circa 1990. I followed some of the team on a walk up the hill, from the top of which you see woods, lakes, distant mountains. Scrappy modern developments surround Castilblanco and Valdecaballeros, but the roads are good because they were built to serve a still-unused nuclear energy plant to the southwest. The big reservoirs are a legacy for which Franco deserves more credit than he gets (see chapter 2). Most of the rest of what's visible must have been the same in 1936—or 1836.

There were some movements below, around the digger. A woman had arrived—not the one Santiago was expecting but an aunt of Marina's, Benilde's only daughter. By the time I joined them, she had been arguing for some time with Marina and her mother. A hundred meters to the northeast of us, there was a low ridge. She had always heard that the grave was in the fields beyond it, closer to Castilblanco. Marina looked dejected. Manuel hunched himself over the levers in his silent cockpit. Santiago and the others wandered in different directions, some of them talking on their mobiles. Feeling like a stranger at a funeral, I moved a little way off, back up the hill. The sun had disappeared some time ago, and once again the women set off for home. Manuel began to fill in the trenches, the volunteers folded up the unused canopy, tools were stowed back in the van. Santiago had decided to abandon Valdecaballeros until he had better information about the grave's location. They would move on to the other potential site he had mentioned, on the way to Guadalupe. The next day, after some inconclusive preliminary inquiries there, the group split up for an unexpectedly free weekend.

Marina remained in Valdecaballeros. For all the arguments I had heard and read—and in many cases sympathized with—about historical naïveté and the need to focus on the future, I didn't feel like recommending her to read this or that book published twenty years ago, or to think about the economy. Anyone who met her would respect her for taking an interest, however subjective, in a cataclysm that had so affected her family; no one could criticize her for trying to do something, however symbolic, while her grandmother was still alive. History isn't a Site of Special Scientific Interest fenced off for professional academics and intellectuals.

Among Spain's strongest and best-known characteristics is its Moorish inheritance, visible in almost every old town, audible in the spoken language and in the music. Islamic Spain (Al-Andalus) has been admired, studied, romanticized, made new by people in every generation from Gautier to Lorca and since. Just as is now happening in relation to the civil war, one "authentic" version supersedes another, and while each myth is being picked apart and reworked, an occasional, more durable element enters the cultural mainstream. I phoned Marina to check a few details: family names, numbers of siblings. Had her great-grandfather ever joined one of the farmworkers' unions? She said she thought her grandmother might know, or perhaps a document might have survived. She hoped that when Benilde was next in Valdecaballeros, she would be able to identify Waldo's grave. I said that, if so, Santiago might try again. She replied "¡Ojalá!"

The expression, originally Arabic, is often heard in Spain. It used to be translated as "God willing," but times change and today it would probably be rendered as "If only" or "I wish." Etymologists point out that, strictly speaking, "law sha'a Allah" implies a subjunctive: "If God were to wish it." But what difference does it make? I said "¡Ojalá!" back.

3

The Alligator's Dams

To the extent that repressive regimes are shored up by propaganda, they are undermined by skepticism. Even when Franco's strategy was valuable and farsighted, its failures, during his lifetime as well as later, were met with a degree of abhorrence that turned them into subversive myths.

One of his unquestionable achievements was a huge increase in Spain's ability to store and distribute water—for agriculture, for industry, for domestic use especially in the expanding cities, and above all for hydroelectric power. Economic historians deplore most of his policies—agricultural protectionism in particular, which in Spain mainly protected the landed aristocracy. Even the revisionist Pío Moa, in his bestselling account of Franco's virtues, has to acknowledge that during the dictatorship, "Inflation ran dangerously high, overvaluation of the peseta hindered exports, overprotected industries required ever-increasing imports of raw materials without generating profits overseas, and currency reserves fell to their lowest historic levels."[1] It's generally agreed, though, that in terms of public works (roads and railways, bridges and tunnels, and especially dams and reservoirs), Franco helped lay the foundations of the relative prosperity that rewarded the last years of his regime and continued through the final quarter of the twentieth century.

In industry, the country had always lagged behind its neighbors, partly because industry needed water and, with it, energy. Agricultural independence also necessitated better harvesting of water and measures to make its distribution less unequal between north and south, and throughout the year. And then there was the new motor of the Spanish economy: tourism. Glad of the sun and also of how much farther their money went in Spain than at home, foreign visitors in the 1950s and '60s were not so grateful, it soon became clear, that they didn't expect modern toilets and showers and clean bed linens and towels. Meanwhile, the indigenous urban population was growing fast. In 1930, fewer than 15 percent of Spanish people lived in towns with a population higher than 100,000. By 1970 the proportion had risen to 37 percent.[2] In the same period, the population of Madrid tripled, creating what Raymond Carr and Juan Pablo Fusi described not long after as "a case of urbanisation unique in Europe, a metropolis that has drained the surrounding provinces, creating a demographic desert."[3]

Big public works are easier to undertake in authoritarian regimes than in those where public consultation is the norm. Besides, Franco, like many other dictators, came from a military background: getting practical things done was part of his training, and he was accustomed to deploying prisoners in the process. In the early years of his regime about a quarter of a million Spaniards were imprisoned on political grounds. Meanwhile, he was able to draw on the resources and expertise of friends in industry and banking—among them, Pedro Barrié de la Maza, whose electricity business, FENOSA (Fuerzas Eléctricas del Noroeste, S.A.), still runs one of the first projects Franco undertook in his home province of Galicia: the brutal-looking dam and network of generators that dominate Los Peares, outside Orense. He also benefited from earlier work by farsighted planners, especially in engineering and the training of engineers. The oldest dams still in use in Europe are in Spain, near Mérida; they date from Roman times. The Moors famously brought their own skills, and new engineering techniques were also developed under the Habsburgs; the Tibi Dam in Alicante, built in the 1580s, held the international height record (46 meters) until the nineteenth century. National projections concerning water use, storage, and distribution were made in Spain as early as 1902, and the Canal de Isabel II, which supplies most of Madrid, was begun more than half a

century before that. By contrast with its reputation abroad, Spain in the nineteenth and early twentieth centuries showed urgency, practical resourcefulness, and consistency in big public projects. The Second Republic was continuing this work when the coup of 1936 brought civil war and a temporary halt to all long-term enterprises. On the one hand, then, Franco's ambitions, in this area as in others, can be seen, like Mussolini's, as a conscious emulation of the achievements of the past, especially of the ancient Roman Empire. On the other hand, much of what he did was based on quite recent plans, including ones made by Republicans. Some of them were started at the time of Primo de Rivera's dictatorship, which should also be credited with the first project for a reliable network of *carreteras nacionales*, state highways.

During Franco's regime, while the national population rose by 40 percent, dam construction doubled and the country's water storage capacity went up sixfold.[4] So closely was the *generalísimo* linked with this work that a popular Colombian song, "There Goes the Alligator," was subversively adapted to refer to him: "*Se va el caimán, se va el caimán / se va para Barranquilla*," the place name being changed to that of whatever local reservoir.[5] The dam-building program depended, though, on a contradiction. In most cases, privately owned hydroelectric companies were told by government, "You build the dams and sell the power, we'll deal with irrigation; the costs can be split between us." But reservoirs that have been run low for irrigation in the dry months between May and September are not much use between October and March, when energy demand is highest and hydroelectric plants need to do most of their work. Again, accumulating large quantities of water in the cooler, mountainous north does not solve the problem of transporting it through the hot and no-less-mountainous hinterland of Spain to the arid south: aquifers are easy to build and cheap to run only if they travel steadily downhill. And then there are the people immediately affected by the construction of big dams. In old rural communities, water is not only a natural resource but a fiercely contested one. If this land is my land, any water on it or under it is surely mine, too. It's a problem, then, that reservoirs, by definition, are built in well-watered areas for the benefit of other regions. They also create microclimates that can change former patterns of cultivation, and they destroy the migration patterns of fish, to say nothing of the farms and villages directly in the way.

In the cause of the huge growth of hydroelectric schemes not only in Spain but across the world during the twentieth century, many communities literally went to the bottom. From Capel Celyn in North Wales to South Australia's former Happy Valley and from Yanakamura in Japan to the Massachusetts townships of Dana, Enfield, Greenwich, and Prescott, established towns and villages have been submerged in the interests of distant modern cities, while displaced residents of the drowned rural settlements have been more or less reluctantly relocated, often to the cities that benefited from their disruption. Admittedly, by comparison with what happened to many European communities in the 1940s, all this was and is next to nothing, but it's not easy to make such comparisons when you have to leave the house you and your parents grew up in, to see the local school and church and graveyard submerged and the landscape disappear forever. Among many such disappearances in mid-twentieth-century Spain, some attained special status as sources of counterpropaganda and as popular rallying points. Just as democratic Spain has come to mourn its unmarked dead, so its attention has turned to the vanishing of whole communities.

Among them are, or were in 1952, a group of windy moorland villages forty kilometers from the northern coast on the border between the regions of Cantabria and Burgos. It's easy to see the fate of these places as a tragedy and to lay the blame at Franco's door. The river Ebro flowed south, near its source, through a high natural basin of land, relatively thinly populated by farming families and their livestock. There was just one substantial local industry in the town of Arija, to the valley's southeast: Cristalería Española, a glassworks that, since 1906, had used sand from the riverbed in manufacturing a wide range of products for scientific and domestic use. Arija, though, stands on relatively high ground. As soon as the civil war ended, work began at the valley's western end to construct a long-projected dam, 30 meters high and 250 meters wide, across the Ebro's path. Republican prisoners were deployed as laborers. The completed reservoir filled up gratifyingly fast: 540 million cubic meters of water covered 6,000 hectares of land on which stood four hundred dwellings and a sprinkling of churches,

the spire of one of which still sticks out forlornly near the southern shore. On August 6, 1952, the dictator, dressed in admiral's uniform, took part in an opening ceremony. The Pantano (reservoir-dam) del Ebro was among the first of his big projects to have been completed.

Two related smaller schemes in the area were less successful. Seven weeks after Franco's visit, a road bridge that had been built to reconnect Arija with its former neighbor La Población, on what is now the lake's northeastern shore, collapsed. And the promised extension of the local railway line to the nearest big town, Reinosa, never materialized. The following year, Cristalería Española moved away, taking a thousand jobs with it. The pompous houses in which some of its managers lived are still there, giving lakeside Arija the feeling of an out-of-season spa town, but one with no season to look forward to, or back on.

How to calculate the profits and losses of the Pantano del Ebro? And how much of the responsibility, for good and ill, lay with the regime? On the credit side, the reservoir guarantees the water supply of much of the region, feeds agricultural irrigation schemes in three provinces, and is a major source of electricity. It is also a beauty spot, a great sweep of water that has attracted new wildlife. All this has to be measured against the introduction of new climatic conditions (dense mists, the exposure of previously sheltered villages to wind and rain sweeping across the lake) and alterations in the ecology of rivers downstream. As for the displacement of families, compensation was paid to those affected in the 1940s and '50s at rates determined in the 1920s. True, Spain was desperately poor at the time, so the money was hard to find and even a little made a difference to the recipients. It's hard to tell, too, how many of those whose property was compulsorily occupied would still have been there if the prospect of compensation had not been held out decades earlier. In this region, you don't have to go to Arija or La Población to see empty houses. The very fact that compensation was calculated so long before the valley was flooded is a reminder that water politics was making itself felt long before Franco came to power. The scheme for the Pantano del Ebro was first proposed in 1913, at a Zaragoza conference on irrigation. It had been nurtured by a local engineer and hydraulics pioneer, Manuel Lorenzo Pardo, then in his early thirties.

Corconte, a hamlet on the reservoir's northeastern shore, embodies

some of the changes to the neighborhood. It remains essentially a farming village: cattle are driven along the single road between the hillside above and the lakeside fields. A short distance away stands a sizable spa-hotel, the Balneario de Corconte, where city dwellers still come to do a little walking, a little fishing, and to take the waters. The village church, meanwhile, speaks of less peaceful times. On its walls, Italian troops drafted in during the civil war carved "*Viva Italia!*" and the Fascist emblem above the word *Duce*. A monument to their occupation of the region was put up on a nearby hilltop after the war and is still there.

Next to the church is a businesslike new information center devoted to the reservoir and its history. Old films and photographs record what was lost. A video installation beautifully communicates water's biological complexity. Posters and leaflets explain how the reservoir fits into Spain's national plans, past and future. Amid all this stands a large, simple set of scales with weights representing various social factors, pro and con; the machine also gives scope for visitors to introduce considerations of their own. Both the balancing mechanism and the museum are indirect products of Spain's earlier failures of balance, not least in consultation and education. One issue, though, is neglected by the display: the socio-aesthetic crudity of Franco's public works; the lack of any creative concern for the places where they were carried out. If the towns beside the lake feel like rundown resorts, it's because no one seems to have considered that, with some attention to planning and architecture, resorts are what they might have become. Instead, the shoreline mingles the poorly designed, ill-constructed houses of a development free-for-all with the melancholy remnants of lost rural communities: empty barns, fallen stone walls, lanes that end in an undignified plunge into the water, where they join a few bewildered-looking half-submerged trees.

The inundation of ancient places on behalf of large-scale modern demands is so richly symbolic that it has inevitably provided a theme for modern writers: for W. G. Sebald in *Austerlitz*, for example, with its recurring allusions to Llanwddyn, in Montgomeryshire, sacrificed in the 1880s to the needs of Liverpool; for Sarah Hall in *Haweswater*, about a comparable situation in Cumbria; and for Anne Michaels, who, in *The*

Winter Vault, employs the Aswan Dam as a metaphor for history's, and memory's, geological strata of dispossession. In Spain, the engagement of writers with dams has sometimes been more direct. Jesús López Pacheco, whose provocative *Central eléctrica* ("Electric Power Station," 1958; see pp. 53–56) was published in Spain at the height of the dam-building program, grew up in the improvised villages where itinerant workers lived with their families, and owed his Communist sympathies to what he saw in those days. The novelist Juan Benet was a successful engineer who, during long winter evenings in the mountains northeast of León, where the Pantano de Porma was being built, passed his time writing one of his most distinctive books, *Volverás a Región*, a strange, ironic narrative of rural isolation and the effects of change (see pp. 234–35). The reservoir he created (now known as the Pantano Juan Benet) had powerful effects on a younger author, Julio Llamazares, whose family home disappeared under its waters. Like many other Spanish writers, Llamazares earns part of his living by writing newspaper columns, and it is in his journalism that he has commented most directly on the effects of this particular dam. He has interviewed people about the destruction of the village of Riaño soon after he was born there, and has described his return as an adult, when the Porma reservoir was emptied for repairs, to find his parents' house "full of algae and dead trout and covered with rust and mud."[6] In another article he told the story of a man who stayed on in his home until the last moment, when the police removed him—one of many episodes in Llamazares's work that focus on conflicts between "progress" and rural conservatism. Most of these elements come together in his short novel *The Yellow Rain* (*La lluvia amarilla*, 1988).[7] The book is based on one true story but has gained resonance from another.

In *The Yellow Rain*, an old man on the last night of his life relates the gradual collapse of his community, the death of his wife and one of their sons, the other son's move to Germany, and his own doomed, lonely battle to survive with his memories and his weakening hopes. Will his son ever return? he wonders, and then realizes the thought's futility:

> If Andrés does come back, he will probably find only a pile of rubble and
> a mountain of scrub. If he does come back, he will find the roads blocked
> by brambles, the irrigation channels choked, the shepherds' huts and

the houses fallen. Nothing will remain of what was once his. Not even the old alleys. Not even the vegetable plots planted by the river. Not even the house in which he was born, while snow covered the rooftops and the wind whipped along the streets and roads. But the snows will not be the cause of the desolation that Andrés will find that day. He will search amongst the brambles and the rotten beams. He will rummage amongst the rubble of the former walls and will find perhaps the odd broken chair or the slates that clad the old fireplace where he so often sat at night as a child. But that will be all. No forgotten portrait. No sign of life. When Andrés comes back to Ainielle, it will be to discover that all is lost.[8]

The passage is clearly part autobiographical, and in a loose sense Llamazares's Ainielle could be many villages. You can't walk far in the southern Pyrenees without seeing the remains of a church amid a huddle of abandoned houses and barns a few hundred meters up from the valley bottom. Though Ainielle (also known as Ainelle) is a real place in the mountains near Huesca, much of Llamazares's story also fits Jánovas, which is sixty kilometers away and, for various reasons, is more famous.

Jánovas is close to a busy road and next to a river. Generally speaking, settlements in the Pyrenean valleys, as distinct from those high on the mountainsides like Ainielle, have prospered from tourism. Ainsa, for example, in the Alto Aragón, and its neighbors Broto, Biescas, and Sabiñánigo, all of which appear in Llamazares's novel, are full of *hostales*, restaurants, and shops selling hiking clothes and climbing equipment. Yet Jánovas is a ghost town, a victim of dam-planning blight. Today you can reach it only on foot, yet it's clearly visible, in all its grand dilapidation, from the main road, to which it was once connected. Though long dead, the village has had an afterlife so persistent that it's no surprise to find both it and the now broken and overgrown tracks that once led to it still confidently marked on some road maps.[9]

In economic terms, Jánovas is perfectly viable. It stands in a fertile plain on the west bank of the river Ara, just upstream from where it is joined by another, narrower watercourse. Cattle graze in the fields. The buildings, though in ruins, show a former solidity common in this once proudly independent region: decorative lintels and porches on the well-

proportioned houses, a sizable school, a mill, and, on a hillock, the parish church. Cars full of weekenders pass on the eastern side of the valley, many of them from France. Families swim in the river. Occasionally a coach stops to decant a group of walkers. The view from the turnout is worth pausing for: on the right, a gently rising plain dominated by the Monte Perdido to the north, its snowmelt pouring into the impetuous Ara; the spectacular ruins of Jánovas in the foreground; and immediately on your left, a high, tight ravine squinting down at the slopes toward Ainsa. This is the landscape that gave Jánovas its long life but that also eventually killed it, along with a dozen or more farms on the other side of the road.

What put everyone in flight was the threat of a reservoir. From a hydraulic engineer's point of view, the area is blessed with *caudal*, an abundant water supply, together with *desnivel*, a good drop. All that was needed, it seemed, was to throw a dam across the ravine. The valley would be full of water; formerly dry, distant land below it would flourish; and far-off cities would be bright with electricity.

The scheme, like many others of its type, was first mooted in the 1910s.[10] José Durán y Ventosa, a prosperous Catalan well connected politically in Barcelona, bid for two water concessions, one of them around Jánovas, the other a few kilometers upstream, in Fiscal. Objections were raised locally, and in 1913, before the case was decided, rights in the scheme were transferred to an industrialist with even more political influence, this time in Madrid. Various aspects of the project were sent back for revision and therefore not made public. Five years having passed since Durán's initial proposal, the rights reverted to him in 1916, by which time he was president of Aplicaciones Industriales, a company that owned similar interests in the Cinca valley, immediately to the east. The rivers Ara and Cinca meet in Ainsa. Subject to various conditions, the Jánovas bid was officially approved in 1917.

Here were the germs of much of what was to follow: the elusive transfer of exploitation rights between different companies; large-scale national political interests operating in the background, together with the openings they provided for individual self-enrichment; opportunities to play off one set of local allegiances against another. Unusually, the outcome was stalemate, though that isn't how it felt to those most intimately affected.

In a context that invites cynicism, it's important to remember that genuine national interests were at stake and that large-scale public works could be the salvation of local communities. Nowhere does Llamazares face up to this question (any more than he deals with the real arguments of the green movement, dismissed in one of his essays).[11] Thousands of young people moved away, like the fictional Andrés, whether to Spanish cities or abroad; many depopulated rural towns in Spain have a memorial to "the Emigrant." For every home the Ara might have drowned, a reservoir here might have saved two or three households on higher ground by bringing paid work for the men as laborers, income from providing accommodation and food for itinerant workers, and, later, if on a smaller scale, jobs at the hydroelectric plant itself. First, though, the project had to be started. Almost immediately, Aplicaciones Industriales came up against the problem besetting most similar schemes in the Mediterranean: the near irreconcilability of the seasonal demands of irrigation and energy. It was also in competition with another company, Hidroeléctrica Ibérica, which had acquired concessions of its own in the nearby Cinca valley.

Hesitations and delays caused impatience in Madrid. In 1928, acting through a new water agency, the Confederación Hidrográfica del Ebro, the government issued a warrant instructing Aplicaciones Industriales to deliver plans for the works for which it was holding concessions. The firm responded with three elaborate schemes, each on a different scale and each involving quite different consequences. They weren't approved but weren't exactly rejected, either, and while they sat on the commodious shelves of the Confederación Hidrográfica, the political situation changed and changed again, from dictatorship to Republic to civil war and back to dictatorship. For fifteen years, nothing more was heard of the plan.

In 1944, when the European outcome of the Second World War had become clear, Aplicaciones Industriales stirred once again, applying for state aid to proceed with its dam at Jánovas. The state, though, was financially broke and badly short of most kinds of building material, and of fuel. The regime refused to help while simultaneously, and with implicit menace, declaring that completion of the project was in the public interest. Aplicaciones Industriales sold its concessions to another new company, Iberduero, itself formed from two previous enter-

prises, one of which was the original firm's competitor in the region, Hidroeléctrica Ibérica. Among Iberduero's main engineers was someone who had been senator for the province, and the firm was fast building up a regional monopoly, exerting quasi-colonial power through its control of a network of nineteen reservoirs. In one village in the Cinca valley, the priest, the doctor, and the schoolmaster were all on the company's payroll. Before long the situation in one of Jánovas's neighboring towns, Boltaña, was similar.

Life in Jánovas itself continued much as before. It had been so long since the dam was first mooted that people had stopped believing it would ever be built. Some people had moved away, but that was true everywhere, and there were still enough children to fill the village school. Families kept their farms going, worked on their houses and barns, stored produce, held the annual fiesta in September. Then, in 1960, a surveyor's airplane began to make low flights over the valley. A year later, owners of the farms were called to a meeting at which they were told that their land had been assessed as being of poor quality and would eventually be compulsorily purchased but that if they sold voluntarily now, they would get a better price. Government in turn brought pressure to bear, instructing some neighboring farmers that their land was needed for forestry and that they must either turn it over to trees at their own expense—in the process inevitably depriving themselves of their livelihood from annual crops on the same land—or sell up. The mayor of Jánovas argued for prices based on recent sales in the area but was ignored. Three times, he and the owners of the most sizable *fincas* affected traveled to Huesca to appeal to the province's governor, but he wouldn't see them. One by one, householders made separate deals with Iberduero and left. At the village fiesta in 1961, the mayor himself fell into conversation with some friends who had come back for the occasion from Barcelona, where they were working for a German-owned business. He told them about the fix he was in and, a few days later, received a telegram telling him there was a job at the firm if he wanted it. He went that September and, once established, was later joined by his family.

In rural Spain, a mayor leaving his village is like a captain abandoning ship. Three of the most prosperous farmers who had so far held out immediately followed him. The money they got for their land was

just enough to pay for a city apartment. One went to work in a factory; another became a taxi driver. The third, Milagros Palacio, head of a family that had been particularly determined to stay, later described their confused feelings:

> We hung on for three years together, seeing what was going on, wondering whether to go or not to go and, if so, where. It was worst before we decided. Making the decision itself was terrible, sure, everyone crying all day, every day, but once we had decided we said: OK, forward march. We were together, that was what was most important. We decided to go to Barcelona and settled in there without any problems. After all, if we had stayed behind we would still have been facing the unknown . . .
>
> Part of what's terrible is being forced to go, is that someone else can choose whether you go today or tomorrow. At least we weren't thrown out of our house on to the street. Yes we were thrown out, but we didn't have to see it like that. And while it was hard not to look back, it also helped us to get to grips with our new situation. We just had to keep our eyes on the future.[12]

Not every family in Jánovas owned property. Emilio Garcés, a shoemaker, with his wife, Francisca, and their six children, and Antonio Buisán, a carter, with his wife, María, and their five, rented their houses and a little land by bartering their labor along with some of what they could make and grow. While the bulk of the village population drained away, they and others hung on. They knew that in places where dams had been built, the sheer physical scale of the operation had, in the end, forced everyone to leave. Here, nothing was happening, so why worry? Whenever anyone from Iberduero harassed the laconic Garcés, he told them not to worry, he wouldn't drink too much of their water.

Thus far, Iberduero had in its own terms made only one false move, but it was a big one. Eager to find an additional, cost-free inducement to owners thinking of parting with their property, it had included a clause in its standard agreement by which—notwithstanding the fact that, on paper, the company would own the farms in question—the vendors could continue to enjoy use of their former lands, rent-free, until work on the reservoir began. As soon as the key owners had sold

up, the firm regretted what it now saw as this overgenerosity. Some of those who, under the clause, were still entitled to farm their old property argued that, to do so, they needed to live on it. The company responded by dynamiting a few houses, claiming that they had become dangerous. Once again, the provincial government of Huesca played its part, this time in the form of posing questions about the village schoolmistress, Cipriana Bartolomé. Told that everyone was satisfied with her work, the education department bided its time. Three other schools in the area were closed down while the one in Jánovas carried on, but in the summer of 1965, Bartolomé fell pregnant. She was granted maternity leave from the beginning of the school year, but a substitute wasn't appointed until mid-November. Meanwhile, it was decided that the teacher's house, on the top floor of the school building, needed to be replaced. Iberduero, the building's owner, vigorously set about demolishing it. The parents of such pupils as remained at the school now feared not only for the educational progress of their offspring but also for their safety.

In 1961, 260 people had still been living in Jánovas. By the spring of 1965, there were only 20, but they were tenacious. Although, or perhaps because, Iberduero was still far from having resolved the financial and technical problems involved in making its dam, the company was incensed by what it now regarded as illegal squatters. If it didn't yet have the means to drown them, it could certainly make their lives difficult, and set about doing so. Roads joining the village to its neighbors were dug up. High-tension electrical cables were strung low above the roofs. A windmill was knocked down, irrigation ditches were filled in, crops were spoiled. With little to lose, and some pleasure in playing David to the company's Goliath, the remaining families still hung on. Years passed. The Buisáns' children grew up and followed some of their friends to Barcelona. Antonio, now a widower, stayed behind and died in the village in 1969.

In 1971, Iberduero applied for a change in the classification of the farms it had acquired, from irrigated land to dry. An official inspection noted blandly that the former irrigation ditches were broken down, and permission was duly granted. So it came about that, sixty years after the first plan to turn this part of the Ara valley into a lake, it was designated a desert.

. Overlooking what was still, to the unofficial eye, a pleasantly fertile region stood the parish church, dedicated to San Miguel. Restored in the sixteenth century and decorated inside with Byzantine-style wall paintings, the building had retained its twelfth-century porch, a Romanesque puzzle of four round arches on pillars. If local resistance to Franco's great hydroelectric schemes seemed to betoken some kind of radicalism, it was countered by Falangist motifs on monuments in the little graveyard, one dating from as late as 1960. Still, the church itself, with its long history, helped to keep up the squatters' morale at least until the winter of 1971, when, shortly before Christmas, a tractor and trailer arrived outside and some workmen carried out the saints' effigies and piled them into the trailer, in Emilio Garcés's words, "like firewood."

It's hard to convey the depth, the intimacy, of such a violation. Spanish processions in Holy Week and on the saint's day of any parish depend on the devout fiction that effigies in some sense actually *are* the holy people they represent, brought back to life. As recently as 2008, in an old town that has long been a sophisticated dormitory of Madrid, I was among a group of visitors refused entry to the parish church during its normal opening hours, the day before Good Friday, because, inside, statues were being dressed for tomorrow's procession. But in Spain's intensity of local feeling, the church and its physical contents matter in ways that don't depend solely on religion. They belong to you and you to them, like soccer cups or regimental insignia; like the family china, too: something bought, owned, and handed down. "They were ours," Emilio Garcés said of the statues. "The village people paid for them, pro rata, after the civil war." Such possessiveness is strongest at times when the saints are particularly needed—especially your own saints, the ones you or your church are named after, each of whom is your particular ally in heaven, like a cousin who works in the town hall. When everyone with power is against you, when even your neighbors have gone, who else can you depend on? Off the saints went, though, in their trailer, and were never seen again. After them, the church's fine porch was dismantled and taken up the road to be reassembled in Fiscal, where it still stands. Ever since, the church has been used as a cattle shed.

Jánovas was now almost utterly deserted. Emilio and Francisca Garcés still lived there, though he was out working all day. Their children joined them at weekends, and some of the Buisán family came back in the summer months. The only other visitors were members of the Guardia and people employed by Iberduero. The provincial governor had stopped the company from dynamiting houses, but intimidation continued. One day, someone blew up the small outbuilding in which Francisca kept her rabbits.

If this sounds like petty feuding, so it may have been. While many local people admired the couple's resistance, others were frustrated by it. There was a feeling that they were the reason the dam was not being built and the surrounding villages were still waiting for the work it would bring. This wasn't true, and in the early 1970s, to the many practical reasons why the project had been held up a new one was added in the form of nuclear power, eagerly embraced both by the aging Franco and by Iberduero itself, partner in a new nuclear installation in Burgos province. Perhaps Jánovas's exiled saints were getting busy. Franco died in 1975, and Spain began its long-awaited but still slow and uncertain transition to democracy. Iberduero's attention, meanwhile, was no longer on the Ara valley. Realizing this, and aware that the most recent concession was about to expire, some of the previous owners and their families formed a group and announced their intention to return to cultivating the lost lands. At ten in the morning on September 30, 1980, fourteen men born in Jánovas drove tractors into the fields. While legal skirmishes continued and Iberduero yet again renewed its pretenses at beginning work on the dam, another new element, more powerful than tractors, took the villagers' side: the media, now free of censorship. In 1984 a national TV program went out as part of a popular series called "Everyday Life." It told the story of a young woman who had chosen to move out of Madrid and make a new life in the Pyrenees, up the valley from Jánovas. All Spain saw footage of the beautiful abandoned village. Members of the indomitable Garcés family were interviewed. Although the conservative local press was censorious of what it described as an attack on Aragón and its irrigation needs, a new ecological organization based in Zaragoza saw an opportunity to show that environmentalism meant protecting human beings as well as other

living creatures. Pressure groups from other parts of Spain, especially ones affected by dams, joined in.

Many issues are still unresolved—particularly ownership of the properties, which a government concerned about future energy needs is perhaps understandably loath to see relinquished. The ratio of involvement by state and private enterprise has shifted, and in the process, Iberduero has been absorbed into another company, Eléctricas Reunidas de Zaragoza, part of the huge, now predominantly Italian-owned, multinational ENDESA (Empresa Nacional de Electricidad, SA). New concerns, particularly environmental ones, have made themselves felt. National legislation in the second half of the 1980s provided mechanisms for imposing socioeconomic and environmental conditions on dam construction.[13] Often, though, projects went ahead without the required investigations, and by 2000 the European Union had taken Spain to the European Court of Justice for failures in implementing its own environmental impact laws. The action gave powerful moral support to local ecological groups—for example, in Navarra, where the concerns of ornithologists were for many years able to prevent the filling of the Itoiz reservoir, its dam built at a cost of 166 million euros in the 1990s. Tourism has played its part, and here, activists have been able to make an impression on government ministers. In two successive years at the end of the 1990s, different officials from the Ministry of the Environment spent holidays in properties at the disposal of the national parks of Ordesa. Jánovas is on one of the two roads leading to the park from the south, and the results of decades of abandonment are visible all around. Despite intense political wrangling and obstruction, the ministry now declared that a reservoir would have a damaging effect on the local environment.

The *Heraldo de Aragón* gave the latest of its verdicts on the saga:[14]

> If Jánovas is a special case, it is not only because all the human cost involved has turned out to have been futile . . . but because the length of the whole process typifies the abuses committed in the Pyrenees in the name of water regulation. It speaks, too, of the deep social problems which have built up over decades and which led to the mistrust and rejection which still meet new hydraulic schemes . . . Jánovas is a lesson which cannot be ignored. Schemes like it cannot be imposed by

one region on another, or treated as a sacrifice to be borne at any price in the name of the general interest.

In focusing on regional rights, the article speaks to its time: one in which Spain's highly devolved political system makes national planning increasingly difficult, at least when what's at stake is redistribution of resources. A hydraulic expert briskly summarized the conservative position to me: "Why should we send water from the north to irrigate farms in Murcia [in the southeast] when the only people it will bring work to there are Moroccans?"[15] The question is not just national but global, and new kinds of discourse, and new technologies, are needed to deal with it. It's all too easy, both from a local point of view and in the cause of nostalgic conservationism, to say that Jánovas and its surroundings should be restored: either give the properties back to their original owners or extend the national park to include them. Like so much of Europe, the place could be a museum of itself. But here as in other ways in the past fifty or sixty years we've surely been too busy with our past, too ready to let it distract us from the present, let alone the future.

Historically, Jánovas is just one manifestation of the continual battle of large interests against small, distant against immediate. But it is also about the tensions between private industry and the state—even at a time when the latter seemed all-powerful—and between ordinary people and the common concerns of both. The story of Ribadelago is the same yet also the opposite.

The people of Ribadelago have always respected the power of water. As is suggested by its name, "Lake Shore" stands a short distance upstream from the graceful Lago de Sanabria to its east. On every other side it is surrounded by the Sierra de la Cabrera. These are the placid highlands along Spain's border with Portugal, north of Bragança: woods, grazing land, and rivers and lakes full of trout. Ribadelago's nearest market town, Puebla de Sanabria, is eighteen kilometers away by what was until recently a dirt road: a serious little castellated place on a hill at the other end of the lake. Now the area is a natural park, and the roads are modern and clearly signposted.

The lake is fed by a confluence of rivers and brooks, biggest among them the Tera, which hurtles down from the Sierra's snowcaps three thousand feet above the village. Though the watercourses are cheerful in summer, they can be fearsome when the snow melts fast or in a rainstorm, so the houses of Ribadelago have always been built of stone, on rocky hillocks high enough and strong enough to send the wildest natural torrent on its way. As if to soften the otherwise defensive impression the buildings might give, many have fragile, timbered upper floors that hang over the narrow streets like staterooms on a galleon. It's an evolved architecture, made for and from its surrounding elements with hard work and long-accumulated local knowledge. What happened to it in 1959 showed the impotence of such knowledge once national technological demands came to dominate even the remotest regions; the fragility, too, of individuals under a dictatorship.

Once again, here was a depopulated mountain range, rainy in the autumn, covered with snow in the winter, squandering millions of cubic tons of much-needed water, with all its potential energy—much of it, in this case, in the direction of Portugal. In the middle decades of the twentieth century, including under the Second Republic, a network of reservoirs was created between Orense and Zamora: Las Portas, Bao, Cernadilla, Prada, Valparaiso, Ricobayo. Toward the eastern end of this zigzag and at its highest point was the Embalse de Vega de Tera, completed in 1958.

Spanish engineers were among the best trained and the most highly regarded in the world, but they were contending with three difficulties. First, although Spain had recognized the need for water regulation early on, it had not kept records of rainfall in any systematic, locally based way. Because the focus was on drought, no one knew quite how *wet* any given place could be. Second, the regime was still short of both money and raw materials. Third, it was in a hurry. The rising dam was linked by two curving walls of mountain to the village of Ribadelago below. At the foot of this giant bobsled run, villagers listened anxiously to stories of poor materials, hasty workmanship, supervision casual to the point of negligence. Soon after the reservoir was filled, the gates designed to regulate any overflow began to rust. The winter of 1958–59 was exceptionally wet, and the reservoir filled up.

Late on the cold night of January 9, 1959, the dam burst. The amount of water tipped down the mountainside could have filled the baths of 32 million people, so the fact that only 144 died says more about Ribadelago's size than about the physical scale of the event. Whole households disappeared: men, women, children, farm animals, pets, furniture, tools, toys, food. One hundred and sixteen of the human bodies were never recovered. Today, scuba divers turn up the occasional chamber pot, but most of what was hurled into Lago de Sanabria, if it hasn't rotted away, is buried deep under silt.

Franco's press reported the event as a natural disaster and focused on a small miracle, one that satisfyingly linked the technological age with a hint of divine protection. According to *La Vanguardia* four days later, a security guard from the electrical installation had dashed to the church and rung the bells as a warning. Although most of the church building was washed away, the bell tower remained. It was left to the skeptical to observe that because church bells are very heavy, bell towers have to be strong. If only the builders of the dam had been similarly prudent! In the trial that eventually followed, ten overseers were found guilty of neglect and given one-year prison sentences, which were soon commuted. Compensation was meanwhile paid at the rate of 85,000 pesetas per man (in terms of purchasing power today, roughly $9,500), 75,000 pesetas per woman, and 25,000 per child. About half the survivors took the opportunity to move away, most of them to Madrid.

A new village was built beside the lake, to house the remaining homeless. With superb insensitivity, someone decided to name it Ribadelago de Franco.[16]

Eight months before the Sanabria dam broke, a young writer who knew the hydroelectric construction industry firsthand published a novel that was shortlisted for the influential Premio Nadal. *Central eléctrica* ("Electric Power Station") is one of many works that contradict the still-widespread idea that Francoist censorship prevented any form of intellectual or creative opposition.

Jesús López Pacheco was in his late twenties, had published two well-received books of poetry and one of short stories, and worked on

a literary magazine called *Índice*. (The title referred sardonically to the Vatican's *Index Librorum Prohibitorum*, a list of books that Catholics were forbidden to read.) In 1956 he was one of the organizers of a formative though short-lived literary pressure group, the Congreso Universitario de Escritores Jóvenes (University Conference of Young Writers). It was suppressed by the regime, and López Pacheco was briefly imprisoned. Yet his new novel was published in April 1958 by Ediciones Destino,[17] and although some of his subsequent work was banned, he was able to publish it abroad and came and went freely between Spain and literary events in the Soviet Union, Cuba, and elsewhere. Perhaps the regime hoped he would leave, as eventually he did—though not until 1968, when he took a university post in Canada.

In a way, the story of *Central eléctrica* tells itself: dam builders come, a community is rehoused, and its former lands and houses are submerged. The conflict between country and town, past and present, poor peasants and entrepreneurial engineers, is ineluctable. Two rebellions are easily dealt with: a gang of men from the village, armed with nothing but stones and flaming torches, makes little impression beyond breaking some of the construction workers' windows, and is seen off quickly by the Guardia Civil; an old woman called Vitorina, who sits obstinately on the roof of her house while the waters rise around her, is carried away in a motorboat, still shouting. These episodes are moving because of their ineffectuality and also because López Pacheco knows his characters' situation so well: the new houses to which they are moved have more bedrooms than they are used to or think they need, while providing hopelessly inadequate accommodation for animals; and the land they are given to replace their poor, dry, but long-worked and deeply fertilized farms is barely cultivable. He also shows that there's little to distinguish the farmworkers from the laborers on the dam; many of the latter, in fact, have taken the work because their farms no longer exist. Ordinary human beings, in this account, are the impotent slaves of remote interests, figures in a calculus that assumes, among other things, that three or four hundred of the labor force will be killed in accidents on a project of this scale during an eight-year construction period, and that the loss of a me-

chanical digger, washed away when part of the dam bursts, is more
regrettable than the drowning of three men.[18] Here again, López Pacheco is good on practical details: how different the earth smells
where there's an unexpected buildup of water; how a rescue party gets
a man and a boy out of a powerful, unpredictable flood; how the itinerant workforce turns itself into a convoy to travel to its next job, its
next home.

The novel doesn't go so far as to say that building the hydroelectric
plant is wrong, though it nowhere gives any sense of the needs of people
far away from the flooded village, and it satirizes government officials
and industrial bosses as complacent, ignorant, and cynically uninter-
ested in the fate of those their decisions affect. Automation of the dam,
for example, will make redundant most of those who have recently
taken jobs there. The project has already had some bad press as a result
of fatal accidents, so it's decided that the new technology can wait until
after an opening ceremony at which local people will be mollified by
long speeches, a fiesta, and a handing out of medals and certificates.
The event backfires: one construction worker can't collect his medal
because he has been imprisoned for taking part in the earlier protest,
so his father uses the opportunity to plead for mercy on his behalf, and
the redoubtable Vitorina, finding herself next to a microphone—an innovation enabled by the electricity brought by the dam—manages to
shout, "You threw us off our lands, you flooded our village," before being hauled away.[19] As far as the reader of the novel is concerned, the
point has been made more fully by the enlightened Andrés Ruiz, forty
pages earlier:

> This dam was made from reinforced concrete and human bodies . . .
> Two men died stuck in the cement and there they'll stay. The pace of
> the work was so rapid that they couldn't pull their bodies out . . . Did
> you hear yesterday that hundreds of men were on the move? Their vil-
> lage and their land were flooded and in exchange they were given jobs
> on the dam. But the work has only lasted eight years and now they
> have no village and no land: the new town made for them is no use to
> them, isn't "theirs," and the land is barren. So they've been given elec-
> tric light and some medals, and we've let some of them be locked up

for what we, on the basis of our own laws and our own idea of justice, treat as a horrific crime. I don't know, but, to me, this doesn't exactly seem like civilization. Something's missing.[20]

It's a sentiment you might find in a work by Arthur Miller or Arnold Wesker. The difference is that it was published under the *dictadura*.

4

• •

Franco's Crypts

Monuments, Museums, Commemorations

Reading the recent past out of (and into) your physical surroundings is hard to avoid in Spain; painful, too. Dams are one example; war memorials, another. Plaques listing the "glorious fallen" are found, of course, in the town squares and village churches of many European countries. To the British, in particular, finding such monuments in Spain doesn't immediately seem odd. But here the names recorded are those of only half the fallen: people who died, in the Nationalist formula, "for God and Spain," fighting, that is, against the government and for the rebel party, whose insignia the memorials usually display, along with the name of the Falangist leader José Antonio Primo de Rivera. Rafael Torres is among many Spanish writers who have commented on this division. From the day the civil war ended, Torres insists, Franco remorselessly divided Spain into winners and losers, and its dead into two corresponding parties: those whose names are engraved on the fronts of buildings and in churches and, "on the other side, the unnamed, those buried in common graves under spadefuls of oblivion."[1]

In terms of a war's immediate aftermath, such a situation is arguably inevitable: as Albert Camus said, commenting on his version of *Antigone*, in which a brother on one side of a conflict is honored and his sibling on the other side left to rot on the battlefield, "Antigone is

right, but Creon is also right."[2] The issue is how long you go on rubbing in the point. Under Franco, this was the job of a national Comisión de Estilo en las Conmemoraciones de la Patria (Commission on the Style of Patriotic Commemoration), founded as early as February 1938. Its members included art critics, clergy, and powerful individuals such as Pilar Primo de Rivera, sister of José Antonio, and it set out procedural and stylistic guidelines that ensured that a stultifying mix of uniformity and militarist pomp was stamped not only on the churchyards, town halls, and plazas of Spain, but also on its wider landscapes. One result was a big abstract monument to the Sixty-Second Division, at the side of the road between Burgos and Santander, described at the time as combining "monolithic weight with a design both futuristic and reminiscent of traditional martial iconography."[3]

Even on the right, what one Falangist called this "monumentalo-mania" didn't find universal favor,[4] and it's easy to imagine its impact on the other side, at the time and later. Many of the memorials were defaced by descendants of Republicans who were killed or imprisoned, and recently, as a result of legislation about cultural memory, most of the more flagrant have been removed. The once-omnipresent equestrian statues of General Franco have been put into cold storage, and new names have been given to streets and squares that previously commemorated him and his generals.[5] But you get an idea of the durability of the divisions involved if you attend a strange ritual that takes place every year on November 20, in a gloomily grand modern temple not far from the Escorial, high in the Guadarrama mountains, a short drive from Madrid: Franco's crypt.

By an ironic coincidence, November 20 is the date of the death not only of Franco in 1975 but also, earlier, of José Antonio Primo de Rivera, killed in a Republican prison in 1936. There are good reasons for thinking that Franco had an opportunity to save José Antonio's life but that, with the ruthlessness toward potential rivals that helped bring him to power and keep him there, he deliberately botched it.[6] Subsequently, however, he contributed to the Falangist's apotheosis as chief martyr of nationalism by having his body dug up and reburied in the palace cathedral of imperial Spain, the Escorial. This was only the first stage in José Antonio's post mortem ascent. From the earliest days after victory, Franco planned, among other celebrations and revenges, to

make the biggest, most religiose war memorial in the world. It stands in a spectacular park. At its highest point rises a 150-meter-tall stone cross. Beneath the cross on one side is a windswept area, something between a plaza and a parade ground, flanked by a Benedictine abbey, a choir school, and a now little-used building that originally housed a Francoist school of social science. On the pinnacle's other side sprawls a vast esplanade giving views over miles of surrounding countryside, much of it now a national park. The two areas are joined by an underground cathedral tunneled into the mountain: the Basilica of the Holy Cross of the Valley of the Fallen. Most of those reinterred there in the 1960s had fought for what Franco and his allies described as "the Crusade"—despite the fact that, as the novelist Juan Benet used to say, "In the civil war there were two Crusades."[7] Later, Franco was persuaded to let in the remains of some Republicans, as long as it could be shown that they were Catholics. But there has never been any mistaking which side the place celebrates. Least in doubt on this score were those who excavated and built it between 1941 and 1959, the majority of whom were political prisoners.[8]

Once the cruciform basilica was complete, the remains of José Antonio Primo de Rivera were moved yet again. His tomb is on the nave side of the transept, between the congregation and the high altar. Opposite it, between altar and choir, lies Franco himself, the only person in the building to have died of old age.

The Falange still has a powerful allure for some Spaniards. Its members quickly became the Nationalists' hard men, the regime using their near uncontrollability as a powerful threat. But in its original form, the movement was philosophically inclined, artistic as well as religious, its patriotism inflected by a strong sense of history. I wondered whether these aspects were in the mind of a serious young monk whom I watched standing in silence beside José Antonio's flower-covered memorial slab on the morning of November 20, 2006.

It was a Monday, and on Mondays the Valle de los Caídos is closed to the public. Whether out of mere adherence to routine, or as a way of heading off a continuation of the neo-Nationalist demonstrations that had filled the basilica that Saturday afternoon and Sunday morning, the main doors of the church were shut. Several miles away, at the entrance to the park from the main road, cars full of blue-shirted men

and women, flags hanging out their windows, were being turned away by implacable police. Inside, though, monks and choirboys gathered in the wide abbey cloister before descending through a series of damp, sloping tunnels joined by an elevator, into the mountain. The other end of this burrow opens into the north side of the basilica's chancel. Two outsiders followed the procession: a young man on a religious retreat and I. We were both staying in the abbey, I as a paying guest. In the windowless basilica, we were the entire congregation for the service of the day, which, though held in private, was a full sung requiem Mass for Franco's anniversary.[9]

It was the only calm ceremony of its kind. The basilica is open at weekends, and Masses are held there every Saturday afternoon and Sunday morning. Both services were packed that weekend: Christmas at London's St. Paul's Cathedral or the Cathedral of St. John the Divine in New York would be fair comparisons. (St. John the Divine is often said to be the longest Christian church in the world, at 186 meters, but Franco's crypt, though much narrower, runs to 260.) The Saturday Mass was a rowdy, jostling affair, some of the participants the worse for drink. Sunday morning was soberer but more menacing. The abbot managed to bring things under control, but only just.

The Valle de los Caídos is run by the Fundación Nacional Francisco Franco (FNFF), a body presided over by Franco's formidable daughter, Carmen Franco Polo, Duchess of Franco. Its stated aims are to spread knowledge about Franco in his "human, political, and military dimensions" and about the achievements of his regime.[10] Among its activities is the organization of the anniversary commemorations. In the 2007 Law of Historical Memory, the valley has a section to itself. Article 16 requires the place to be run "strictly along lines applicable to places of worship and public cemeteries." It prohibits, everywhere in the valley, "acts of a political character and celebrations of the civil war, its leaders, and of Francoism." (An earlier draft would have obliged the FNFF to include among its objectives "honoring the memory of everyone who died as a result of the civil war and of the political repression that followed it, with the aim of deepening an understanding of this historical period and the celebration of peace and democratic values," but this clause was dropped.) The foundation had already made some effort to demilitarize the November 20 commemorations, for example,

by issuing an instruction that, beginning in 2006, flags, military-style uniforms, and other predemocratic insignia were not allowed in the basilica. Despite a heavy police presence at the gate, though, and airport-style security at the main door, scores of people dressed in the Falange uniform of navy blue trousers and shirt with a red tassel, black boots, leather belt, and beret, paraded at both services. Most were men of all ages, but there were also uniformed women and small boys. At the Sunday morning Mass, several carried banners and stood in the front rows of the nave, having peremptorily ejected the elderly citizens sitting there. Everyone sitting farther back was prevented from seeing the high altar by a line of Nationalist flags.

During the Sunday service, a uniformed column moved slowly down the central aisle in pairs and took turns standing at the corners of José Antonio's tomb. The rotation was organized by a young man at the front. Four uniformed people fell in behind the previous honor guard, which gave a fascist salute, turned, and marched toward the back of the line. The new guard stepped forward to take its turn at the tomb, each member raising his right arm in salute. As the ritual proceeded, some old men and women in the congregation, not in uniform, offered to take part. Despite the smirks of the uniformed youth, there was a poignancy about these Francoist survivors, not least because they were so small in stature. Even more than in most countries, the young in Spain tower head and shoulders above working-class people of their grandparents' generation.

Outside the basilica after both weekend Masses, old anthems and chants—"¡Viva Franco!" and "¡España una, grande y libre!"—were loud, along with cheerful roars of "Za-pa-tero, hi-jo de puta" ("Zapatero [then prime minister], son of a whore") and other, newer slogans. As the Sunday service began, though, there was a crucial showdown inside. The elderly abbot, Anselmo Álvarez, broke away from the procession to the high altar and walked over alone to the big, uniformed men lined up facing it. There was an urgent-seeming conversation. I learned afterward that the abbot was telling them that their demonstration had to be silent: no chants, no singing. They argued with him. Several others joined in, until more than a dozen surrounded him: a threatening sight, with their rolled-up sleeves and bull necks. They beckoned over some of the oldest men in uniform, as if trying to match

the abbot's authority. He kept shaking his head. Eventually, with a pantomime of reluctance and injured pride, the neo-Falangists gave way and the service continued. The congregation, its older members long habituated to such collisions, was expressionless.

The abbot's dignified if belated action was a clear response to the mood that lay behind the government's proposals. So, too, was his sermon, which, to the annoyance of right-wing commentators, made no mention either of Franco or of José Antonio. Quoting Isaiah's words about the Lord's house being established on the top of the mountains, Don Anselmo said that the cross above the basilica is a symbol of peace and reconciliation. The dead being remembered today, whether buried there or anywhere else in Spain, no longer belonged to any side. To God, there were no losers or winners; His message was: live in harmony, get over your rivalries. The abbot went further: "Leave this place in peace: let it go on being a space for peace and spirituality."

There was more, including a highly debatable defense of the use of political prisoners in the construction of the crypt. (They were paid, the abbot said; they also earned remission of sentence; above all, they were free to choose whether to work on the project. In today's open Spanish society, only a monk could get away with calling that freedom.) He defended the religious values embodied in the valley and criticized the secularization of contemporary society, saying that in this respect as in others, reconciliation has to be a two-way process. And he directly addressed the issue of recuperating historical memory, arguing that in the Valle de los Caídos, memory has been alive and well for almost half a century. (The abbot, along with several other monks there, joined the community while Franco was still alive.) "We can't wipe away what has happened, pretending we got here from nowhere." Much of this was what anyone would have expected. But the abbot's pointed refusal to mention the old regime and his insistence on a bipartisan approach to history, modest enough in cold print, came across as a powerful reproach to the massed uniforms and flags, not to speak of what went on outside the basilica: the parade ground drill, the soccer crowd roars, the sight of some of the burlier men racing off afterward in a black Humvee.

After the weekend, the abbot spent some time talking to me. He rightly feared that the Law of Historical Memory represented, among

much else, an attack on the abbey, part of a wider attack on Spain's still deeply entrenched ecclesiastical power. On the teaching staff of the abbey choir school, laypeople now far outnumber monks. But the church has managed to hold on to the teaching of "citizenship" in state schools, despite the Socialists' attempts—overwhelmingly supported by public opinion—to hand the subject over to lay teachers.[11] Tussles between church and state are a well-established aspect of Spanish history, and one of the advantages of electoral democracies, from the point of view of long-lived institutions, is that their governments come and go. Don Anselmo didn't say this, or at least not in so many words, but some of what he did say showed that he and his supporters were playing a long game. He came across as a shy, intelligent, quietly passionate man, treated by the schoolboys as a favorite uncle while communicating unmistakable authority in the abbey's chapel and silent dining room. He was also as shrewd as one would expect of someone in his position. They had considered moving the monastery away from its present site, he volunteered disarmingly, but everyone wanted it to stay; it was regarded as central to the place. Besides, what was all this talk about monuments? Most European cathedrals and public places are full of statues, many of them to objectionable people. "When I show parties around the Valle de los Caídos, I say to them, 'Do you see any statues?' They are astonished: there are none."

Literally speaking, he was right. There is no effigy either of Franco or of anyone else—though among the basilica's adornments are some muscle-bound expressionist figures in granite, representing different branches of the armed forces. The point is that the whole place is a monument. From the imposing entrance gates, via four unfinished columns quarried in the sixteenth-century reign of Spain's emperor-king Carlos I and moved to the valley by Franco, across a long viaduct up to the basilica, its colonnaded abbey, and the cross visible from Madrid, it's surely the most imposing piece of fascist landscape art and architecture still in active use anywhere. Even the light fittings in the abbey entrance hall echo the Falangist symbol of a yoke and arrows. A guidebook to the site mentions that there was an early plan to include a military base there, a notion evident in the final design, which represents what the book calls "the last link in the chain of great temples to which the alliance between Church and conservative bourgeoisie gave

rise from the mid-nineteenth century, and of military-Nationalist monuments of the same period."[12] To a layman's eye, it is not unlike a bunker.

Could the Valle de los Caídos just be left alone, as the abbot pleaded? More than one of the monks pointed out to me that the demonstrations, which they seem genuinely to deplore, happen only once a year. For the rest of the time, the abbey carries on its quiet work of prayer, study, and teaching; the basilica acts as a parish church for the surrounding area; tourists come and go, though in much-diminished numbers; and the wooded hills and valley provide the politically unsqueamish with a spectacular picnic destination. It is, after all, part of Spain's *patrimonio nacional*. But herein lies part of the problem. Should a place supported by public funds be allowed to continue representing a disgraced regime? And, if not, what can be done with it?

There are difficult questions behind these, to do with representation, interpretation, and the role of the state. Put in the baldest terms: Is it a democracy's job to protect its citizens from works that embody antidemocratic attitudes? If so, how can it differentiate that process from totalitarian censorship, whether of the right or the left, ostensibly aimed at saving people from corrupting influences? Isn't it better— more democratic as well as more pragmatic—to trust people to form their own judgments? On the other hand, surely a phenomenon such as the Valle de los Caídos is a special case: an unambiguous celebration of military values as well as of the Francoist victory. What is there to interpret about it?

Even the most blatant memorials lose their historical resonance with the passing of time. Few French tourists in London care, or even notice, what Waterloo Station once stood for in terms of Anglo-French relations. As for the Gare d'Austerlitz in Paris, it took a German writer living in late twentieth-century England, W. G. Sebald, to give it back its original associations with a Napoleonic victory and to place them within the entire bloody context of European conflict. As many artists have shown, imaginative contemplation of a historical outrage can shake later generations out of indifference and into an understanding of what Primo Levi called "the nature of the offense." The most interesting suggestion about the Valle de los Caídos is that it should house a museum and study center devoted to the civil war.[13] On the face of things, the

idea is readily practicable. Without any loss of room for the normal number of worshippers at the heart of the crypt, much of the basilica could be used as exhibition space. There is also the long, atmospheric set of tunnels between basilica and abbey. A still more obvious site is the handsome building on the far side of the abbey plaza. Now an underused conference center, it once housed a center for social studies that, according to the abbot, trained some of those who negotiated the transition to democracy. What could be more appropriate than to turn it into a Spanish civil war research center?

Among other things, such a center could assist one of the more scholarly aims of the Law of Historical Memory, which concerns acquisition and care of archival materials, and improved access to them. It could also help coordinate and monitor related regional activities. The abbey might have a role in all this. Whatever the merits of separating religion and state, the church played an all-too-powerful part in the civil war, providing not only much of the support for Franco but plenty of the war's victims. Most of the monks I met were clever, well-educated, and good-hearted men, young as well as old. Involving them in a major work of commemorative reconciliation would be of symbolic as well as practical value.

What in Spanish is sometimes called the *musealización* (realization in museum form) of the civil war is revealing both in what's there and what isn't. While commentators have grumbled about the lack of anything in Spain to compare with the many museums throughout the world devoted to the Jewish Holocaust or the galleries in the Imperial War Museum given to Britain's experience of the two world wars, little attention has been paid to what actually exists. First and oldest is the archive and museum in Salamanca, the city that was and to some extent still is the intellectual hub of Spanish Catholic conservatism. Here, when in 1936 the liberal intellectual Miguel de Unamuno, supposedly *rector perpetuo* of the university, spoke bravely and directly against Nationalist glorifiers of war, he was shunned by his colleagues, hounded from his post, driven into virtual house arrest, and died a few months later. Here, too, early in the civil war, Franco established his headquarters with his brother-in-law and leading adviser Ramón Serrano Suñer,

who moved his family into the bishop's palace. As town after town fell to the Nationalists, troops transported local records en masse to Salamanca, on the basis of which card indexes were compiled of Republicans and trade unionists, together with a separate index of Freemasons, to facilitate future investigations and reprisals. There's some overlap: different pieces of information about an individual sometimes result in there being more than one card for him or her, but that scarcely diminishes the scale of the endeavor. The "Social Political" files contain 2,527,052 cards, augmented by 155,305 in the Masons' boxes, and a further 41,147 in a special list compiled for the Tribunal Especial para la Represión de la Masonería y el Comunismo (Special Tribunal for the Repression of Freemasonry and Communism). Setting aside collections of other kinds (for example, of photographs and military identity cards), the total number of items is 2,751,021.[14] They are still housed where they were compiled by Franco's secretariat, in a room next to what is now the archive's directorial office.

In 1938, Franco boasted to a British journalist that two million people had been indexed and that the list contained "proofs of their crimes." The Republican prime minister, Juan Negrín, had promised that if his side won, there would be a general amnesty. Franco said the opposite: he believed in what he called "the penalty of labor," a penalty that, thanks to the index, many would pay. Here is a card for Lorca— "Poet[;] his works treated of popular poems [a mistake for "themes"?]. Died in - - Granada" (how tantalizing the dashes are!)—along with ones for Ramón Sender, Max Aub, and Arturo Barea. Not everyone who offended made it into this specialized but arbitrary *Who's Who*. There's no card for Diego Ruiz Schacht, though there's one for a José with the same surnames, identified by a busy clerk as a "*Suboficial*," or NCO, in the Republican infantry. Waldo Ruiz Belmonte is missing, too, though it's tempting to wonder whether his fate was the result of a mix-up with Antonio Ruiz Belmonte, a *campesino* alleged to have been affiliated with the Communist Party. Even if you try to ignore the possibility of such mistakes, handling these cards chills the heart.

On my first visits, in the early years of the millennium, nothing about any of this appeared in the public display cases downstairs, which offered a somewhat perfunctory selection of leaflets, identity cards, and other materials. There was a heavy emphasis, however, on

the history of Freemasonry, presented (more or less in accord with Franco's opinion) as one of the chief enemies of Catholic, Nationalist Spain. An entire Masonic lodge had been relocated there as a trophy of war. A useful display of international involvement in the war, especially on the Republican side, was undermined by the fact that the captions were exclusively in Castilian (not even in Catalan, though it was from Catalonia that much of the strongest opposition to Franco came). Visitors did learn that there was a funny side to nationalism: its propaganda. One postcard of the time showed Spain as an island defended by three soldiers against an invasion from the east by pig-faced fat devils with green bodies and webbed feet, whom they were throwing back into the sea.

The raison d'être of the Salamanca museum, though, was and is its archive. An inevitable consequence of the end of dictatorship was that places that had lost their papers asked for them back—because they were theirs but also because they contained information specific to their communities. The long-running battle that ensued is among many illustrations of the local, devolutionary character of Spanish feeling about the war. Franco's nationalism was explicitly opposed to regional differences, including linguistic ones.[15] Democratic Spain, by deliberate contrast, is exceptionally respectful of them.

Barcelona, as the capital of Catalonia, was vociferous in demanding the return of what are in effect state papers, but successive claims were met with equally fierce opposition from Salamanca's conservative authorities, supported by public demonstrations. In 2006, copies having been made of a large portion of the Catalan material, the originals were returned to Catalonia, but regional feeling about the matter in Castilla-León ran so high that the street where they had been housed, known since the fourteenth century as the calle de Gibraltar, was officially renamed calle del Expolio, "Plunder Street." This was rectified in 2011 as part of a deal by which the remaining archives, continually reinforced by new acquisitions and housed for the most part in an extension to what's now called the Documentary Center for Historical Memory, was promised a nationally funded extra space together with the files of the Spanish Communist Party to put in it.[16] The collection's hard core, though, remains its rows and rows of drawers packed with typed or handwritten cards, each bearing someone's name and a note on his or

her political details, with references back to the documents from which they were gleaned.

The card files stay put in Salamanca because they were compiled there. Where historical documents and other materials "belong" is of course a question that affects all museums and historical collections. Greek statuary, Italian Renaissance paintings, African fetishes that once held religious power—whose are they and where and how should they be looked after? Notions of the museum itself, of what it does and for whom, have also been changing. Pedagogical concerns are involved, as are movements in the visual arts. New technology plays a big role, along with the development known to sociologists as "hypersegmentation"—a focus on increasingly small groups and areas—which is in turn facilitated by the Internet. All these tendencies can be seen in new museums intended to commemorate, inform about, and in some cases re-create aspects of "the experience of" Spain's civil war, places that in their very nature reflect the local cultures from which they have emerged.

Among the more successful in its own terms is in Cartagena—appropriately enough, given the city's role in some of the Mediterranean's most ancient conflicts, including the wars between the Roman Empire and the Carthaginian one from which it took its name: in Latin, Carthagonova, New Carthage. Cartagena is rich in historical sites and collections, among them the beautiful Museo Nacional de Arqueología Subacuática (National Museum of Underwater Archaeology) in the port, a vivid narrative display central to which are once-sunken Carthaginian galleys and their cargos of lead and silver mined in southeastern Spain. Powerful groups, we are reminded, have always exploited the less powerful; and industrial innovation, not least in means of extracting resources from the earth, has always involved brutality as well as courage and risk. In more recent times, mining, like agriculture, was one of the activities in which rich and poor came into conflict, and where the latter, influenced by the new ideas that had been spreading throughout nineteenth-century Europe, began to organize themselves. Miners' strikes in Asturias, on the opposite side of Spain, were among the first big manifestations of the conflict that would become civil war.

When war came, engineering skills that had been developed in

mining were to be used in an unexpected way: to protect civilians against an entirely new form of warfare—bombing. The port of Cartagena was the Republican naval fleet's main base; food and military supplies arrived here for the defense of Madrid, so it was an important target for the Nationalists. In October 1936, three months after the military rebellion began, city planners included among their main defensive projects the construction of a series of underground air-raid shelters. The biggest of these, designed to hold 5,500 people, was dug into the side of the hill on which the city's castle also stands.

Like the castle, the air-raid shelter is now in a sense a museum of itself: just going inside the *refugio* works powerfully on the imagination. But of course visitors don't necessarily know much about what it is they have to imagine, so there are wall displays with informative, if very basic, texts about the civil war, Cartagena's role in it, the construction of the shelter, and the kind of life that went on outside. A model of the city can be lit up to show where the other shelters were. There are a few (too few) objects from the period, but a short documentary film fills out some of the local detail. Then there is a room, or rather a chamber of the catacomb, in which drawings and paintings by today's local children are displayed in the hope of encouraging aspirations toward peace.

Two elements work particularly well: the experience of being in the tunnels themselves and an appreciation of community, of people working and fighting and taking shelter together and somehow surviving. Other aspects that are foregrounded seem more questionable. While it's true that Franco depended heavily on Italian and German air support, so did the Republican government on planes from the Soviet Union. There's a risk, in the way that Germano-Italian attacks on Cartagena are stressed, of encouraging an idea that Spain was attacked not by one side of itself, but by external powers. Second, the pacific nature of the shelter, emphasized in the display's use of the phrase "passive defense," combined with the sentimentalism of the children's art section, distracts attention from issues concerning the powerful attractions of conflict, its longevity as a human phenomenon. It might be more stimulating, if less "positive," to draw attention to the site's role in a continuum of human violence involving the castle above it and the naval ships that still use the harbor.

Similar doubts are raised by another *refugio-museo* farther along the coast, in another Republican stronghold, Almería. Here the visit is more strictly controlled—visitors have to book and are taken through the tunnels by a guide—but the rewards are greater. The journey is a kilometer long, and you emerge in a different part of the city, having been reminded, all along, of what it is you are standing below: this church, that plaza. The catacombs were particularly well constructed under the supervision of the municipal architect and two engineers, one a specialist in mines, the other in canals. They are lined with benches on which people could sit or sleep, and entrances and air shafts were thought out in terms of crowd control and of the possible effects of blast. Deeper chambers provided space for food storage and, notably, an operating room. The project was vast: four and a half kilometers in total, able to hold more than thirty-four thousand people (almost 70 percent of the town's population at the time), and because it was so well made, its contents are in near-perfect condition. Where today's children have provided Cartagena with artwork, those of 1930s Almería scratched their own drawings of airplanes in the refuge walls, where they can still be seen, just as the fully equipped operating room is still stained with blood. Again, though, too much is made of the site's peaceful character and of the fact that the airplanes that attacked the city were German. To call Almería "*un auténtico Guernica*," "a real Guernica," is to enter into a contest that embodies Spanish regional competitiveness at its worst. The town suffered, but it also played a powerful active role in the war and took part in its share of atrocities. You have to go back outside to the cathedral square to find any acknowledgment of the fact that the bishop of that time, Diego Ventaja Milán, whose statue is there, was murdered by Republican militias almost as soon as the war began. He had expected as much, and had rejected an opportunity to escape on a British ship.

Still, at least in Almería, both sides have their monuments. In some other Spanish towns, local divisions have resulted in a kind of commemorative paralysis. One of the most ferociously fought-over areas was Teruel, east of Madrid, a town held by initially weak Nationalist forces against which the Republicans mounted an offensive in the bitter winter of 1937. The aim was to deflect an anticipated attack on the capital. Initially this succeeded, but strong Nationalist reinforcements,

combined with infighting among Republican military leaders, led to the town's being recaptured a couple of months later. Losses on the two sides during the brief but savage campaign came to more than a hundred thousand. Visitors to the town today, though, learn nothing about any of this. In terms of public works as well as tourist information, the emphasis, instead, is on Mudejar architecture: buildings of the later Middle Ages whose craftsmen incorporated Muslim elements into Christian commissions. The great towers of Teruel's cathedral, churches, and market, with their elaborately interconnected, decorated arches, have been beautifully restored, and the social coexistence they embody, or at least can be thought to symbolize, deserves emphasis. Still, the fact that seventy years after the battle of Teruel, nothing—no substantial monument or museum display—commemorates the people of the town killed on both sides confirms some of the worst suspicions of the campaigners for historical memory.

Recently there have been thoughts about making a museum of the civil war in Teruel, with an ambitious plan, sponsored by the province and by a group of social scientists at the University of Barcelona called *DidPatri* ("Teaching and Heritage"), for a study center dedicated to peace and representing the entire war in innovative ways informed by comparable museums elsewhere in Europe and in North America.[17] In the current economic situation, though, such schemes have been more often announced than completed. Seville, which already has a military museum, announced in October 2008 that the former headquarters of the Nationalist general and propagandist Queipo de Llano were to be given over to commemorating the civil war, but little more has been heard of the plan.[18] So it's all the more impressive that, with next to no fanfare, a range of projects, including the completion of three local museums, one of them devoted to the civil war, has been going on in the small Andalucian town of Almedinilla, between Granada and Córdoba.

They owe their existence to an imaginative synergy between the local authority and a young historian trained as a classical archaeologist, Ignacio Muñiz Jaén, who spent childhood holidays in the area. Almedinilla has been growing fast, and while there's nothing to be said for the pompous chalets proliferating on its outskirts, the restoration of buildings in the picturesque center is being carried out with

sympathetic care. There was a motive for this in the existence of the remains of a sophisticated Roman villa, but those involved have gone much further, for example, by restoring an old olive oil mill as a museum of, among other things, the role played by the olive in the region's economy and ecology. The mill stands beside the river Caicena, and the display shows, too, how water has been deployed locally over the millennia. Attention is also paid to the region's flora and fauna. Some of the most formidable exhibits, though, come from two periods of wealth: the Roman era, during which Almedinilla, on the evidence of what archaeologists have found at the villa, was governed by an exceptionally cultivated and spiritually minded family; and the late nineteenth century, when machine presses made by a Spanish industrialist and, eventually, motor manufacturer of British descent, Ruperto Heaton, were used in the production of olive oil.

A particularly original aspect of the museum is housed separately, in another former agricultural building, at the foot of the slope on which the mill stands. This is the Aula del Campesinado, the Agricultural Worker's Hall, and what it exhibits is the role of activism by farm laborers in the growth of republicanism, and the movement's fate during the civil war. "Exhibits" is inadequate, though, to what the project does. "Museum," too, at least as traditionally understood, conveys little of what has been happening there. Together with colleagues and volunteers, Ignacio Muñiz has brought together archaeology and oral history, environmentalism and archival research, in ways that have been inspired by the work of the Association for the Recovery of Historical Memory and also—as in the cases of the association's founders and many of its members—by his own family background. Muñiz's paternal forebears were Republicans: his grandfather was an officer in the Garibaldi Battalion of the International Brigades. Like many Spanish families, they are divided: the woman Muñiz's father married had relatives on both sides. With these sensitivities in mind, he set up a series of summer camps for young people whom he and his helpers organized to record interviews with elderly residents of Almedinilla about their early memories. Meanwhile, the town's substantial archives were catalogued and investigated.

Muñiz read extensively in histories of the region: accounts of the civil war and of the relations between landowners and agricultural la-

borers over the previous century and the spread of socialist ideas. Crucial to all this was what happened there before and during the Second Republic. Inevitably, much of the story is similar to that of other regions of Spain. What fascinates, though, is the precise ways in which Almedinilla differed. The *ayuntamiento*, local authority, has almost always been characterized, if to varying degrees, by an enlightened liberalism, which it still displays. Historically, this attitude was reinforced by the number of relatively small property holdings in the area. *Latifundios*, feudal estates, existed, as throughout southern and western Spain, and their aristocratic owners—here, mainly the Marquess of Priego—built up their holdings by expropriating what had previously been common land, but what was less usual was that they were not Almedinilla's main agricultural employers. In the early 1920s, 86 percent of the town's permanent households owned some property. Small-scale ownership resulted in a variety of employment practices that benefited both residents and itinerant laborers. There was also more freedom when it came to where proprietors sold their produce. Again, these smaller employers being much closer to their workforce than were the Madrid-based aristocracy, the poor could count on a degree of local sympathy in hard times. Like the rest of Spain, Almedinilla endured frequent famines in the nineteenth and early twentieth centuries. In these circumstances, the *ayuntamiento* adopted two main policies—repressively liberal in the Gramscian terms that have influenced Ignacio Muñiz, but clearly well intentioned and, to the recipients, a lot better than nothing. It set in motion programs of public works—especially road building and the construction of municipal water supplies—to provide employment. And it sent strongly argued, even impassioned appeals to the bigger farmers not to divert produce away from the town for the sake of higher prices.

Almedinilla had its share of strikes, demonstrations, arrests, and seizures of land by one side and then the other. Not surprisingly, given its high proportion of property owners, it returned as many conservatives (chiefly, members of the Unión Monárquica Nacional) as Republicans to the local council in 1933. The mayor was a Catholic and a conservative, albeit moderate—"*nicetista*," after Niceto Alcalá-Zamora, first president of the Second Republic. But when farmworkers went on strike that summer, he wrote to his landowning constituents about

their responsibility toward what he called "the wretched predicament of our neighbors." He used the word *convecinos*, fellow neighbors, which implies something still more communitarian than *vecinos*, and went on to call them "our friends." In words that reverberate today, he said that these people were "besieged" by their sheer lack of any means of making a living. Children were begging for charity and, in this crucial phase of their lives, building up hatred for a society that paid no attention to them. The mayor pointed out that any troubles that had arisen so far in Almedinilla were mild by comparison with what was going on in neighboring towns. "All I can hope is that our more important landowners and farmers will heed my call to them to give work to those who need it, in a friendly spirit and without either side trying to stand on its rights."[19]

Many Spanish people at the time, particularly agricultural workers, had fallen for the simultaneously perfectionist and defeatist idea of the nineteenth-century Russian thinker Bakunin that to take part in established political processes such as elections is to capitulate to the system. Anarchism of this kind appealed to the lazy as well as the rebellious and individualistic, and by encouraging many of the poor to withhold their votes, it had the effect of making a vulnerable coalition of conservative landowners, churchmen, and military officers look stronger than it was. Muñiz disagrees with this interpretation of his work,[20] but many visitors will see it as one of the lessons the museum teaches, along with that of the inexorable widening of inequality in early twentieth-century Spain and the political polarization of rich and poor. By tracing these patterns in a relatively stable, amicable community, Muñiz poignantly suggests that what happened was needless. Even by the early months of 1936, the local branch of the Falange had attracted only thirty members, but after the coup, this number went up tenfold. Politically active Republican men were arrested and murdered. The wives and daughters of some of them had their heads shaved and were sexually molested, given purgatives, and paraded half-naked, helplessly shitting. Stories like these were told by survivors to Muñiz's volunteers, who recorded them. The fact that there is nothing special about them is what makes them so moving.

Most of those who spoke up were unwilling to name their persecutors, even if the latter were dead. Muñiz respects those decisions,

and there is nothing vengeful about his museum or about the book he has written out of his researches. But he is a historian, and details, including names, matter to him. His narrative lists, for example, every violent crime recorded by the *ayuntamiento* from the end of the nineteenth century, along with the culprits' names, partly as a way of showing that in normal times, Almedinilla was a reasonably peaceful place and one where politically motivated violence had been more or less unknown. It would have been inconsistent, then, to anonymize the civil war years, and while Muñiz doesn't breach his informants' trust, he does give the names of everyone who belonged to the seven Falangist squads that ran the town by 1937. Both the museum and his book achieve their impact by a mixture of objective juxtapositions and a reflective, in some cases poetic mood. One of the museum's exhibits, alongside agricultural tools of the time and political documents and newspapers, is a recent bronze sculpture titled *The Spanish Labyrinth*, after Gerald Brenan's famous 1943 account of the civil war.

The turbulent river Caicena, over which the Museo del Campesinado looks, formed part of the front line between Nationalists and Republicans in the civil war. These projects in Almedinilla are characterized by an imaginative receptiveness to the environment—from the values embodied in some of the artifacts excavated from the Roman villa to the imposition of Falangist emblems and street names in the formerly liberal town. The river has been a strong element in itself, one that formed the focus of a traveling exhibition about its role in the life of the region, and that figures, as a metaphor as well as in reality, in a documentary film shown in the museum. The day before I visited, there was a storm, and the river burst its banks, pouring mud, branches, and leaves into the streets of the town and breaking one of the museum's windows immediately above a model of the landscape showing where civil war troops had been based. If the museums of Almedenilla constantly remind us of the geophysical basis of the town's history, that environment still has unmediated ways of asserting itself.

There are, of course, more traditional ways of recording Spain's recent past. The house where Lorca grew up is well set out, both in terms of restoration and furnishing and as an exhibition of the artist's work,

pictorial, dramatic, and poetic. Exhibitions of local civil war photographs are common: a recent one in Lérida/Lleida brought home the actualities of conflict in the streets outside seventy years before. It's often the case in Spain, though, that the most powerful sites of memory are those where what has happened is *not* drawn attention to. The little bull brooding silently and enigmatically on top of its pillar in the center of Teruel can seem an apt enough symbol, and there are similarly potent ambiguities, evasions, and outright absences in many other places. Badajoz, near the southern border with Portugal, is one instance: an ancient strategic city where, in revenge for Republican activism, not least a particularly active approach to land redistribution, the Nationalists committed one of the civil war's first atrocities, rounding up any likely Republican sympathizers they could find, driving them down through the narrow streets toward the bullring and on through the tunnel by which, for centuries, the bullfight parade entered the arena, and machine-gunning them. The number of victims is disputed, but Jay Allen of the *Chicago Tribune* reckoned at the time that 1,800 were killed in twelve hours. The resulting lake of blood, he wrote, was "palm deep."

With a commemorative schizophrenia not uncommon in Spain, the former headquarters of the Sociedad Obrera "Germinal" in Badajoz, which now boasts a memorial plaque, stands in calle Regulares Marroquíes ("Moroccan Regulars Street"). I found no plaque, though, at the site of the massacre. Even the bullring itself was elusive. Standing close to where it should have been, I showed an elderly man the map bound into my copy of Richard Ford's 1845 *Handbook for Travellers in Spain*. He didn't seem surprised that the book was so old: physically, the centers of Spanish provincial towns tend not to change all that much. Still, there was a hint of embarrassment. Ah, yes, until recently the Plaza de Toros was where the map showed. But it had been moved. Now it was here, to the right of the map. The former Plaza de Toros had been pulled down and redeveloped as a conference center.

Where there have been arguments about physical monuments, they have centered, inevitably, on Francisco Franco himself, and particularly on the Pazo de Meirás, a late-nineteenth-century baronial house on raised ground in the middle of seven hectares of park not far from La

Coruña, in Galicia. Fully visible from the country road that runs in front of it, the façade is flanked by square, mock-medieval towers of unequal height. *Pazo* means "palace" in Galician, but it is often used for a more modest building—a grange, say. However you describe it, it is less good to look out from than up at. The surrounding country, close to the coast and within easy commuting distance of the regional capital, La Coruña, has been haphazardly built over, and a far-from-vernacular new housing development just outside the park wall to the northeast has obliterated the remains of a fourth-century castle. Not that the view is one that outsiders, until recently, had much chance of experiencing. Nor were they able to browse in the library, some of the contents of which were left by the house's most literary occupant, Emilia Pardo Bazán.

Spain's first important woman novelist and critic, and also its first vocal feminist, Bazán was nonetheless intensely conservative in various ways. A fervent Carlist and a terrific snob, she was delighted when in 1908, in her late fifties, the king gave her a Spanish title slightly grander than the papal one she had inherited, along with the estate, from her father. Often misleadingly described as a Spanish Zola, Bazán was, like her younger contemporary Yeats, particularly absorbed by the paradox of great old houses in the hands of unworthy owners—a theme she explored in one of her first successful novels, *Los pazos de Ulloa* (1886). It's not clear which of the book's characters we should sympathize with most: the innocent chaplain of the remote Galician castle, with his efforts to make order of its chaotic archives; the frail, passionately religious young woman who has married into it; or the children who grow up semi-wild there. At any rate, Bazán certainly doesn't have much patience with the hunting, shooting, hard-drinking philanderer ostensibly in charge.

What, then, would she have made of a ten-page spread in *¡Hola!* in August 2008? Here was the now-bulky figure of the former international long jumper José Campos, big white shirt jacket hanging over his black trousers, together with a model and TV presenter and various handsome, swarthy men in tailcoats, one of them tucking sunglasses into a white silk waistcoat and another, with hair on his shoulders, carrying a jeweled brown leather saddlebag. They and three hundred others had

come together for the wedding of one of the descendants of Francisco Franco, conducted in what the magazine described as "the strictest intimacy," in the chapel of the Pazo de Meirás.

By intimacy, what seems to have been meant was that *¡Hola!* wasn't invited—any more than was the bride's father, estranged husband of one of Franco's granddaughters. The family is celebratedly dysfunctional. José Campos, he of the long jump, is the latest of the numerous partners of the bride's aunt, María del Carmen Martínez-Bordiú y Franco, whose son Luis Alfonso de Borbón has taken to claiming to be king of France. One of Luis's Franco cousins, Jaime, has spent time in prison for domestic violence. All of which was cause enough for the family matriarch, the dictator's only child, Carmen Franco y Polo, Duchess of Franco, to have wanted to keep the press at bay.

But there was another reason, one to do with the house itself, which in 1938 became the first component in a portfolio of property acquired by Franco as spoils of victory in the civil war. In the initially rocky transition to democracy after his death, no measures were taken to recover any of this. Indeed, quantities of more portable property—including gold and silver medals bestowed on the *generalísimo* wherever he traveled in the course of his long reign—found their way into Swiss bank vaults. The duchess herself once suffered the embarrassment of being stopped by airport security on her way to Lausanne when a metal detector was activated by a large number of such decorations in her handbag. Once historical memory established itself on the Spanish political agenda, the family's houses and lands began to set off alarm bells, too.

How the Pazo de Meirás came into the Francos' hands is a story that could have been written by Emilia Pardo Bazán herself. She inherited the place from her father in 1890. Married in its chapel when she was seventeen, she had two children, but her increasing feminism and perhaps also her literary fame were hard for a conservative Spanish husband to take, and the couple lived separately, Emilia much of the time in Madrid, where she became the lover of the great Republican novelist Benito Pérez Galdós. She wrote prolifically—novels, hundreds of short stories, books of criticism, polemical journalism, especially about women's education—and was if anything more at home in the radical intellectual world of Unamuno and Azorín than in the aristo-

cratic one to which she aspired. She became the first woman chair of the literary section of the Spanish Athenaeum and in 1916 was made professor of romance literature at the city's Central University, though the male students routinely boycotted her lectures.

On her death in 1921, the Pazo de Meirás was inherited by her son, Jaime Quiroga y Pardo Bazán, an army officer who spent much of his career in Spanish Morocco. Jaime was married, with a son of his own, and also had an illegitimate son whom he refused to acknowledge, by a girl described by Pilar Faus in her two-volume biography of the novelist as "*de posición social inferior.*"[21] By a melodramatic twist that curiously echoed the plot of Pardo Bazán's novel *La tribuna*, this illegitimate son joined the Republican militia and, under cover of disturbances in Madrid as the civil war began, turned up with some other men at his father's house and killed both him and the legitimate half-brother.

Emilia's distraught daughter-in-law, who inherited Meirás, in due course sold both house and contents—including the library containing the writer's papers, Pérez Galdos's letters among them. The buyer was a consortium set up in 1938 by the governor of La Coruña and an industrialist. Their intention was to provide Franco with a country seat, partly to reward him for saving Spain from communism, Freemasonry, and international Jewry, partly to ensure that he would not lose touch with his native Galicia, and partly to enhance their own careers. (The governor subsequently became head of the *generalísimo*'s household; the industrialist, in addition to benefiting from a number of public works commissions such as the dam at Los Peares, became Count of Fenosa, a nonce title whimsically made from the initials of one of his businesses.[22]) Local mayors throughout the region were instructed to calculate how much everyone in their communities should contribute to a *subscripción popular* and, by way of encouragement, to make it clear that they would keep lists of those who did so. Once the purchase was complete, a few peasant families who lived inconveniently close to the *pazo* were bundled into military trucks, taken to a nearby lawyer's office, and told to sign over their properties. From then until his death, Franco spent part of every year in Meirás, using the house as a family retreat and also for government meetings and official entertainment. He called it his "little pocket parliament."

Not that he lacked choice of accommodation. Reluctantly dissuaded,

at a time when many people in Spain were starving, from making his main home in the 240-balcony Bourbon Palacio de Oriente in Madrid, he moved instead into the not-much-less-grand former royal hunting lodge, El Pardo. One of his aristocratic supporters, meanwhile, the Count of Las Almenas, made him a gift of a modern mansion, previously the home of a prime minister, in Torrelodones, midway between the city and the Escorial. Later, when a historic town house in the old part of La Coruña came on the market, that, too, was discreetly acquired by Franco's Ministry of Education, which in turn sold it by secret auction to another aristocrat, who had the dictator's wife's name put on the deed.

After Franco's death in 1975, his family gave up El Pardo; and when his widow died, they sold the Torrelodones place for a gratifying 300 million pesetas. But nothing was taken from them. Much of the success of Spain's transition to democracy depended on a combination of realpolitik with an admirable determination not to replicate the vindictive triumphalism that had characterized the caudillo in victory. Amid a prevailing, though far from unanimous, wish to forget if not to forgive, very many people who had served the former regime, from national and local politicians to soldiers and policemen, stayed in place. As far as the Pazo de Meirás was concerned, this meant that until quite recently, the family enjoyed the support, on the one hand, of the local mayor—who, handily, was also their pharmacist—and on the other, of a still-more-powerful figure, Manuel Fraga, architect of Spain's tourist boom under Franco, one of the authors of the 1978 constitution, and a founder of the conservative Partido Popular in both its current and earlier forms. By a happy stroke of fortune, Fraga became premier of Galicia in 1990, when he was in his late seventies.

Both men, though, along with many others broadly sympathetic to the Francos, were ousted in the new millennium. Nationally, Zapatero's left-of-center PSOE came to power in 2004. Galicia, meanwhile, is one of the regions that, after Franco's death, gained the kind of autonomy he had always proscribed and in 2005 acquired a socialist president. The *ayuntamiento* that controls Meirás was taken over in May 2007 by the left-wing separatist Bloque Nacionalista Galego. As it happens, the BNG's official spokesman belonged to one of the families evicted seventy years earlier from houses adjoining the Pazo de Meirás.

Among the dictator's most visible legacies were statues. It pleased
Franco to be depicted like great emperors of the past, on horseback,
and during his time in power a cavalry brigade of equestrian monuments to him was scattered throughout Spain. Over the thirty-odd
years since his death, they have gradually been taken into hiding—
including, in 2005, the one tourists had gotten used to seeing in Madrid's Plaza de San Juan de la Cruz. A particular problem was caused
by its counterpart in the central plaza of the Galician naval and fishing
port where Franco was born, El Ferrol. There's no shortage of residents
there who believe that the harm Franco did has to be weighed against
achievements they value. Some think that keeping Spain's troublesome
regions together was better than allowing devolution, just as they think
that defending Catholicism and the traditional family was better than
not doing so.

You don't have to be an admirer of Franco's to believe that remov-
ing all trace of an uncomfortable past is not the best way of dealing
with it. Still, the statue was a problem for El Ferrol, if only because
people kept painting it red and there were occasional attempts to blow
it up. Besides, the *ayuntamiento* had other matters to deal with. The
decline in shipping and in the fishing industry had brought unemployment while leaving behind an industrial coastline difficult to adapt to
tourism. The town's narrow, sloping streets were increasingly clogged
with traffic, especially around the Plaza de España. Underpasses were
needed, parking garages, new amenities.

Sometimes one solution brings another. A way of attracting visitors, it was suggested, might be to exploit El Ferrol's maritime history.
There was a handsome group of disused buildings around a dockside
courtyard that could be turned into a naval museum. A museum needs
a park, and there was one across the road, the Plaza Antón, that could
be tidied up. Such a park might benefit from modern works of art—
sculptures celebrating freedom of expression, for example, and honoring local heroes killed under the repression. The necessary plans and
commissions were put in hand. Along with them went major roadwork
in the town center. To make an underground parking garage and a
traffic underpass, the Plaza de España had to be dug up. Fortunately,

the Plaza Antón—now renamed the Plaza de la Constitución—with its new statues and cafés and its future museum, gave people somewhere else to go. While most eyes were on these changes, Franco's equestrian statue was respectfully lifted by a crane, to make way for the excavation of the old plaza, and carried to the security of the naval museum's courtyard.

No one could be offended by its having found a home there. Ironists enjoy recalling that Franco's first, unfulfilled ambition was to follow his father and brother into the navy, a dream echoed in his preposterous part-autobiographical, self-propagandizing novel and film, *Raza* (see pp. 199–201). He has made it at last, and by means that showed democratic local Spain at its adaptable best.

As for the Pazo de Meirás, Socialists in Galicia were determined to have the place declared a site of cultural importance (Bien de Interés Cultural, or BIC). The connection with Emilia Pardo Bazán alone provided ample grounds for this, but it's also the case that important decisions were made in the house under Franco, and important people stayed there. Furniture and paintings collected by Franco's wife were of interest, too, though much disappeared in 1978, when a mysterious fire at the house was followed by a lengthy to-ing and fro-ing of trucks. The denomination BIC makes various requirements of private owners, among them that they should maintain the building and its contents to a high standard. The benefit is that the property becomes eligible for grants. The downside is that it has to be opened regularly to the public— normally, four days a month.

Feudalism lasted longer in Spain than in any other European country, and there is no tradition there of public access to big houses—those, that is, that have not been turned into museums or hotels. Besides the fact that Carmen Franco Polo owns the Pazo and, since her early teens, has spent part of every summer there, she was concerned about her security: it's not much of a stretch from bombing a statue to bombing a *pazo*. For eighteen months she used a combination of appeal procedures and strong padlocks to prevent the initial surveys required by the BIC process. In March 2008 a legal judgment forced her to give in to this first stage, but she continued to complain noisily both about the invasion of privacy involved and about the expenses to which she would be put if the house had to be opened.

At one end of the spectrum of opinion in all this was the view that the Pazo de Meirás should be returned outright to Galicia. The public subscription that had paid for it had been far from spontaneous, and its purpose had arguably been to provide the dictator with an official residence on his home ground, not to enrich his descendants. At the other end were those who said that a gift is a gift; that, seventy years on, it was a bit late to be having second thoughts about it; and that it had taken some courage for the family to stay in Spain after Franco's death and that they should be left alone.

Carmen Franco Polo had only three possible ways through. The most obvious, at least to outsiders, was to accept the situation gracefully, negotiate an agreement by which opening days would be bunched at certain times of the year and then only under strict security conditions, and stay away from the house at those times. This would, though, have required a degree of humility and diplomacy not hitherto visible in the Franco gene pool. Another option would have been to put the house on the market. The third was what in fact happened: a series of delaying tactics that, at the cost of ensuring that the Francos were continually excoriated in the leftist media, maintained the possibility that another change of regime might have enabled them to keep not only their doors closed but also—and this may have been the main reason behind the duchess's obduracy—their land potentially available for development. Whatever her thinking, it was overtaken by events. In January 2009 the Xunta of Galicia officially declared the Pazo de Meirás a Bien de Interés Cultural.

Throughout the dispute, the duchess continued to encourage displays of suzerainty such as the Franco-Jiménez wedding. Whatever was made of these provocations by the shade of Emilia Pardo Bazán, the side of her that liked to write about comic, festive aspects of rural life might have enjoyed the carnivalesque demonstrations that went on simultaneously outside. In one of these—a mock wedding held in August 2008—a figure dressed as the *generalísimo* strutted up and down brandishing a sword, while his stout wife, in black dress and mantilla, allowed a stern-faced man in bishop's robes and miter to squeeze her bejeweled breast. The cheerful crowd shouted, "Franco! Franco!" but what the banners prophetically announced was "The Pazo de Meirás Returns to the People." The house eventually opened to the public in March 2011.

Slowly, then, the physical record of the Spanish dictatorship has been changing. The triumphalist, one-sided war memorials are still there, but there are new monuments to the losers, and new museums give accounts of the past that differ from, while not wholly replacing, what was previously understood and to a degree imposed. While there's still some bickering about what streets should be called (see pp. 277–78), this seems to be settling into a kind of regional game, a verbal form of *bolos*, the skittles tournaments once played in streets where you wouldn't have wanted to be in the way of the wooden ball. Most of the commemorative work done has been imaginative, relatively small in scale, and solidly executed: money was spent at a time when there was an illusion of wealth, and whatever comes next, these particular projects should last. The elephant in the room, though, remains Franco's crypt, in the Valle de los Caídos.

5

Art's Abstractions

The dictatorship left visible marks on the Spanish landscape and in the cities. What about painting and sculpture? A familiar version goes like this:

Spain had been at the heart of experimental modernism. Picasso, Juan Gris, Miró, Dalí—these and other artists returned their country to the position of world leadership in the visual arts that it had lost (among much else) in the seventeenth century, with the death of Velázquez. Their achievements, though, were at first more valued abroad than in Spain itself, and many of the artists chose to emigrate. Picasso and Gris spent most of their lives in France, and other adventurous visual artists abandoned Spain, especially after the victory of nationalism, with its limited sympathy for avant-gardes of any kind. Just at the point when the Second Republic had briefly made the country a place fit for artists to live in, the military uprising and the ensuing dictatorship threw away one of the strongest claims Spain could make for international cultural respect. While the civil war generated an artistic life of its own, particularly in the form of posters, photographs, and cartoons, and some talented people remained behind after the Republican defeat, bravely huddling together in groups such as Pórtico in Zaragoza, Dau al Set in Barcelona, El Paso in Madrid, Equipo Crónica in Valencia, they enjoyed no state funding, had few ways of communicating

with artists outside Spain, and couldn't keep abreast of, let alone participate in, what was happening elsewhere.[1] The Spanish authorities, meanwhile, imposed their own philistine, outdated criteria: patriotic, religious, neoclassicist. Spain's artistic landscape was left uncultivated.

This last metaphor (taken from a twenty-first-century account of the situation[2]) is oddly inappropriate to a historical context in which not only were hungry Spanish people returning to the land but landscape painting was among the most vigorous forms.[3] In a country impoverished first by civil war, then by a combination of economic mismanagement and the consequences of the Second World War, it's true that there was not much, at first, in the way of material support for artists. International high-cultural contacts weren't easy—though in the first half of the 1940s this was the case in most parts of the world. Yet the underlying story of Spanish art during Franco's regime is more complicated. It illustrates the limitations of the dictatorship, especially when faced with dissidence from right as well as left; bears witness to the robustness of the creative spirit; and confirms the ability of art, particularly but not exclusively nonverbal, nonrepresentational art, to outwit political or moral interpretation. More interestingly still, it shows that, in time, the regime itself came to recognize these limitations, to learn from its opponents, and to give artists their head.

In 1960 a big exhibition of Spanish art was mounted in Barcelona. Franco had been in power for more than twenty years—almost twenty-five if you count from the military rebellion—and was beginning to leave much of the management of the country to other people while carrying on himself as something between a monarch and a tough, autocratic, though often out-of-touch military commander. His staggeringly costly Valle de los Caídos had been ceremonially opened the previous year, a time when unemployment was rising and wages were being held down. So what could be expected of the Exposición Nacional de Bellas Artes (National Fine Arts Exhibition), a biennial event held that year in Barcelona at the Palacio Nacional de Montjuic[4] under the auspices of the Ministry of Education and the Council of Fine Arts?

Franco himself attended the opening, and his patronage is ful-
somely acknowledged at the beginning of the catalogue—a fusty, poorly
printed document that starts with a long list of members of the selection committee, all given their elaborate titles, from "Exc[elentísi]mo
S[eño]r D[on] Antonio Gallego y Burín; Barón de San Calixto," a
Falangist art historian who had become a leading political figure both
in his native Granada and nationally;[5] and "Excmo. Sr. D Juan de Con-
treras y López de Ayala, Marqués de Lozoya," one of the main custodi-
ans of Spanish art throughout the changes of the 1930s and '40s and
now head of the Spanish Academy of Arts in Rome; down to "Secre-
tario: S[eñori]ta Josefina Cáceres," the only woman directly involved.
Yet these discouraging signs were deceptive. In the first place, the show
was the result of a big national program of art subsidy in the form of
eighty-six prizes ranging in value from 6,000 to 100,000 pesetas but
averaging around 15,000 (in terms of average Spanish incomes at the
time, about three months' pay). A third of the prizes were national, the
rest being funded by, and to some extent linked to the art of, regions
and individual cities: 50,000 pesetas from sophisticated Barcelona and
Granada (half, in each case, from the province, half from the city), 3,000
from impoverished Cáceres.[6] In all, the state put up 585,000 pesetas;
the separate regions, 454,500—just over a million pesetas, then, eight
times more than the annual acquisitions budget of the national Museo
de Arte Contemporáneo (Museum of Contemporary Art).[7] No bonanza but—combined with the many teaching jobs available to artists,
a fair sprinkling of curatorial and arts administrative posts, and a
range of bursaries of various kinds—better than nothing.

Was it the case that these rewards went only to artists whose work
promoted the regime and its ideals? Naturally, some did. The pieces
shown included a bronze head of Franco by the venerable Ignacio
Pinazo Martínez, who had won the first of his many prizes in the 1899
National Fine Arts Exhibition, when he was sixteen. There were also
various religious figures and scenes; a wide range of more or less conservative canvases depicting the Spanish countryside and village life;
portraits of aristocrats and officials; and a small *corrida* of depictions
of bulls. In any art show, though, what stands out is by definition
what isn't predictable, and there was plenty of more compelling work
on display. Four grimy, unsmiling men stare accusingly out of a

lithograph titled *Obreros* ("Workers"), one of three pictures by the Barcelona artist Francisco Vila Rufas, then in his early thirties and later known internationally as the cartoonist Cesc.[8] Cesc was one of several participants who had been children during the civil war. Another of them, Julián Pérez Muñoz, who contributed a beautiful postcubist figure of a woman sitting at a desk,[9] was born into a working-class family in Extremadura in 1927, studied in Madrid, and in the mid-1950s won a bursary from the Fundación Rodríguez Acosta to study in Italy. The slightly older Joan Josep Tharrats, one of the founders of the avant-garde Catalan school Dau al Set (but in 1960, like all Catalans, still obliged to appear under the Castilian version of his name, Juan José), was represented by a violent, dark, scratchy expressionist oil whose impact on at least one viewer can be gauged by the marginal note in a surviving copy of the catalogue: "urff!"[10] Similar grunts of disapproval were elicited from this unknown connoisseur by the fierce abstraction of a young Burgos painter, Luis Sáenz,[11] some of whose apocalyptic canvases were later exhibited in Japan and the United States, and by work representing other painters at early stages in subsequently successful careers.[12] A powerful oil of a scrapyard (*El cementerio de camiones*, "The Truck Graveyard") by the up-and-coming colorist Francisco Echauz escaped without comment in this catalogue,[13] but the more traditional Salvador Rodríguez Bronchú was accorded a small tick, as was a painter at the heart of the Spanish establishment, Miguel Rodríguez-Acosta, for his uncompromisingly titled *Virtudes teologales* ("Theological Virtues"). Yet even boundaries as apparently strong as those between the last artist and young Julián Pérez Muñoz were often crossed. Rodríguez-Acosta ran the eponymous family foundation that had sent Pérez Muñoz to Italy. Later, he did a portfolio of illustrations for Lorca's gay *Sonnets of Hidden Love* (*Sonetos del amor oscuro*), unpublished, and unpublishable, in the Spain of 1960.

Only five of the exhibitors were women, but they included Carmen Arozena Rodríguez, who had recently studied in Paris with the British painter and printmaker Stanley Hayter, founder of Atelier 17, and had shown in South America and Switzerland as well as Paris before becoming one of the prizewinners in the 1960 Exposición Nacional.[14] Among other established figures, the architect José Antonio Coderch de Sentmanat was represented by a clean, bold set of unrealized but none-

theless prophetic designs for a coastal hotel complex near Girona.[15] If any kind of painting dominated, it was landscape, by painters who were then at the height of their powers and who command serious prices today.[16]

ART IN *LA POSGUERRA*

This was 1960, of course, not 1940. In the immediate aftermath of the civil war, official taste dominated and innovative Spanish artists suffered. Revisionist historians have made valuable attempts to put their predicament in perspective, but in terms that can seem strained. Out of a total of 668 art teachers in postwar Spain, Javier Tusell tells us, 550 experienced no official difficulties whatsoever. But what about the other 118? And what about the three ("only three") graduates of the Escuela de Bellas Artes (School of Fine Arts) in Madrid who, he tells us, were politically unlucky?[17] One of these was Aurelio Arteta, a Basque Nationalist who was in his mid-fifties when the civil war began.[18] As a young artist, Arteta won scholarships to work in Paris and Rome. In 1924 he became director of the new Museum of Contemporary Art in Bilbao but was fired after he criticized the dictatorship of General Miguel Primo de Rivera. Stuck in Madrid at the time of the 1936 military uprising, he managed after a few months to escape to Republican Valencia, where he was active in negotiations with the Basque leadership. When Franco's victory became inevitable, Arteta made his way via Barcelona and the decreasingly hospitable refugee camps of southwestern France to Mexico, where he was taken under the wing of the newly arrived former Republican minister Indalecio Prieto. In 1940 another Basque politician, the writer Julián Zugazagoitia, was captured by the Gestapo in Paris, handed over to the Nationalists, and executed in Madrid. Shocked by the news, Arteta and his wife decided to drive out into the countryside, but he crashed the car on the way and was killed.

In these early days of the *dictadura*, the Falangist leader Rafael Sánchez Mazas had set the official tone in a famous speech at the national Museum of Modern Art in Madrid in 1940. We are not asking artists for patriotic pictures, he said, let alone for adulatory ones, but for pictures that "bring to the mind and the senses the luminous glow which

we want for the whole Fatherland."[19] He urged his listeners not to waste their time on "obscure local episodes," on Spain's "blemishes," or on "gathering a lot of domestic rubbish in some sort of subversive chaos under the name of Still Life," but to remember that "our Mediterranean art is an art that holds its face to the sunshine"—"Cara al Sol," the title, of course, of the Falangist anthem that Sánchez Mazas himself had helped to write.[20] A decade later the rhetoric had not changed much. The education minister Joaquín Ruiz Giménez, whose brief included the arts, opened a major new exhibition series devoted to contemporary Hispanic (including Latin American) art by asserting the need for strong ties between art and society. To him, one of the crucial tasks of education—in Spanish as in Latin, the word means "upbringing" or "formation" in all positive senses, not just "schooling" (and manners, too: *bien educado* means not "well-schooled" or "knowledgeable," but "good-mannered")—was to cultivate an aesthetic sense, a major responsibility for "the great educational authorities, the Church and the State." Intellectual formation is not enough, he said. "We also have to stimulate the spirit that creates forms" and "the capacity to understand and respond to them" (*vibrar ante ellas*, literally, "vibrate in front of them"). This was the only way of achieving a fully integrated human education, which he defined as one that combined "the true, the good, and the beautiful."[21]

The formation of most twenty-first-century Western art lovers has been based on different assumptions, especially that it's the duty of an artist to shock and subvert, but the ideas of these Nationalists were part of a long historical tradition from which the majority of the works we still regard as great derived and that continues today in many parts of the world. Besides, statements made by people in authority were sometimes no more than a matter of party line and were often ignored or evaded in everyday practice. A case worth considering is a conservative attack on the policies of the Spanish national Museum of Modern Art published in 1943.

The critique was presented as a "graphic and spiritual" guide to the collection.[22] Its author was Francisco Pompey, a successful realist painter and prolific author of books on Spanish art and artists, several of them published by the regime itself. Pompey's argument was that a museum, as distinct from a private gallery, has a didactic, expository responsibility to choose and arrange its work historically so as to demonstrate

"a lasting development." Instead, he claimed, the Museum of Modern Art, although it had been founded in the nineteenth century, now seemed concerned only with contemporary fads, an approach he regarded as "essentially *antimuseal*, revolutionary and sectarian."[23] It was an odd thing to say about a collection that many others at the time and later thought distinctly old-fashioned. Pompey may have had in mind the museum's brief role as a center of avant-garde internationalism under the Republic.[24] Or perhaps his motives were personal: since 1939, the museum's director had been Eduardo Llosent Marañón, a poet associated with the 1920s avant-garde and now part of a group determined to keep artistic innovation alive. Begun in 1942 by Eugenio d'Ors, this group was known as the Little, or Brief (or Short-Lived), Academy of Art Criticism (Academia Breve de Crítica de Arte). *Brava*, "brave," would have been a better adjective.

The story of the Academia Breve is fascinating in itself, and Eugenio d'Ors is among the unsung heroes of twentieth-century art. Three facts stand out here. First, d'Ors, Llorent, and others of their circle were in many ways supporters of the regime—though artistically radical, they were politically conservative. Second, Pompey's theory of the proper function of a publicly funded art museum wasn't without validity and is still voiced today. Third, not only was the debate to which it contributed held under a dictatorship supposedly stifling to intellectual life, and during its most repressive phase, but also it had important practical consequences.

In 1951 a new national Museum of Contemporary Art was opened in Madrid, the holdings of its predecessor being divided between it and a more historically based museum devoted to the nineteenth century. The creation of the Museo de Arte Contemporáneo (now the Museo Reina Sofía) suggested, and was intended to suggest, that philistinism was not in charge. So, too, did the first of a series of big biennial exhibitions of Spanish American art, also held in 1951. Neither of these ventures satisfied everyone, least of all Spanish Communists living in exile. While the respective curators (the forty-year-old José Luis Fernández del Amo at the museum and the forty-two-year-old Leopoldo Panero in overall charge of the Biennial) favored experimentation, they weren't interested in social realism of the more propagandist kinds preferred by the left. Besides, anyone continuing to work within

Spain had, as far as the opposition in exile was concerned, self-evidently sold out. An "anti-Biennial" manifesto appeared in Paris with Picasso's support, and in Mexico the painter Josep Renau denounced what he saw as the rehabilitation of the decadent aesthetics of Falangism.[25] It's still hard to see through the dust kicked up by these scuffles, and once again, personal hostilities were involved. No one at either political extreme would let himself sympathize with those who steered a less partisan course. Among the latter, and particularly hard to pin down, was the cosmopolitan Panero. Educated at Cambridge in the 1930s, he was a member of the Falange, yet he had been published by one of Franco's most vociferous opponents, the Chilean poet Pablo Neruda and, working in London in the early postwar years, had befriended anti-Francoist exiles such as Luis Cernuda.

The biennial exhibitions and the Museum of Contemporary Art were crucial in supporting living artists, whatever their politics, and in opening the eyes of those who saw the work on display. Who, reading out of context Fernández del Amo's moving memo about what he wanted from a museum of contemporary art, would guess that it was written not only under but for the Franco dictatorship?

> It will have an experimental character, regularly showing anything that's interesting, even if the interest proves momentary. These [temporary] shows will help us choose work that will figure [more lastingly] in the museum, which as a result will be a living entity. My ideal would be to set up a network of active units: a library, a cinema, even . . . a little open theater where dance can be explored and studied as a plastic form and where artists can discuss and defend their work to the general public. Because one of my ambitions is to make contemporary art popular.[26]

PUBLIC COLLECTION, PRIVATE VALUES

The realization of such aims was a slow process and involved many different people: successive directors and their advisers, liberal-minded politicians, critics, and teachers. Their efforts have increasingly been recognized in Spain, where art historians skeptical of received opinions

have in the past couple of decades been focusing on factual materials—budgets, bureaucracies, diplomatic links, decision-making processes, acquisitions, touring exhibitions—in ways that have changed and complicated a once-familiar, falsely simple story. In a phrase heard more and more often from cultural historians and from imaginative writers and artists, "There were not two Spains but many Spains."[27]

The point is made vividly by the Museum of Contemporary Art's collection itself, as it had become by the time Franco died.[28] For example, the famously pro-Soviet Mexican Diego Rivera had been there since the early 1960s with his fabulous *Flower Seller* (1949), a composition like a flower in itself, though the brilliant foreground half-conceals some less cheerful motifs: two working women and a man carrying baskets, that of the man supported by a band across his forehead, the browns of their skin picked up in the color of a bowl of bulbs in the bottom foreground. The picture met with disapproval from members of the museum's committee, not on grounds of its quality but because of the artist's political views.[29] Still, it was acquired. Also in the museum, despite the regime's attacks on him, were a dozen works by Picasso. And there's the famously seductive, Japanese-influenced painting of a woman lying by a pool by the Catalan postimpressionist Hermenegildo Anglada Camarasa, who had hidden in a monastery throughout the civil war, and afterward escaped to France. Anglada eventually returned to Mallorca, which, like the other Balearic Islands and parts of the mainland coast, was becoming a haven of cosmopolitan bohemianism. Among the artists then living in Mallorca was Miró, who had also gone back to Spain despite the fact that of all important Spanish painters during the civil war, he was among the most unambiguously pro-Republican in his art as well as his opinions. Work by him, too, was in the collection, though not the propagandist paintings that, like versions of Picasso's *Guernica*, became part of it later.[30]

The gallery's Hispanic brief was extended to include some of the many foreign artists who made their homes in Franco's Spain: the Romanian Pic Adrian in Barcelona, the American Mil Lubroth in Madrid, the German Will Faber in Ibiza, the French Liliane Ranceze in Gijón. A couple of small bronzes by Henry Moore, who had called on the British government to support the Republic, also found their

way into the collection. Its main strengths, though, were in work by twentieth-century artists who not only were Spanish but had spent most of their lives in Spain. Some, such as the cubist María Blanchard, whom Lorca elegized, had died before the military rising; several spent the war abroad but returned soon afterward; others carried on in Spain through the late 1930s as best they could, whether or not openly taking sides. Daniel Vázquez Díaz, by then in his fifties, was simply a celebrated painter who happened to be in Republican Madrid during the Nationalist siege. His former student Rafael Pellicer, though an avowed Republican, was changed by his wartime experiences and subsequently devoted most of his artistic efforts to religious subjects. By contrast, the Andalusian expressionist Rafael Zabaleta, one of those who, under the Republican government, had the job of trying to protect Spain's cultural treasures during the civil war, was at first less fortunate. Denounced in 1939 for having worked for the wrong side, he was imprisoned by the Nationalists in their notorious selection camp at Higuera de Calatrava, near Jaén, from which thousands of Republicans went to their deaths. It's customary to say that these prisoners were shot, but a different story is told by the records patiently examined by a Spanish historian: "Daniel Delgado Fresneda, 36 years . . . Asphyxia by hanging . . . Lorenzo Daza Rosales, 61 years, builder . . . Asphyxia by hanging . . . Francisco Ortega Díaz, 22 years, day laborer . . . Internal hemorrhage . . ." Among other causes of death commonly listed are "starvation," the usefully ambiguous "blockage" (*atresia*), and all-purpose "weak heart."[31] It seems that Zabaleta wasn't so unlucky after all. Perhaps out of respect for his professional standing, or to make him an exhibit in himself, he was transferred to another prison, where he was obliged to do a painting or series of paintings, now lost.[32] Quite soon he was transferred to house arrest and then exonerated. He resumed his work, which can be seen in various galleries today, among them a museum named after him in the town where he was born and died, Quesada, in Jaén province.

Art historians who believe that nothing good can come out of what they see as political compromise have duly found ways of running down Zabaleta's work. His main subject was the rural working class. "Impoverished peasants!" jeers Michelle Vergniolle Delalle, in a lively, well-informed, but tendentious book about painting under Franco.

"How pointed a novelty in a period when people only painted the land-owners. Still, how picturesque they are in their *alpargatas* and straw hats! These are happy peasants with clean clothes . . . strong bodies and round, friendly faces."[33] So some of them are, indeed, though unmistakably suffering faces look out from Zabaleta's work, too. But what Vergniolle Delalle ignores is that Zabaleta's flat, geometrical canvases satirize the posed imagery of totalitarian "realism," whether of the right or the left. To her, Zabaleta is a piece in a larger argument against his patron, Eugenio d'Ors, whose taste must have been bad because he, too, operated within the regime. It has to follow, then, that the painter "fell slowly into silence and oblivion after d'Ors's death in 1954"—a claim that would have been news to the curators of the Colección Banco Central Hispano, which bought his *Peasants in the Granada Mountains*— finished in 1959, the year before he died—and to those who included him in exhibitions in Madrid in 1961, Barcelona in 1984, Valladolid in 1996, and in the Bilbao Guggenheim's first show of contemporary art from Spain in 1998. The fact that one of Zabaleta's paintings of rural life was sold at Sotheby's in 2010 for about $150,000 may say nothing about its quality, but along with these other marks of esteem, it contradicts the idea that his work has been forgotten.

Zabaleta knew from his wartime experiences that most great art collections embody painful stories, not only about the lives of those whose work they contain or the ownership and acquisition of the pieces themselves but also about the collections' sheer survival. The same is inevitably true of the Spanish Museum of Contemporary Art in Madrid, where some of his own pictures are housed. Above all, though, it's the early careers of those who started out after 1940 that are recorded in its initial holdings. Four names in particular stand out: Eduardo Chillida, Antoni Tàpies, Manolo Millares, and Antonio Saura. All are internationally renowned and all lived and worked in Franco's Spain.

CHILLIDA, TÀPIES, MILLARES, SAURA

Work by Chillida—in stone, in wood, in alabaster, above all in iron— can be seen today outside I. M. Pei's concert hall in Dallas and the

Federal Chancellery in Berlin, and inside many of the world's leading galleries, from the Art Institute of Chicago to the Kunsthalle Basel. Along with Claes Oldenburg, Bruce Nauman, and Louise Bourgeois, Chillida was a winner of the Wolf Prize for Sculpture; he shared the Andrew W. Mellon Prize with Willem de Kooning. But more than anywhere else, he is to be seen in Spain; and in Spain, more than anywhere else, in his native Basque country. Best known of all, perhaps, are his tough "Wind Combs" gesturing to each other across the rocks in which they're fastened at the western end of a beach in San Sebastián, the city for whose soccer team Real Sociedad he kept goal in the early 1940s. The sculpture, executed immediately after Franco's death, was first planned as early as 1952[34] and takes part in its physical surroundings in many ways, one of which is the region's long history as a source of iron and ironwork. Like some other sculptors of the post-industrial age—the American Richard Serra, favorite of the Bilbao Guggenheim, is another—Chillida draws on, pays homage to, and at the same time acknowledges a sense of inferiority beside the huge practical enterprises of the nineteenth century, in this case shipping: his three circular claws cemented into the rocks at San Sebastián seem to half-offer a safe mooring yet also, because the rings are open, half-refuse it; and though majestic in some photographs, they look touchingly small and vulnerable in their natural context.

Chillida knew what real ironwork could be. After training as an architect in Madrid and as a sculptor in Paris, he returned to the Basque country and apprenticed himself to an old blacksmith in Hernani, once a port on a now-disappeared tidal river in Guipúzcoa. The decline of shipbuilding in the region and its longer history of embattlement—French invasions, Carlist wars, the proud nationalism that even Franco was unable to suppress—inevitably had their impact on him. In 1980, working (as before on *Wind Comb*) with the Basque architect Luis Peña Ganchegui, he completed a public memorial to the defense of "*los fueros Vascos*," the name for the Basque legal system associated with independence, abolished by the Spanish government in 1878. The sculpture, an evocation of another Basque symbol, Guernica's ancient oak tree, is ensconced in an architectural maze, itself within a (to my eye, sadly brutalist) grouping of plaza, amphitheater, and a high wall, in Vitoria-Gasteiz, an inland city between Bilbao and Pamplona.

Basque nationalism—rejected in its extreme forms by the over-whelming majority of the region's population—has provided a motive for some of modern Europe's most violent acts of terrorism. Attempts to contain it are among the links between the dictatorship and ensuing governments of both parties. While Chillida's brand of nationalism was arguably not very much more dangerous than playing soccer for a Basque team, it was enough to persuade the authorities of the city of Seville initially to reject his 1982 *Monument to Tolerance*, a commis-sion by the Fundación Sefarad (Sephardi Foundation). The piece mourns Spain's expulsion of the Jews in 1492 and was intended for and finally installed by the Triana Bridge over the Guadalquivir. At its inauguration, the sixty-eight-year-old sculptor made a speech that showed how far democratic Spain had traveled from its National-Catholic past: "I don't want to pretend to set myself up as an example to anyone but it would be perfect if one day the Jews, Arabs and Chris-tians of Seville could go back to holding hands with one another. That's the ideal this monument reflects."[35]

This brush with the artistic pitfalls of Spanish politics came late in a career that, like that of Chillida's contemporary Antoni Tàpies, had been marked by very rapid success. Young artists, in fact, found plenty of opportunities in Franco's Spain, despite what's supposed to have been a uniformly traditionalist and repressive official culture. Many were helped by chances to study in Paris, winning French scholarships and enjoying the support there of a large Spanish artistic community. Tàpies benefited from both, and by his late twenties, his work was being shown not only in Barcelona and Paris but at the Venice Biennale, the Carnegie Institute in Pittsburgh, and commercial galleries in Chicago and New York. The 1950s brought him worldwide recognition.

A decade earlier, Tàpies had become friendly with the charismatic Joan Prats, a close friend and former fellow student of Miró's who, al-though (or because) he had resigned himself to working in his father's prosperous hat-making business, was at the social and promotional heart of the Barcelona art world. Through him, Tàpies met Miró. He also borrowed the French arts periodicals Prats had collected in the 1930s. Soon he won a scholarship to study in Paris and went there armed with a letter of introduction to Picasso. According to the English surrealist Roland Penrose, who was friendly with and wrote biographies

of both men, Picasso discussed communism with the young Tàpies and warned him that "Watchwords and tendencies can never turn a bad painter into a good one."[36] Like many other foreign supporters of the Spanish Republic, Penrose had had a crash course in what Soviet communism entailed, but in other ways he sympathized with the political and, more deeply, spiritual and humane yearnings expressed in Tàpies's work.

Tàpies's background and upbringing involved discords typical of his time and place: a royalist grandfather; an atheist, Catalan Nationalist father; a strictly Catholic mother; a church education disrupted by anarchists who, on one memorable occasion, dressed up in priests' vestments and danced around the school before making a bonfire of its contents. The boy was tubercular, and suffered a cardiac illness in his teens, followed by a period of depression. Simply in terms of health care, this was no time to be ill in Spain, but the convalescing Tàpies read and dreamed and found his way into Zen Buddhism. So his radical, intensely exploratory approach to physical materials has dimensions that go beyond the puritan aesthetic associated with *arte povera*. The effects on his work of the 1950s and '60s are seen at their best in the simultaneously heavy and malleable-seeming lumps of gray and brown, disturbed by abrupt slashings, of his "superpositions" in the Reina Sofía, the Bilbao Guggenheim, and, above all, the Museum of Spanish Abstract Art, in Cuenca. Here, his 1959 *Marrón y ocre* ("Brown and Ochre") is hung opposite a window through which, on entering the room and before we encounter the canvas, we see the cliff opposite the gallery, its rock interrupted by a long, straight, almost horizontal crack. As a result, turning to face the Tàpies, we see it as a landscape painting—albeit abstracted, and depicting a harsher version of the land than the impressionists, say, cared to look at. It's important, then, not to overintellectualize his work, even when it becomes more overtly symbolic and, indeed, verbal, as it did (arguably to its own detriment) later in his long career. Still, he was susceptible to social-political ideas, or at any rate feelings, and sometimes found himself in situations that prompted conservative attacks. A retrospective exhibition of the Dau al Set group, which Tàpies, like his cousin Modest Cuixart, was part of, was closed down by the police in 1951; in 1966 he was among thirty people arrested, fined, and briefly jailed for taking part in a

radical meeting organized—a sign of a powerful new current in the Church—by Capuchin monks. As late as the 1970s, Catalan nationalism was still being repressed in ways against which some of Tàpies's work overtly protested, and Penrose describes the results with typical passion:

> A theme that haunts him throughout is the injustice and oppression that has been imposed for many years on his native Catalunya. It appears as a writing on the wall akin to graffiti scrawled at night by clandestine hands with the only means at their disposal, their blood. Elsewhere he may express forlorn hopes in a scrap of newsprint that has littered the streets and which becomes the central feature in a sombre landscape at each side of which he inscribes arrows extending the horizon beyond our view. Or he may use a black rectangle, the negative value of which he cancels by vigorous red strokes crossing it out.[37]

In all this, his work goes well beyond what can be taken from it by way of literal, programmatic interpretation. "Magic," as Penrose is the first to insist, is more important to it than message. In this and in other ways Tàpies resembles his younger contemporary Antonio Saura.

Born in 1930, Saura, too, was a frail, tubercular, intelligent child whose health wasn't helped any more than his formal education by the civil war. He experienced the bombing and shelling of all three of Spain's most powerful cities, Madrid, Valencia, and Barcelona, where his family lived successively between 1936 and 1939. His father was a lawyer, his mother a pianist; the four children—Antonio was the eldest—included the future filmmaker Carlos Saura (see pp. 211–15). Antonio Saura taught himself to draw and paint and, like both Chillida and Tàpies, he spent a few years in Paris, in the mid-1950s. But he had already in his late teens begun the long, at first derivatively surreal, but soon more distinctive series of depictions of the female form half-respectfully, half-skeptically called *Damas* ("Ladies") that gave his career its strong central current. (They were shown together at the Fundación Juan March in Madrid in 2005.) With Manolo Millares and others, Saura founded the El Paso group in Madrid in 1957, and he showed with Chillida and Tàpies at the Venice Biennale in 1959. Like

them, he was more interested in what any artwork was, physically and visually, than in what it "said," though he attributed some of his style in the late 1950s to his response to the brutal suppression of student riots in Madrid at the time of his return there. There's an unmistakable line of succession and cross-influence between some of Miró's "savage paintings" of the mid-1930s, Julio González's series *Montserrat gritando* ("Montserrat Shouting"), Picasso's *Guernica* and its "postscripts" of crying women, and Saura's 1959 *El grito no. 7*, which was among the Spanish Museum of Contemporary Art's earliest Saura acquisitions.[38] The unforgettable half figure in the top right of *Guernica* has arms and hands outstretched, the desperate face uplifted like that of someone falling into a pit. The creature in *El grito no. 7* (see illustration on the cover of this book), part human, part wolf, is similar, but there are important differences. Like most of Saura's paintings, this one is in black and white, but what is unmistakably blood drips (bursts) from the figure's unprotected head and left hand. Its teeth, as in some of González's sketches for his *Montserrat*, are bared, and the face and body, shown in full, are moving forward rather than down, legs and feet windmilling, tail swinging— sheer fury in action. The painting's title is usually translated as "Shout," but the noise of *El grito* is surely a yell, a scream, a howl of rage.

Any political reading of *El grito no. 7*, though, is in danger of being overdetermined by the hints Saura gave about it. He was to write in a less specific way that a canvas "is a limitless battlefield. Facing it, the painter engages in tragic and sensual bodily combat, his gestures transforming inert materials into a cyclone of feeling that radiates cosmic energy forever."[39] If these words are more about the physical and psychological process of making a work of art than about, say, democratic protest, you only have to juxtapose *El grito* with the in many ways startlingly similar *Brigitte Bardot* of the same year (or the earlier *Bailaora*, "Spanish Dancer") to see that the names artists give their works can be as opportunistic as what they say about them.[40] The variety of Saura's titles, in fact, can seem whimsical beside the grim reiterativeness of the canvases themselves.

While Chillida, Tàpies, and Saura were affected, then, by the political-historical situation in which they grew up, it didn't hinder them, or seriously affect the majority of the work they did, except in ways that are hard to interpret unambiguously. To discuss them in

terms of protest or dissidence isn't wrong; it just doesn't do justice to their miraculous energy and fertility, their sheer superiority. The same is true of Manolo Millares. To the ten-year-old, his father was "the civil war's first casualty." Juan Millares Carló had wanted to be an artist, but in order to make a secure living for his family, or so he hoped, he became a university teacher. A liberal in politics, he was deprived of his job when the Nationalists took control of his native Canary Islands at the war's outset.[41] It was twenty years before he got it back. The vicarious humiliation never left his son.

The family was, once again, a cultivated one; in a society that had been so feudal for so long, not many twentieth-century Spanish artists came from the working class. (Julián Pérez Muñoz is among the exceptions.) Millares's great-uncle was a painter who did a portrait of the novelist Galdós. There were writers as well as academics among his older relatives, and two of his brothers became poets. While teaching himself to paint surreal versions of the surrounding landscapes, Millares helped start a literary magazine in Gran Canaria. And he spent time in the museum there, becoming increasingly fascinated by the Canary Islands' aboriginal art, particularly its mummies. He found something he could use imaginatively in their coarse shrouds—"fabrics made of twine, tarred and torn, with their dirty, burnt-ochre color, their rough weave."[42] His description fits some of the work with which he's most associated, inflected as it often is, too, by the shapes of human remains, and of wounds. Where Tàpies draws the side of a spatula through his built-up paint, Millares rips the canvas itself, nowhere more movingly than in the black-and-loam-colored *Cuadro 61* (1959), in the La Caixa collection in Barcelona. Here, the center of the canvas is a dreadful horizontal gash that has been so roughly stitched together, with painted sackcloth tied partly across, partly beneath the rest, that it's unclear what came first, which fabric is being used—futilely, desperately—to repair which. Before the end of the dictatorship, the Spanish Museum of Contemporary Art already had three of these stunning mixed-media *arpilleras*, "burlaps"—among them the 1966 *Asesinato del amor* ("Love Murder").[43] Millares, his reputation already established by work selected for shows in Latin America as well as mainland Spain, had moved to Madrid in 1955 and helped found the El Paso group there. By 1980 he was represented in collections throughout the world.

Millares, like Saura, came to describe his work in terms of angry political rebellion. In one of the avant-garde publications edited by the high-conservative Camilo José Cela, he wrote that one has to break with the past in order to build the future.[44] But this was the rhetoric of the time, whether you lived in the Soviet Union, the United States, or Europe. It can't be taken as having anything specific to say about the role of an artist in Franco's Spain. So we're left with the dilemma acknowledged even by critics most keen to connect a country's politics with its art:

> On the one hand, the regime prohibited every form of thought which didn't serve it and was incapable of conceiving an innovative artistic project: a situation which should have stifled the arts. On the other, by the time the dictator died, Spain was one of the European countries with the largest numbers of artists who were internationally recognized and involved in the main contemporary artistic movements. Besides, while in the nineteenth century all the talented painters had to emigrate, in the Franco period they were once again living on the Peninsula. Did this unexpected development occur because of or despite the regime?[45]

The answer to the last question is: neither and both. Governments don't bring about art; artists do. And while many individual artists are helped by being at odds with their political and cultural surroundings, many (some of them the same artists) benefit from whatever positive support they are offered. We've seen examples of all these phenomena, but it's worth pausing on the work of Eugenio d'Ors and the Academia Breve.

ADVENTUROUS PATRONS (1):
THE ACADEMIA BREVE, 1942–54

Among the consequences of the work d'Ors and people like him did was that Spain didn't succumb to the insularity of its own ruling order. Francoist critics described Miró's work as infantile and Picasso's as satanic. Modernism in general was attacked as a betrayal not only of classical traditions but, worse, of Spanish national identity, brought

about (of course) by Jewish-Masonic cosmopolitanism.[46] If these yelps and groans achieved anything, it was to attract audiences to the many international exhibitions held in Spain in the 1950s, under the auspices of the French embassy and the Museum of Modern Art in New York, among others—shows that engendered many ironies and conflicts. Several French artists who had been willing to exhibit in Spain at the height of the repression there in the early 1940s, when France was occupied by pro-Franco Nazis, developed democratic qualms in the 1950s.[47] Some of their Spanish counterparts, meanwhile, found it hard to decide whether to accept invitations to appear in the Venice Biennale— one of the most prestigious of international showcases, of course, but also of use to official Spanish national self-aggrandizement.

Would they have been easier in their minds if they had known that Franco himself really didn't care much either way? At one of the Spanish national Biennials, a group of nervous officials stood with him in front of some pictures by Tàpies. "Excellency, this is the revolutionaries' room," one of them is said to have explained. "So long as this is how they carry out the revolution," he cheerfully replied.[48] Tàpies himself told this story, though he wasn't always reliable, whether factually or in his loyalties. It's well known that whether in telling the truth, expressing gratitude, or being kind about their friends behind their backs, artists are no more to be depended on than other people, yet despite this, their statements can command disproportionate respect—the more so the more famous they become. Tàpies is one of those who tend to be quoted on the work of his fellow Catalan d'Ors, whose taste he said was mistrusted by Catalan intellectuals and whom he criticized for his closeness to the regime.[49] Early accounts of Tàpies's career, meanwhile, generally omitted the fact that in one of the last exhibitions put on in Madrid by the immensely influential d'Ors, the latter chose Tàpies—then in his twenties, a member of the radical Dau al Set group, and unknown outside Barcelona, where d'Ors had seen some of his work. The old man deserved better from those he had helped. In Spain, sixty years after his death, his reputation as a serious thinker and patron (rather than as an essayist) has still to recover. Elsewhere, he is almost unknown.

His biographer Antonino González is concise about the reasons. D'Ors's standing as a philosopher has been occluded by "his work as a

journalistic pundit, his politics, his focus on literary and art criticism and also his tough writing style, which put a distance between him and academic philosophy."[50] All this, as far as d'Ors was concerned, was a matter not only of choice but of conviction. His activities were immensely diverse. He stands at the historical point where the dilettante, in the best sense, turned into the interdisciplinary "public intellectual," but with the important difference that he actually ran things—the Catalan public education system, for example, and later the Spanish national body charged with supporting the visual arts—as well as writing, lecturing, and talking. He was also consistent in his beliefs and loyal to his friends. The life of the mind, he believed, is indistinguishable from life of other kinds. It is communal, gregarious, communicative; thought, indeed, doesn't become thought until it is shared. D'Ors wrote in *La filosofía del hombre que trabaja y que juega* ("The Philosophy of Someone Who Works and Plays," 1914)[51] that thinking is "a form of love, it lives on talk, on society, and on human companionship." Reason, he believed along with some philosophers of the Enlightenment, is much more limited than intelligence, which is "the active faculty that gives us an overall vision of the world, made up not only of rational elements but also of experience, intuition, feeling, and *taste*"—*gusto* (he underlined the word), which also means "pleasure."[52]

He was a man of his time and background: middle-class, well-educated, sociable. In the course of a long life, he got to know many other gifted and powerful people and didn't hesitate to involve his friends in whatever he believed in, especially since one of the things he believed in was friendship. His senses were strong—when he recalled his childhood in late nineteenth-century Barcelona, it was the smells he wrote about—and so were his ambitions. In his early thirties he applied for the chair in psychology at Barcelona University and luckily didn't get it. Soon he was lecturing at the Residencia de Estudiantes in Madrid, a kind of liberal, cosmopolitan think tank that brought him invitations from all over western Europe and South America. Meanwhile he wrote the daily newspaper column, or "glossary," that he began in 1906, when he was in his mid-twenties, and was still writing when he died in 1954. The *Glosario* is a lifetime's collection of essays, or *pensées*—intellectual diary entries on whatever caught d'Ors's attention.

Being conservative, classical, and elitist in his thinking, he was a natural supporter of the Falange and, as soon as the Nationalist victory was certain, was taken on by the new Ministry of National Education as the head of everything to do with the arts. This included museums. One of his first tasks was to organize the return of works from the Prado that had been sent to Switzerland by the Republicans for safekeeping while Madrid was being bombed by the Nationalists. So he had a professional sympathy with Rafael Zabaleta, who had been one of the Republicans involved in similar work.[53] In any case, d'Ors was too intelligent a man (in his own rich sense of intelligence) to let differences of past political allegiance come between him and anyone whose work he liked. In the early 1940s, the years of Spain's impoverished, repressive *posguerra*, what mattered most to him was that imaginative life should not be stifled.

A very simple, practical idea came to him, though one difficult to execute. What if a group of friends, people from many different walks of life but with a common passion for the visual arts, were to organize an annual exhibition, each of them choosing and championing the work of one artist? He put together such a group: eleven people, ranging from the aristocratic feminist María Campo-Alange to Eduardo Llosent, the editor of an arts periodical whose friends included the Communist poet Rafael Alberti. One was a physician; two (including the Japanese ambassador) were foreign diplomats; another was a former academic, a friend of Unamuno's who, in 1939, had been deprived of his professorship at Salamanca for being on the wrong side. The eleven made up the Academia Breve de Crítica de Arte, which, over time, put on, among other shows, eleven "Salons of the Eleven," plus one extra in memory of their founder when he died.

It was a brilliant outcome of d'Ors's philosophy, one that incidentally suggests how ways of supporting the arts today might be transformed. The Academia Breve provided the opposite of collective compromise and secret cronyism: its decisions were made by named individuals, each of whom was required to write a defense of his or her choices in the catalogue. In political terms, it represented several kinds of coalition, including at a personal level. (Llosent, to take just one example, was married to a right-wing novelist.) Inevitably the results were mixed, both in style and quality, though no more so than would

have been the case with the choices of a committee; variety, in fact, was one of the pleasures on offer. Works selected had to be modern, but the artist didn't have to be alive. So, for the first salon, held in 1943, the Countess of Campo-Alange's choice was her mother, the cubist María Blanchard, who in the 1910s had shared a Madrid studio with Diego Rivera but spent most of her adult life in Paris, made her reputation there and in other parts of Europe, died in 1932, and had not been shown in Spain since 1915. The Academia Breve's secretary, Enrique Azcoaga, on the other hand, championed a traditional portraitist, Pedro Bueno; while the architect and poet Luis Felipe Vivanco (perhaps nudged by the academy's president) went for Zabaleta. D'Ors himself chose a somewhat derivative, Matisse-like double portrait by the Catalan émigré Emilio Grau Sala of two women—or are they, like Goya's Majas, the same woman?—one naked, one demurely dressed. Two working men standing at a bar are the subject of a realist canvas by another artist in his early thirties, the generally more decorative Eduardo Vicente, selected with due diplomacy by Ambassador Yakichiro Suma.

If the show was mixed in terms of originality, everything in it was well executed, much was new to Spanish viewers in 1943, and it attracted big audiences. One has to imagine the state of the city through which they passed to get to the gallery: ruined buildings, flattened bomb sites, Falangist graffiti. The salon was an oasis, and its sheer catholicity was a recreation, an education, a source of hope. People drawn in by the familiar found themselves looking at newer, more challenging work, some of it done abroad. Established artists hung beside newcomers. For the second show, d'Ors's choice was the Uruguayan constructivist Joaquín Torres García, who had spent the early years of the Second Republic in Madrid. José Gutiérrez Solana, who late in his career had made a point of depicting "the most sordid aspects of the Spanish *posguerra* . . . with its resulting starvation and misery, physical and moral,"[54] was included in 1945, the year of his death. Meanwhile, a self-taught twenty-five-year-old landscapist called Agustín Redondela made his first appearance that year, and in 1949 it was the turn of Tàpies, who, along with an even younger Catalan, the neosurrealist Joan Ponç, found himself exhibited beside Miró and Dalí. For all the unease Tàpies later claimed to have felt about taking part, he became almost as regular an element in the salons as Zabaleta had

been earlier, and was soon joined by three other artists who were to become internationally known: Josep Guinovart was chosen by a new member of the Eleven, Cesáreo Rodríguez-Aguilar, an expert in Islamic law who had fought on the Republican side in the civil war; Manolo Millares was the selection of a Falangist journalist, Pedro Mourlane Michelena; and Antonio Saura was brought in by one of the most hardworking members of the original group, María Campo-Alange.

D'Ors died in 1954, and the Salon of the Eleven, having put on the eleventh of its shows that year, mounted its final one as a tribute to him in the winter of 1955. Seventy years since it was founded, the Academia Breve and its founder are still seen as politically tainted, their dedicated work on behalf of young Spanish artists during a dozen bleak years as compromised. The artists themselves, meanwhile, not only kept on working but in many cases almost immediately found a new patron: the cosmopolitan Fernando Zóbel, himself an important painter, and of their own generation.

ADVENTUROUS PATRONS (2): FERNANDO ZÓBEL AND "THE MOST BEAUTIFUL MUSEUM IN THE WORLD"

Born in 1924 into one of the richest families in the Philippines, Zóbel was educated at Harvard. He was an addicted collector—of postage stamps, old coins, books, china—but according to his own account, his tastes were transformed by a chance visit to an exhibition of abstract art at a little gallery in the center of Madrid in 1955. The artists shown included Saura, Chillida, and Tàpies, and Zóbel later recalled having been instantly ("*de golpe y porrazo*") won over by a combination of the vitality of their material and the modesty of its surroundings.[55] As a result, both his collection and his friendships were transformed. Zóbel was a writer as well as a painter and connoisseur, and the diary he kept over the following years makes a vivid story out of the increasingly complex mix of social, intellectual, instinctive, and financial processes involved.

By the early 1960s, Zóbel had already decided that he wanted to find a permanent Spanish home for his acquisitions. In October 1963,

the by now well-established Millares, who had a show coming up in New York, called him to say that there were two pieces he wanted Zóbel to see before they crossed the Atlantic, because he was eager that at least one of them should find a home in Spain. He proposed an exchange with one of Zóbel's own works (perhaps as a way of avoiding any accusation that he had done his art dealer out of money). "Five years ago," Zóbel wrote, "I wouldn't even have done a swap with Rembrandt," but he went round to Millares's studio with another painter, Gerardo Rueda, and the three chatted casually, Millares showing them some pieces from his collection of ancient Roman and Inca objects. Eventually, Millares produced the first of his two new paintings: "A triptych, very well made made, all bums and corsets, referring to the Profumo scandal"—the resignation of a British cabinet minister who had been entrapped by the Russians through a beautiful prostitute, Christine Keeler. Zóbel found this picture "very unlike Millares, too topical," but was taken with the other one:

> A big diptych of the sarcophagus of Philip II or somebody like that. For all its poverty and the roughness of its material, it's powerfully elegant. The difference between pop art and Millares is that Millares makes something beautiful—he composes. The shock effect isn't the point—it's an extra. He said it himself: "Neo-Dada doesn't interest me in the least."[56]

They did a deal, and before long Zóbel acquired another piece by him. This time supper was at Millares's house. Rueda was there again, and also a kinetic artist who talked about how much he admired Buñuel's film *Viridiana*, which had caused a fuss in Spain a couple of years earlier (see pp. 201–204). ("Trendy, pretentious," was Zóbel's comment.) Discussion turned to the state of the French art market, which Zóbel said he found "hysterically nationalistic"—in general, he was sure that what was happening in Spain these days was infinitely more interesting. Rueda said he thought the mechanisms of selection in France had failed; Zóbel trenchantly responded, "No doubt. But the French painters have failed, too. Why, yet again, are the French painting so badly?" Millares, by contrast, he told his diary, seemed to have widened his horizons while still using the same technique. The collector found

something lyrical in the new work: "He's never painted better. Round, tranquil pieces. And then a series of objects, something between painting and sculpture, fierce, bellicose."

Again and again Zóbel found not only the best works by his new friends, but also the right words to describe them. He told Tàpies he was the only artist he had come across who was "capable of painting dust."[57] He bought a small piece of marble with lead inlay by Chillida and met him soon afterward through Saura, finding the sculptor "direct, friendly, obviously intelligent and very well informed . . . He adores Greece—never stopped talking about the Greeks. He thinks their art . . . is a direct result of the quality of the light (but if the quality resides in the light, why did their art dry up a couple of thousand years ago?)" Zóbel was still thinking about how and where his collection would be housed, and he commissioned a piece in wood from Chillida with a particular place in mind.

At the Venice Biennale in 1962 he had met the painter Gustavo Torner, a native of Cuenca, 170 kilometers southeast of Madrid, on the road to Valencia. Torner brought him to the ancient city, its rugged citadel fringed on one side by then-dilapidated houses hanging over a spectacular ravine through which flows the river Huécar. Zóbel had rejected various potentially grander settings. He kept thinking about something the American artist Mark Rothko had said, about preferring his work to be shown in houses rather than in big galleries, where they just looked like postage stamps. He immediately saw the potential of these strange spaces, their solid stone entrances leading into a maze of interconnected, irregular-size rooms, some of them gazing vertiginously at the cliffs opposite.[58] In June 1964 he spent a couple of days in the city and had a meeting with the enlightened mayor, Rodrigo de la Fuente, who had nothing to propose, Zóbel wrote, "except assistance and solutions. We had a look. We could make a terrific museum of the Hanging Houses. 20–30 years at a nominal rent and the paintings remain my property." The hanging houses were already being restored by the city. Work on turning some of them into a gallery began almost immediately, under the direction of Torner, helped by Zóbel himself and by Rueda. The resulting Museo de Arte Abstracto Español (Museum of Spanish Abstract Art), described at the time by Alfred Barr, director of the Museum of Modern Art in New York, as the most beautiful

museum in the world, is now well looked after by the wealthy Juan March Foundation, to which Zóbel donated his collection in 1981.[59]

Chillida's poplar woodblocks, rings and knots exposed in their angular joints, are the first thing you see today as you go upstairs into the museum. The elegantly arbitrary-seeming formation, like that of some crystal, anticipates the gallery itself, with its planned surprises of level, space, and color. It's common in Spain to hear a house described as a jewel, but rarely has the metaphor been more apt than to these multifaceted little spaces, glinting not only with natural light but also with their brilliant and diverse, and now immensely valuable, contents. When it was commissioned, Chillida's piece would already have sold for more than 350,000 pesetas—a third of the total prize money offered annually by the Exposición Nacional de Bellas Artes—but the sculptor let Zóbel have it for half that. Everyone wanted their work to be in Cuenca. Zóbel found himself besieged by offers. "Every fifth-rate abstract painter in Spain wants to GIVE me a picture. I'm becoming an expert at writing saccharine refusals. If I had a crystal ball I think I would see my future filled with bearded enemies in sandals."[60] Many more rejections and a few more purchases later, the museum was opened in June 1966. After first one and then another piece by Chillida—the latter, the elegant marble-and-lead tablet that hangs on the right as you move into the next room—visitors encountered pieces by Millares, among them that black-and-white *Sarcófago para Felipe II* ("Sarcophagus for Philip II") and an exceptional range of work by Tàpies, including the *Marrón y ocre* rock formation of 1959. Instead of the sober marble floors that have gone before, the high room containing the latter work, which faces over the ravine, is painted gloss white underfoot and prepares for the startlingly opposite experience of a softly carpeted black space, the Sala Negra, showing individually lit items by Antonio Lorenzo and others, which in turn gives way to some rooms that, while they have no natural lighting, are full of color. In terms of how the collection is hung, this is a new element: the primary reds and blues and yellows of the New York–based José Guerrero, one of the few artists shown who no longer lived in Spain, and the more muted, changeable tones that his fellow native of Granada, Manuel Rivera, achieved by painting thin layers of wire netting stretched over, but separated from, a flat panel.

The names Guerrero and Rivera hint at some of the ways in which Zóbel's choices went beyond, while overlapping with, those of d'Ors and his friends. These were partly negative—put at its simplest, Zóbel's taste was anti-figurative—but they were also a matter of his more thorough-going immersion in the international currents of the time. Other artists he favored included the Valencian Manuel Fernández Mompó, who had worked in Paris and Amsterdam before, in 1958, winning a scholarship from the Juan March Foundation that enabled him to develop his enthusiasm for mosaics, the effects of which were subsequently developed in his work in the Balearic Islands and in Madrid. Tàpies's cousin Modest Cuixart (who *had* been chosen by the Eleven)[61] was also here, as was Saura with his astonishing *Brigitte Bardot*.

Between them, did d'Ors and his friends on the one hand and Zóbel and his on the other miss any serious talent? Inevitably so. Women artists, in particular—represented though some were in the annual national exhibitions—were neglected, indeed arguably shouldered aside, by these mainly masculine groups, at least in their operation as groups. (Individually, some of the men behaved differently.) María Blanchard was included in the first of the salons, but she was already dead, and it seems to have been best for a woman artist not to be a threat to any up-and-coming men. The cosmopolitan Olga Sacharoff, who had settled in Spain in 1915, was well into her fifties when the salon included her. It's true that Renée Aspe, who was in the salon's tenth (1953) exhibition, was both relatively young and distinctly glamorous, often photographed with bare shoulders or on horseback or both—but then, she was French and, though widely traveled, spent little time in Spain. It was by other routes that Spanish women painters such as the Basque landscapist Menchu Gal and the younger Carmen Laffón made their reputations, the former nonetheless becoming the first woman to win the Spanish national prize for painting; the latter finding her way into what is now the Reina Sofía, as well as into the Juan March collection.[62]

More names could be added. But clearly any notion that Franco's Spain was an artistic desert is the opposite of the truth. Naturally, this is how some artists themselves tended to describe their environment—not only in Spain but also, as María Bolaños has shown in an

absorbingly anti-parochialist essay, throughout Europe and North America.[63] Our backward gaze always flattens the landscape. At the time, when intelligent people in Spain looked ahead, it was to the rich variety they hoped for in a post-Franco future. But by the 1950s and '60s, Franco's Spain was already living that future. As the novelist and essayist Juan Benet wrote, Spanish culture began to be post-Francoist well before the end of the dictatorship, "experiencing something like a clandestine democracy, even though democracy didn't exist." As for the merits of the work being produced, we have not only the evidence of our own eyes but the verdict of the collector who, more than any other individual, enabled us to look at it. Spanish artists of his own generation, wrote Fernando Zóbel in the introduction to the Cuenca museum's catalogue on its opening, represented "the continuation of the artistic renewal initiated by the era of Picasso, Juan Gris, and Miró."[64]

ART, POLITICS, AND THE VICARIOUS

An old question, but one that won't go away, is whether artists are ever in any serious sense of the word political, let alone powerful. The most often discussed examples, in the case of mid-twentieth-century Spain, are Picasso, Miró, and Dalí. A huge amount has been written about all three, but the relevant points can be summarized quite simply. Despite the left's appropriation of surrealism, Dalí refused to denounce fascism and was content to live in Franco's Spain. Miró put some of his work explicitly at the service of the Republican side in the civil war, during which he lived in France, but he went back to Spain in 1940. Thereafter, although his immensely varied output, like that of Picasso, includes representations of suffering (the *Barcelona* series in particular), the limpid elegance of his *Constellations* is equally true to him, and he had nothing specific to say about politics, in his art or otherwise. Picasso called himself a monarchist and, as a guest of José Antonio Primo de Rivera, found him *"muy simpático."*[65] While he criticized Francoism, very little of his huge oeuvre engages with it, and his series of cartoon-style etchings *The Dream and Lie of Franco*, though unmistakably satirical at the *generalísimo's* expense, is conservative in that what it

attacks him for is the destruction of traditional Spain. The *Guernica* series, meanwhile, speaks about the horrors of war and, in context, the Nationalist bombing of the Basque capital, but even this great work, with all its global impact, hasn't saved anyone from being bombed. Poetry, W. H. Auden famously concluded in 1939, "makes nothing happen," yet what he wrote about that "nothing" sounds like something— albeit something not exactly measurable in political terms—and his words are applicable to all the arts:

>   . . . it survives
> In the valleys of its making where executives
> Would never want to tamper, flows on south
> From ranches of isolation and the busy griefs,
> Raw towns that we believe and die in; it survives,
> A way of happening, a mouth.

To say that art is ineffective politically, though, does not mean that political art, or art prompted by political events or feelings, is no good. Being in opposition can give an artist new energy; the difficulties and dangers of censorship can send him or her in previously unimagined directions, whether of language or materials or form. And the sense of shared, albeit vicarious experience that any viewer is bound to feel when faced with the *Guernica* is, as d'Ors and many others have argued, among the gifts that art, any kind of art, at its strongest offers. This is true of novels and films, too. The issue of vicariousness raises a different question relevant to all the arts. What exactly is the experience being shared? Picasso, after all, was not in Guernica when it was bombed but safe in his Paris studio, working on his as-yet-untitled project for the International Exhibition's Spanish Pavilion. Not even the newspaper reports on which he, like most of the rest of the world, relied, were firsthand, though they were written on the basis of interviews with eyewitnesses. Some visual artists, it's true, sought to record "direct" experiences of the war, but we know that even the photographs of Agustí Centelles were often posed. The drawings of Antonio Rodríguez Luna, meanwhile, contained their own kinds of satiric-surreal editorializing. Caricature and cartoon, in fact, are the forms in which visual art came closest to telling us what the war was "like": Goya was

inevitably a big influence, as was the anti-Nazi German artist George Grosz, especially on Luis Quintanilla, whose series *La España negra de Franco* ("Franco's Black Spain") memorably depicts a timid little Franco with a chain through his nose, being pulled along by a giant wearing a swastika. In the early 1960s, Millares did a vivid, atypically representational series of anticlerical cartoons now in the Reina Sofía, *Los curas* ("Priests"), one of which shows a big fat priest with his cock out, about to bugger a boy under an apparent pretense of playing leapfrog. This was the period, too, of Estampa Popular (The People's Image), a loose national network of politically engaged artists committed to making affordable art, much of which took the form of satirical prints. Again, though, one has the uncomfortable sense that these examples of, in Sartre's terms, direct engagement are either inferior work by the best artists or the best work of inferior ones.

The writer W. G. Sebald (born in Germany in May 1944) argued in an essay called "The Natural History of Destruction" that in descriptions of war, authenticity is no guarantor of vividness; indeed, generally the opposite. On the one hand, he quotes research that has found that those who have had traumatic experiences, though they may wish to tell their stories, are often unable to recall accurately what happened to them. On the other hand, he points out that the skill of an artist lies in making things vivid in ways that most of the rest of us, with our proneness to cliché, generally can't:

> Even Victor Klemperer's diary entry on the fall of Dresden remains within the bounds of verbal convention . . . The death by fire within a few hours of an entire city, with all its buildings and its trees, its inhabitants, its domestic pets, its fixtures and fittings of every kind, must inevitably have led to overload, to paralysis of the capacity to think and feel . . . The accounts of individual eyewitnesses, therefore, are of only qualified value, and need to be supplemented by what a synoptic and artificial view reveals.[66]

It should follow from this that artists far removed from a historical event or period with which they want to engage not only can but are more likely to succeed. Do they? The question is more pressing in the case of narrative art forms—especially fiction and cinema, for which

historical subjects provide so much material—than in that of painting, at least as we know it today. Spanish artists of the post-Franco era have found plenty to draw on in their traditional culture—whether in rural poverty or religious practices and iconography—and like artists elsewhere, they have used new media as ways of, among other things, commenting on newness itself. On the whole, though, they have not been preoccupied with "historical memory" in the narrow sense of dealing with the Francoist past, and indeed history in the fullest senses of the word is hard for art to communicate. When a critic complains, for example, that Miró's *Reaper* substitutes "an idealized view of 'the people' for a historicized investigation of the difficulties, false starts, confusions, and triumphs of real people," or that painters such as Picasso "evoke the horror of Spain's war . . . shockingly well but they are less successful at eliciting its causes or how it might be avoided," the problem is the medium's, not the artist's: the demands being made would be more appropriate to historians or novelists.[67] How have these dealt with the Franco era?

PART TWO

STORIES AND HISTORIES

6

History's Wars

The civil war and its aftermath dominate Spanish publishing like no other topic. Bookshop tables are laden with titles such as "Loyalty to the Republic," "The Firing Squads of Almudena," "War and Memory in Contemporary Spain," "We Murderers," " 'If you want to write to me': Songs of Politics and Combat from Spain's War." But what's in some ways the most impressive work of history published in Spain in the millennium so far is one you won't find in bookstalls. Spain's dictionary of national biography, the *Diccionario biográfico español*, the first twenty-five volumes of which (from "Abad" to "Hernández Rodríguez") appeared in 2011,[1] is a vast project, its handsome sky-blue bindings bearing the grand crest of its originator, the Spanish Royal Academy of History. Subsidized by the Ministry of Education and by a cultural charity, the Fundación Botín, set up by the family that runs Banco Santander, the *DBE* was designed to complement the national biographies of other European countries, chief among them the British (now *Oxford*) *Dictionary of National Biography*, begun in 1881 by Virginia Woolf's father, Leslie Stephen. What the Spanish dictionary instantly achieved was something different: a political-sectarian row of a kind that was particularly revealing about the legacy of Francoism and that eclipsed the project's value and distracted attention from other questions it raises. Yet the *DBE* is a valuable resource, conservative in methodology

but wide-ranging in its choice of subjects and contributors and ambitious in its associated aims.

The dictionary includes living people, so there are expert entries on José María Aznar, conservative prime minister between 1996 and 2004, as well as on the sixteenth-century Alonso Abad, "Conquistador"; on the longest-serving of Spain's prime ministers, the socialist Felipe González, as well as on Gesaleico, Visigothic king of Spain in the sixth century; on the film director Pedro Almodóvar as well as on the Andalusian emir 'Abd al-Malik b. Qaḍan al Fihrī (A.D. 654–741; very full coverage of figures from Spain's long Islamic era is one of the dictionary's triumphs). We aren't surprised to find Emilio Botín here, head of Banco Santander and of the foundation that helped fund the *DBE*, though his career-banker daughter and heiress apparent, Ana Patricia Botín, whom *Forbes* has listed among the most powerful women in the world, does not appear. We can read, however, about a cultural impresario of a different kind, Antonio "Botín" González, a lover of books who in the 1960s revived the fortunes of what's said to be the oldest restaurant in the world in continuous operation, the sixteenth-century Sobrino de Botín in Madrid. (He's rare among *DBE* entrants in that he doesn't, at least as I write, appear in Wikipedia. The restaurant does.)

The contributors are in most cases among the best that could have been found. Antonio "Botín" González is written about affectionately by one of the main promoters of gastronomy and tourism in post-1960s Spain, Pedro Galindo. A long, absorbing entry on Goya is contributed by Manuela Mena Marqués, director of the 2008 Prado exhibition, *Goya in Times of War*. The novelist Manuel de Lope proves keenly appreciative of the austere fictions of Juan Benet (see pp. 234–36). Miguel García-Posada does justice to the performative aspects of Lorca's personality as well as of his works. The French historian Bartolomé Bennassar writes on the conquistador Hernán Cortés, his biography of whom appeared in Spanish and German as well as French around the time the *DBE* was begun. With King Ferdinand of Castile and Aragón, Luis Suárez Fernández—a key figure in the project, of whom more in a moment—is on ground he made his own with half a dozen books published between the 1960s and 1990s. So it's regrettable that the dictionary is best known for embodying less impressive aspects of how,

almost four decades after the death of Franco, history is still done in Spain: that, politically, it remains extraordinarily polarized and that, in some quarters, Spanish historians have clung to a degree of seclusion from worldly concerns that would have been the envy of medieval monks.

The Royal Academy of History—motto: "While Spain's light shines, history's will not go out"—is a self-electing body founded in 1738, consisting today of a dean and thirty-three "numerary members," or fellows, all of whom are distinguished professional historians. Inevitably, given that fellowship is awarded in recognition of achievement and that numbers are restricted, most are pretty senior in age as well as status: few fellows are under sixty, which means that almost all had their university education as well as their earlier schooling under the dictatorship. Another reflection of the social history of their profession is that only three, at this writing, are women. Most of the academy's work is based in a handsome old building in the calle León in central Madrid, which houses the library, a "cabinet of antiquities," and a simultaneously intimate and imposing formal meeting room for the fellows, often mischievously described as a Gabinete de Antigüedades in itself.

What the academy is for is a little hard to identify. In addition to electing fellows, it puts on a sprinkling of lectures, and there are occasional exhibitions, though the most recent of these was in 2007. Its most regular activity is publishing: the academy brings out about a dozen books a year. A recent list included monographs on taxation and royal power in medieval Castile; on the Celtic god Toutatis; and on Lucius Cornelius Bocchus, who lived in what is now Portugal and wrote in Latin about natural history, though not much of his work survives. These books can be bought online, and if the topics look a little fusty, the academy's website does its best to enliven things by offering its own bestseller list—No. 1, "Mints [in the sense of coin manufacture] in the Roman Provinces of Spain"; no. 6, "Queen Isabella the Catholic and Her Time"—though actual sales figures aren't given.[2] The *DBE*, then, is by far the most sizable, as well as the most readable, of the academy's publications and, as we learn from its preface, represents the fulfillment of part of one of the institution's founding aims in the eighteenth century, which was to produce a "Critical-Historical Dictionary of Spain."

To be told that these volumes, themselves only reaching the letter *H*, will, even when they are complete, represent just one aspect of what was originally intended, and took 271 years to appear, may seem discouraging to readers who have seen Wikipedia grow up in little more than a decade, but academies have their own sense of time. It wasn't until conservative prime minister Aznar put on some pressure while offering additional government funding that the academy's fellows announced in June 2000 that they were going to pull out their engraved cuff links, roll up their sleeves, and get the job done, and actually did it. Here are more than forty thousand entries, the forgivably triumphalist preface tells us—as many as in any comparable publication. The *DBE* is indeed an enormous project, and it's not surprising that not all the hopes invested in it—for an online version, a research center, a journal—have so far been fulfilled. Still, some things *are* surprising. One is that the dictionary contains next to no information about its own procedures, past or future. How, for example, will entries on living people be kept up-to-date and made available? Another oddity, at least from an outsider's perspective, is the distinctly cap-in-hand note of deference that is felt throughout. These issues are more connected than they may seem. The enterprise is in every way old-fashioned—nowhere more than in its unspoken assumption that biography is intellectually and methodologically unproblematic.

Just how was the dictionary compiled? From the scanty information given in the opening pages of each volume, we learn that it was based on the work of a number of group "commissions," the members of which were presumably entrusted with requesting (commissioning) the entries themselves. Most had between three and six members, the exceptions being military history (eight) on the one hand and, on the other, a catchall "commission on history (various) and entertainment" consisting of one solitary member with responsibility for what are somewhat offhandedly described as "biographies of sports people, bullfighting, cultural leadership (patrons, collectors . . .), gastronomy, theater, cinema, and similar matters." As for the contributors themselves, they are for the most part named at the end of their essays, but there is no full list of them, let alone of the subjects any individual has written about, and a few articles are anyway semi-anonymous. These anonymous articles appear over the signature "Diccionario biográfico es-

pañol,"[3] an attribution that leaves us in a Borgesianly circular situation in the matter of responsibility, which we're firmly told lies with the authors: "The Academy has not wished to change [any entries] even though there may be occasional discrepancies between their contents. It only ensured that they complied with established presentational criteria."

This statement, which comes at the end of a brief note of thanks printed in every volume, was frequently called in aid in the months after publication, but before turning to the reasons why, it's worth noting what these scanty editorial preliminaries do attend to. If procedural questions are ignored—how people were chosen for inclusion; what guidelines, if any, were followed in selecting contributors; why, as we now know, it wasn't thought necessary to submit what they wrote to any form of scrutiny (whether anonymous peer review or just the critical gaze of a skilled editor)—careful attention is paid to matters of social status and hierarchy. There's an antique charm about this. The preface, by the academy's director, Gonzalo Anes y Álvarez de Castrillon, acknowledges with some formality the "great honor by which the Dictionary enjoyed the patronage of His Majesty the King" and the efficiency and generosity of the director and president of the Botín Foundation, "don Rafael Benjumea Cabeza de Vaca, Count of Guadalhorce . . . and don Emilio Botín-Sanz de Sautuola García de los Ríos." In this and other ways the dictionary gives a true picture of one facet of Spanish culture; and if we think of the project as, among other things, a roll call of the great names in Spanish history, then the more rollingly sonorous they are, surely the better. But those who give deference tend also to expect it, which has led to some difficulties.

It would be fair to say that the academy's publications had not previously attracted much media attention, but this one was bound to, and one entry everyone was sure to look up was "FRANCO BAHAMONDE, Francisco. Ferrol (La Coruña), 4.XII.1892–Madrid, 20.XI.1975. Generalísimo and head of the Spanish state." The biography that follows takes up just five double-column pages—the same as for the bullfighter Juan Belmonte, one column more than for ex–prime minister Aznar. The tone is neutral but not entirely without irony: we learn early on that Franco was always keen to emphasize the upper-class connections on his mother's side of the family. The brilliant military successes

of his early career are recounted with quiet emphasis, while his role in repressing working-class rebellion is downplayed: the crushing of the miners' strike in Asturias in 1934, in which thousands of people were killed and tens of thousands imprisoned, for example, is passed off as Franco's having "assisted in quelling the revolt without taking part in the operations," which is a bit like saying that Lord Kitchener took part in the First World War but didn't actually shoot anyone. This technique of questionable negative extenuation is used often here. Franco's civil war generalship is described as "authoritarian but not totalitarian," and the involvement of Nazi Germany and Fascist Italy are passed off as the consequence of economic links forced on Franco by the hostility of France and Russia. Spain's neutrality in the Second World War is praised, not least for having made possible the escape of some European Jews through the country, but nothing is said about Franco's having tried to persuade Hitler to let Spain take part in the war on conditions Hitler rejected,[4] or about his routinely anti-Semitic outbursts or, for that matter, about the escape routes (not to speak of career opportunities) the country offered to many fleeing Nazis after 1944. Again, the United Nations' condemnation of the regime in June 1946 is presented as a consequence of an "Anglo Saxon–Soviet" alliance that Franco cunningly "knew about" and therefore took no notice of—as if the alliance hadn't been a well-publicized fact and as if there had been nothing to condemn. A more pressing matter—that Franco was opposed and indeed hated on many counts, his regime's grim violations of human rights among them, and that these issues still burn today—might also have been worth mentioning at some point, but is overlooked.

And so the story goes on, Franco moving slowly but surely toward anything good (such as the restoration of monarchy) and away from anything bad (such as right-wing extremism among his allies). By 1950, we learn, the legitimacy of the regime was internationally recognized and world leaders found him "a head of state one could rely on"; he succeeded in persuading the Vatican to agree to a more tolerant approach to Jews and Protestants, began the work of decolonization that would occupy him for much of the next quarter century, "gave the green light" to Spain's negotiations to join the European Common Market (a wonderful way of spinning the fact that the EEC gave the red light to

Spain), agreed to liberal economic reforms that by 1963 made the country "the seventh most prosperous in the world," did his best to persuade U.S. president Lyndon Johnson against the war in Vietnam, introduced a national constitution, and in his last illness made a brief will in which he called on the Spanish people to unite around the king.

All this was both too much and too little for the critics. *El País* was quick to point out that the article's author, Luis Suárez Fernández, had always been so openly sympathetic to his subject that Franco's daughter had personally allowed him access to restricted archives held by the Franco Foundation, which she heads.[5] Suárez is president of the *hermandad* (religious fraternity) of the Valley of the Fallen. And he has evidently been a powerful element in the dictionary's commissioning network—a member on five panels (more than anyone else), including political and administrative history, and literature and humanities.[6] Not only the Franco article, *El País* pointed out, but several others by Suárez lacked objectivity, in religion as well as politics. For example, in his piece on Josemaría Escrivá de Balaguer, founder of the Catholic organization Opus Dei, Suárez writes, "While [Escrivá] was celebrating Mass on February 14, 1930, God told him that [the movement] should also include women." This is almost certainly Suárez's belief—he is a member of Opus Dei—but wouldn't a distancing phrase ("it seemed to Escrivá that God . . .") have been appropriate here? In a similar way, the *DBE*'s biography of a Nationalist priest killed by Republicans describes him as "martyr in the civil war," a designation not used of Republicans.[7] Similar biases were attributed by *El País* to other contributors, among them one José Martín Brocos Fernández, who consistently refers to Republican troops in the civil war as "the enemy" and describes Nationalist brutalities in cities they invaded as a process of "normalizing civilian life."[8] The eminent historian Santos Juliá, meanwhile, published a devastating list of factual errors in the *DBE*'s entry on Manuel Azaña, first prime minister of the Second Republic, of whom Juliá has written a full biography.[9]

Such criticisms quickly spread. The Ministry of Education, which under the conservatives had committed 6.4 million euros to the project but at this point was run by the PSOE, called for the correction of "any biographies whose contents do not show the objectivity proper to academic studies," a demand that the culture minister, Ángeles

González-Sinde, reiterated while also complaining that only 8.8 percent of the dictionary's subjects were women. Some members even of the PP came out against the work. "Respect for the Academy's institutional independence and the authority of its researchers," said its cultural spokesman, "is not incompatible with the fact that most Spanish citizens consider Franco to have been a dictator."[10] And a Catalan senator predictably deplored the fact that Suárez had failed to mention either the Francoist ban on the Catalan language or the atrocities committed in the region by Nationalists. All twenty-five volumes, he urged, should be withdrawn.[11] Hostility was also turned on the academy itself, with allegations that in his role as one of its more senior fellows, Suárez had always proposed right-wing historians for election, that the fellowship was heavily weighted toward early historical periods at the expense of the twentieth century,[12] and that it had resisted calls for modernization along lines adopted by the more prestigious and broader-based Spanish Royal Academy.[13]

Others were quick to come to the defense, or rather to the counterattack. "Left-Wing Totalitarianism versus the Academy of History," read the front-page banner of the conservative La Razón on June 3, 2011. Inside, among various claims about an orchestrated campaign if not to destroy then at least to harass the academy, one of its fellows, the nonagenarian classicist Francisco Rodríguez Adrados, blamed Spanish educational curricula for having created a general belief that the Republic was a blameless utopia.[14] The academy itself debated whether to revise the entries that had caused controversy, and decided against.

Three months after these arguments began, the newly ennobled director of the academy, Gonzalo Anes, stirred himself not exactly to enter the lion's den, but to do what must have felt much the same: submit to an interview in his office by a couple of El País reporters. It soon became clear that Anes, author of the dictionary's deferential preface, was neither impressed by his interlocutors nor disposed to any form of diplomacy. Have the criticisms bothered you at all? he was asked. No, he said, "not in the slightest." Did he feel any responsibility for them? "I was responsible for organizing the project. I can't control forty-three thousand entries." Did he think the Franco article was objective? "I don't want to judge." But shouldn't there have been some kind of editorial pro-

cess, as there was for the *Oxford Dictionary of National Biography* and its Italian equivalent? "Possibly, but there wasn't—period ["*y punto*"]."

Another question: the director had said that in every case, the best biographers had been chosen. In that case, why had the article on a former minister, Bibiana Aído, been lifted from her ministry's website, and why had all the information about the princesses Elena and Cristina, sisters of the heir to the throne, the younger of them married to someone under investigation for large-scale financial corruption,[15] been supplied by the royal household?

"Because we couldn't find any books about them."

Now things began to heat up.

Q: That isn't exactly scientific rigor.

A: Look, these people are in because Bibiana Aído had to appear because every minister is in and we couldn't exclude her. You follow?

. . .

Q: Did it really never occur to you that you ought to read what the entry on Franco said?

A: Look, I lived through the Franco era and know perfectly well what it was like so I wasn't curious to—I was concerned with other matters and it was other people I was interested in.

Q: Presumably you've read it now and can tell us—

A: No, not at all.

Q: What?

A: I haven't had time. What do you want, that I should sit down and read it now, while we're talking?

Q: Do you believe that Franco was a dictator?

A: He lived through various periods and behaved in different ways during them. There were several Francos and I didn't like any of them.

Q: But was he a dictator or not?

A: Look, I'm exhausted. I have to go.

. . .

Q: One more question. Do you think the Royal Academy of History is obsolete?

A: No, that's what *you* think. The academy is a very conservative institution in its customs. I respect those customs. But the fact that we

respect our customs doesn't mean that we aren't extremely innovative in our methods of research.

Q: What's missing from the academy?

A: More women. There are plenty who are ready [for election], but not as many as there are men. It's a problem: a historian has to spend many hours working on documents in the archives. And unfortunately, women devote those thousands of hours to bringing up their children and being housewives.

Game, set, and match to the interviewers, many readers thought. Were they wrong?

First, while it's true that the Franco entry is only one of forty-three thousand, there are anyway things to be said in its defense, some of which have by now been said often enough by the author himself. It's possible for reasonable people to disagree about the meanings of the expressions *dictatorship*, *authoritarian regime* and *totalitarian regime*. Suárez has defined the first as a situation where "a high official takes charge of all state offices for a fixed term to restore order"—a debatable view, to be sure, but a clear one.[16] Besides, he points out, while Miguel Primo de Rivera called himself a dictator, Franco never did.[17] Suárez has said that he will not rewrite the article: he stands by everything in it and points out that there is such a thing as freedom of expression. Asked why he wrote this particular piece in the first place, he answered reasonably enough that he is the author of scores of entries in the dictionary and, in any case, was the best person for this particular task, having recently brought out the six-volume *Franco: Crónica de un tiempo* ("Franco: Chronicle of an Age," 1997–2007), in preparation for which he was allowed an unprecedented degree of access to some of the archives.

As for making moral judgments, that's not a historian's job, Suárez has said. He could have gone further. In many though far from all its entries, the *DBE* is something between a work of record and a celebration. The authors are often people linked to their subjects by admiration as well as interest. Plurality is the essence. Many articles refer unequivocally to the Franco regime as a dictatorship, and those on left-wing figures such as Lluis Companys, the Catalonian president shot by the Nationalists in 1940, or Felipe González, the socialist leader who was

prime minister between 1982 and 1996, are sympathetic and expert. The Francoist censors' mutilation of some films by Luis García Berlanga is firmly dealt with by Francisco Perales Bazo (who takes the opportunity to digress enthusiastically on the rock music career of the director's son Carlos, with groups such as Kaka de Luxe). Controversial living figures are often dealt with in a similarly inward, relaxed way. The cultural historian Luis Alegre Saz, for example, describes the 1980s "Madrid movement" led by Almodóvar as "a playful phenomenon that arose as a reaction against Francoist morality" and gives a clear if brief account of the filmmaker's political engagements, not least against the Aznar government's sending Spanish troops to Iraq. In terms of whether historians should judge their subjects or consider controversies they have aroused, Luis Suárez's view is the opposite of that taken by fellow academy member Juan Pérez de Tudela in an article on Cristóbal Colón (Christopher Columbus) that is frank about the discrepancies between the old image of Columbus as a superhuman adventurer and Christian missionary, and the actions of a viceroy "bloodily dedicated to enslaving Indians."[18] As for complaints about a shortage of women subjects, there are full articles on—to take names almost at random—the feminists Concepción Arenal and Clara Campoamor, the cubist María Blanchard, and the anarcho-syndicalist Teresa Claramunt. Cross-referencing the *DBE* with online lists of distinguished Spanish women in a range of fields confirms the impression that the dictionary has done a thorough job.

As for the delay in publishing the second tranche,[19] it may be at least partly attributable to authors' having wanted to look again at their work in light of how the first half was received. For the tragedy of this great but flawed project is its failure of anticipation: anticipation of readers' questions about procedures, anticipation of future (not to say existing) intellectual developments and technological needs and possibilities, anticipation of criticism—anticipation of the fact that after two generations of democracy, Spanish citizens feel entitled to give their opinions on how public money is spent. Asked whether he had expected the reactions to his Franco entry, Suárez replied that he neither expected nor understood them. Such detachment may be a virtue among the Brothers of the Valle de los Caídos but is surely a mixed blessing in a historian of the modern world.

The *DBE* is in several ways a microcosm of the Franco legacy in Spanish culture. The pro-Franco entries, both of themselves and in the peremptory ways in which those responsible have defended them, show that an authoritarian approach to knowledge continues to function in some quarters. The absence of information in the dictionary about its procedures is itself part of this process. To attack what looks like a lack of editorial control, as some have done, is to treat the unspoken as if it didn't exist: Luis Suárez himself is not only one of the dictionary's main writers, but also among the most powerful figures in its labyrinth of commissioning panels. But in Spanish culture as a whole, some aspects of the traditionalism that might seem in Suárez's case and that of others like him essentially an adherence to youthful loyalty on a par with, say, Eric Hobsbawm's having remained a member of the Communist Party after 1956, are actually stronger and more pervasive. The dictatorship reinforced Spain's long-established tendency toward Manichaeism and away from its opposites—away from a skeptical willingness to entertain opposed points of view, away from collegiality between intellectual opponents—and the habit has not disappeared under democracy. In 2012 the pro-Catholic Spanish daily *ABC* reported a debate about the existence of God held in Oxford between Richard Dawkins, author of *The Selfish Gene*, and the then-archbishop of Canterbury, Rowan Williams, chaired by the philosopher and ex-priest Anthony Kenny. The article focused admiringly not on the arguments but on the even-tempered, sometimes playful mood of the event. While the reporter exaggerated in saying that "the English . . . are the only members of the species who talk educatedly, passionately and at the same time with dignity about matters which, in countries that prefer Goyaesque ferocity to intellectual gymnastics, take a much less civilized course," the implied criticism of Spain wasn't unfair.[20]

The country's tendency toward voluble, emotionally charged partisanship is partly religious in origin but, with increasing longevity, also generational. Those who came off worst in the row over the dictionary were in their eighties and nineties. To Luis Suárez (born in 1924) and the project's academic coordinator, Quintín Aldea Vaquero (1920–2012), the dictatorship of Miguel Primo de Rivera and the ensuing Second

Republic were living memories. The early childhood of Gonzalo Anes (born in 1931) was dominated by the civil war, and the Franco regime had begun by the time he was eight. All three men had conservative, religious upbringings—Aldea Vaquero became a priest as well as a university teacher—but for almost everyone of their age, Spanish education was Catholic, patriotic, and nostalgic about Spain's lost imperial greatness. Children learned about the glories of the past—the Romans, the Visigoths, Ferdinand and Isabella, and the conquistadores—within a context of intense religiosity. Something similar was familiar in Ireland, where it was anatomized by James Joyce in *A Portrait of the Artist as a Young Man*, and it had Protestant parallels in British education, particularly in the boarding schools of Victorian England. In Britain, though, much of this changed as a result of the First World War and of a spread of socialist ideas and habits before and during the Second. In Spain, by contrast, an ancient conservatism, social as well as political, survived more or less intact into the 1970s. Just as everyone there who reached their fifties in 2013 had their primary education under Franco, those in their mid-sixties or above were well into their careers by the time he died. Many of these believed what their teachers told them and still find it hard to accept a version of events in which the civil war was not justified by anti-Nationalist atrocities committed by "the red hordes" (real though those atrocities were); the greater number of casualties was not suffered by the right; and the virtues of the *dictadura* in stabilizing Spain have to be weighed against the costs, among them loss of individual freedom and the perpetuation of a feudal economic and political system. Only now can it be said, for the first time ever, that the formation of the majority of teachers in Spanish schools and universities took place under democracy.

THE HISTORIANS' HISTORIES

Facts like these have many causes and implications. Before the late 1960s it was difficult for graduate students in Spain to do politically balanced research into contemporary history. Who would have supervised their work? Few Spanish academics could claim the expertise. Even the most independent of historical writers tended to steer clear of

recent topics. An example is the liberal intellectual Gregorio Marañón (1887–1960), a physician and essayist who had opposed the Primo de Rivera dictatorship, helped to draw attention to the plight of Spain's poorest inhabitants,[21] spent the civil war and early 1940s in Paris, but returned to Madrid as an incorrigible provocateur—anticommunist, but a proponent of national reconciliation when Franco was determined to keep old wounds open, and a representative, through his sheer presence as well as through his books, of attitudes (especially about political and personal freedom, including in relation to sexuality)[22] detested by upholders of the regime. When Marañón died in 1960, one of the biggest crowds in Madrid's populous twentieth-century history gathered for his funeral.[23] The books he wrote under the dictatorship were distinctively his own, and their take on the past, particularly on "the Spanish outside Spain,"[24] had plenty to say to his own age. But the past was mainly what they were about, and besides, Marañón had some enviable advantages. He was too well known to care about pleasing people who weren't even his masters: he had no university job. Not only that, his son was head of Franco's political secretariat. The case was different for many others.

The British Hispanist John Elliott, who did his first research in Catalonia in the 1950s, has described the hardships faced by his Spanish colleagues. Most had too much teaching to leave time for their own work, and those who managed to write faced the sack if the results displeased the authorities. Elliott collaborated with a Catalan, Jaume Vicens Vives, who, like him, took a revisionist view of the history of the region's nationalism—a position that wasn't intended to suit Madrid but of course did. Vicens was rewarded with a chair in modern history at Barcelona University. Among his predecessors there was Ferran Soldevila, no less learned—and, in his day, no less controversial— but during the Republic, a leading figure in Catalan Nationalist historiography. After the Francoist victory, Soldevila lost his job and, with it, his access to archives. Elliott describes a walk in the country in 1954 with Soldevila, whom he persuaded to sing an old harvest song associated with the 1640 Catalan uprising and banned under Franco. Soldevila wept as he did so, and Elliott realized, "I think for the first time, what it really meant not to be free."[25]

Still, one way or another, some people managed to keep up their

research and to follow where it led. Among them, as so often in the period, was a former Falangist: José Antonio Maravall. Born in 1911, a liberal conservative and a fellow of the Royal Academy of History, by the 1960s he had grown interested in social and political change and how it comes about, a preoccupation that put him at the center of contemporary developments. For Maravall, this had been a matter of purely intellectual curiosity, but for some of his students it was a basic condition of belonging to the *posguerra* generation. An example is Javier Tusell, who died prematurely in 2005. Born in 1945, Tusell did his *bachillerato* (eleventh and twelfth grades) at a church college in Madrid and went on to study history and politics at Complutense, where he became a militant member of the Union of Student Democrats and the Union of Young Christian Democrats, was disciplined by the university authorities, but managed to continue to a doctorate. In 1977, still in his early thirties, he was appointed to a chair in contemporary history at Valencia. His research, meanwhile, broadened in scope, moving from studies of electoral procedures under the Republic to the history of Spanish democratic movements in general. His appointment at Valencia coincided with the publication of his groundbreaking account of democratic resistance to Francoism. Tusell's next books were on other aspects of the regime—its dealings with the Church and with Italian Fascism, the restoration of the monarchy, the transition to democracy, Spain's international relations in the twentieth century, and also its arts. These are by general consent works of deep authority and ideological responsibility, their fair-mindedness of a piece with the spirit of the Transition.

In 1981, Tusell moved on to UNED (the Universidad Nacional de Educación a Distancia—National University of Distance Learning— begun in the early 1970s), Spain's Open University. If the Royal Academy of History represents history as an exclusive form of social mummification, UNED is its opposite. The head of the department of history there was the slightly older Santos Juliá. Eminent and increasingly vocal, Juliá had never been much of a student radical, but he typifies his generation in another way: in its belief that serious journalism in any medium is as important a vehicle for ideas as book publication. Born in El Ferrol (Franco's home town) at the beginning of the dictatorship, Juliá was educated in part at a seminary in Seville of

which a contemporary has given a vivid account that could apply to many similar places at the time, including in its more unexpected details: the wide social mix; the influence of the liberalism of Pope John XXIII on the boys, despite or because of the fact that it was ignored by most of the Spanish ecclesiastical establishment; in particular, how far the boys were able to withstand the official presumption that they were heading for ecclesiastical careers. "It's difficult today," according to the author, Francisco Sánchez-Blanco,

> to understand the psychological atmosphere in schools like it in the 1950s [and '60s], where an imposed religiosity coexisted with a great deal that broke with traditional culture . . . We brought out a cyclostyled journal that satirized the rhetoric of Francoism and of the little monarchist groups that were arguing about the succession . . . We had a "yé-yé" group and made a crime movie in super 8. And we hung out in bookshops that stocked prohibited material.
>
> There was more and more bad conscience about the social inequalities and misery we saw in the city outskirts. We knew that the Franco regime and traditional Catholicism had been complicit in letting all this happen . . . One thing is certain: the majority of people who decided to go into seminaries at the time believed that the church was going to change . . . We suffered a lot of disillusion before losing this hope.[26]

In Sánchez-Blanco's recollection, few of their teachers were particularly clever, let alone progressive, except for a philosophy master who, as an amusement, got the boy with the strongest rural accent to read out passages from a notorious nineteenth-century Spanish tract called "Liberalism Is a Sin," chortling and commenting sardonically while he did so.[27] But the brightest pupils were inherently skeptical about the regime's "Nationalist harangues," a point worth remembering in any context, Spanish or otherwise, where official doctrine tends to be treated by later generations as if everyone accepted it. Santos Juliá and his friends passed from hand to hand illicit novels and French-published works of Marxism and existentialism. They went to talks given in the city by leading intellectuals, some of them at the archbishop's palace, where discussions between Christians and Communists were organized. Among those who took part was Manuel Giménez Fernández, who had

been agriculture minister of the Second Republic and in the 1950s and '60s ran a Christian Democrat group in Seville.

Juliá later studied theology at Salamanca and sociology at Madrid and became friendly with members of the democratic-socialist Workers' Commissions. He read Marx and Weber, was in Paris during the *événements* of 1968, spent a year at Oxford studying the industrial revolution, and, at a time when recent Spanish archives were inaccessible, did research at Stanford in the now-famous collection of Spanish material that had been put together by a wealthy British Republican sympathizer, Burnett Bolloten. This led to a book about life in Madrid under the Second Republic—a period that Juliá summarized as having begun as a street party and ended in class warfare—and then one on Spain's longer social and economic history. In these works, he reacted against what he saw as the oversimplification of sociology by exploring the effects of phenomena such as demographic change over a much longer period than had previously seemed relevant.[28] And while this involved analyzing the roles of organizations and groups, especially political parties and trade unions, Juliá, unlike many left-leaning historians of the time, also took account of the power of individuals. Among his books that have reached an audience outside universities is his biography of the Republican prime minister and president Manuel Azaña.[29]

Juliá's cosmopolitanism is characteristic of the formation of these historians. (Tusell was unusual among them in not having spent substantial periods abroad.) José Álvarez Junco (born 1942), whose early work on Spanish anarchism was supervised by the ex-Falangist Maravall, went on to senior positions at Tufts and at Harvard. Juan Pablo Fusi (born 1945), author of books on different versions of nationalism in Spain and on the nature of Franco's power, also taught in the States and, with the English Hispanist Raymond Carr, at Oxford before returning to Madrid. International careers of these kinds represented a professional as well as personal reaction against nationalism, as did the sheer fact of researching into the movement itself. Another historian of the period, Mercedes Cabrera, has written that the Transition was a time when

> despite those determined to talk about a *"pacto de olvido o desmemoria,"* there was an outpouring of books, articles, seminars, confer-

ences and exhibitions on the 1930s, the Republic and the civil war . . .
We were all involved in it, academics and politicians, as well as a large
proportion of ordinary citizens and many of those who had until then
stayed silent, both inside Spain and abroad.[30]

Yet in their professional relations it hasn't been easy for these scholars
to bridge the divisions they described and analyzed. From the vantage
point of people who were now their senior colleagues and who had
spent the Franco years working their way up within the system, intellectuals of the *posguerra* generation were and still are rather frightening. What should have seemed admirable credentials—their intelligence,
idealism, and international perspective; their access to public media;
their connections with the new political order—posed a threat, living
proof that orders of all kinds change. Mercedes Cabrera Calvo-Sotelo,
professor of the history of ideas and of social and political movements
at one of Spain's most prestigious universities, is the niece and great-
niece of two conservative leaders yet has been a key figure in the PSOE.
As minister for education in the final Zapatero administration, she was
in a sense the employer of all academics and teachers. And she is a
woman.

Cabrera is not a fellow of the Royal Academy of History. Nor are or
were any of the other leading modern historians I've mentioned—not
Juliá, not Tusell, not Álvarez Junco, not Fusi. Perhaps it doesn't matter.
History, as the exhumations campaign shows, is not just a matter of what
happens in academies and universities. It's taught to everyone at school.
And it's a subject of live engagement by journalists and polemicists.

AT SCHOOL

What do Spanish children learn about the past?

One answer might be "what their teachers tell them," and it's true
that teachers at state schools in Spain, like anywhere else, while between them representing a wide range of opinions, tend in the nature
of their work to side with what they see as social justice—a position
reinforced by the historical fact that a disproportionate number of the
victims of Nationalist murders were teachers, just as those of Republi-

can ones were priests. Another answer, though, as in the case of Juliá and his fellow pupils at the seminary in Seville, is that some of the most important things children learn are the ones they find out for themselves and teach one another. Formal curricula, national or otherwise, are limited in their effects, and if they reveal something of an agreed orthodoxy, albeit ultimately the orthodoxy of the teachers' and parents' generation rather than the children's, the heat of any debate about such matters is often proportionate to the ignorance of the participants. When the historical academy's Francisco Rodríguez Adrados claimed that Spanish romanticism about the Second Republic is a consequence of the new national school curriculum, apart from implicitly exaggerating the impact of curricula in general, he must have forgotten that in order to have followed a syllabus for eleven-to-sixteen-year-olds introduced (by the conservative PP) in 1996, you had, at the time when he was interviewed, to be younger than twenty-six.

But what about the syllabus itself? An easy way of countering Rodríguez's charge would be to describe school texts approved by the education ministry in the early years of the Franco regime, with their drawings of children giving the fascist salute, and their authoritarian catechisms ("He who takes responsibility must also have power. This is the reason why the state has all the power . . . Our sole duty as subordinates is to obey. We must obey without discussion. He who gives orders does so because he knows what he is doing."[31]) A more fruitful approach, though, is to look at what today's set material actually consists of.

History is one school subject within a program followed by everyone between the ages of twelve and sixteen, leading to the school-leaving certificate ESO (Educación Secundaria Obligatoria). Local regions have a degree of autonomy in what is taught, and within that, schools themselves choose among approved textbooks. A lot of material is also available on the Internet. But there's some consistency in what's offered.[32] By the end of the fourth and final year, students are expected to have covered, albeit somewhat superficially, fifteen main historical topics, about half of which are pre–twentieth century, among them the Birth of the Modern State (the Catholic Monarchs, European Expansion and Colonization), Renaissance and Reform, the Age of Enlightenment, and the Industrial Revolution. While the emphasis is on Spanish history, there's always a wider context; in the twentieth

century, for example, a section is devoted to communism, both under the Soviet Union and in China from Mao to the present day. (Islam—a more important topic in world politics today, as well as in the Spanish past—is neglected.) Twenty percent of the history curriculum is given to the main Spanish conflicts between 1920 and 1980, one section being devoted to the period of Alfonso XIII, the Second Republic, and the civil war; another to the Franco era; and a third to everything after it: "The transition, the constitution of 1978, and the statute of autonomous regions, democratic governments, and integration with Europe."

Given that history is just one of the subjects on the curriculum, studying the Second Republic takes up only a tiny fraction of students' time. And like everything else, it is presented by the textbooks in neutral, factual terms. Both books and approved Web materials include, for example, graphics representing the election results of 1931, clearly shown as a wide prism in which no individual party won as much as a quarter of the seats. There are also time charts setting Spanish events in the context of world affairs ("Proclamation of the Second Republic/ Japan occupies Manchuria"). In the printed example I'm drawing on here,[33] the main body of text is complemented by boxed quotations from authoritative sources on matters such as votes for women and reform of agriculture and education. And while it's explained that Republican measures were opposed by a range of vested interests, the left's internal difficulties are also highlighted. The anarchist-led rural uprising in Casas Viejas in 1933 (the "January Revolution"), for example, is attributed to the Republic's delays in carrying out its own policies[34] and is in turn presented as one of the reasons for the conservative victory later that year, a swing to some extent reversed in February 1936, though the diagrams again make clear how much new ground the right still held, by democratic means, at that point.

From the point of view of balance, it's clearly wrong, then, to assume that the curriculum treats the Second Republic as a utopia. But perhaps more sinister influences are at work in Spanish education. What about the Internet? It's instructive to look there, but not for the reasons conservatives might suppose. If you go to Spanish Google and key in *"ESO historia textos II Republica"* ("school certificate history texts Second Republic"), you are, it's true, quickly led to images of smiling women at the ballot box.[35] Another educational site on the first

page, though, offers an article by Fernando González Meléndez entitled "The Other Face of the Second Republic," stressing the baneful influence of the Soviet Union on Republican politics.[36] And if you return to the Google.es results and scroll down another few lines, you'll find a polemical commentator, César Vidal, declaring that the 1931 constitution was like that of the Weimar Republic in that it was "put together by professors" and "failed at the moment of truth because professors are theorists rather than practical people."[37] Vidal uses a good example to illustrate what went wrong: an early proposal to separate church and state was abandoned and was recklessly, damagingly replaced by the dissolution of the Jesuits. Quite right—and these facts are there, too, in the standard textbooks.

The situation, in marked contrast to that under the dictatorship, is not one in which Spanish schoolchildren are being fed a distorted, unitary version of history. On the contrary, both the official material and other sources readily available to them offer an energetically pluralist introduction to a complex set of facts they are asked to interpret. Indeed, the main distortion in this particular case turns out to be a criticism made by a senior scholar in a respected daily paper. Can it be that Spain's problems in dealing with its own twentieth-century past are in part the result of a combustible mix of quarrelsome academics and media greedy for controversy? If so, one of the more inflammatory elements is a disillusioned radical who writes as Pío Moa—his real name is Luis Moa Rodríguez—and has become a bestselling defender of Francoism.

PÍO'S PROPAGANDA

Pío Moa is a skilled propagandist, very busy on the Web as well as in print.[38] He derives some of his impact from the well-tried ploy of presenting himself as an isolated figure battling against the might of institutions that exclude him from their discussions, a posture resembling that of the British historian David Irving, though the similarity ends there. Moa doesn't deny the worst things about the dictatorship. Although his best-known book exasperated his opponents with its title, *Franco: Un balance histórico* ("Franco: A Historical Balance Sheet,"

2005), its success has a lot to do with the fact that in terms of weighing the more extreme pros and cons, an almost histrionically adroit impression of balance is exactly what it provides. Like a professional tightrope walker, Moa is skilled at making what he's doing look more difficult and hazardous than it actually is: we're so busy watching him adjust the pole, swaying unexpectedly before continuing his elaborately measured steps, that we forget about the technicians working away unperturbed in the more inaccessible heights of the big top. If one element in the performance is solitude, another is elusiveness. Few writers apparently so self-confident and so eager to engage in debate have been so resistant to being interviewed, or to taking part in events of the kind where new work by professional scholars is delivered and discussed. It's tempting, then, simply to accept the repudiation of his output by historians on the left, but that would be to ignore what readers like in it and what makes it worthwhile.

Outside the Hispanic world, Moa's many books have been praised by some well-established mainstream conservative historians, among them Henry Kamen and Stanley G. Payne, but have otherwise made little impact. They aren't available in English. Much of what he says (and Moa rarely hesitates either to repeat or to quote himself) is based on three main arguments. The first is incontrovertible: that Stalinism was a dreadful tyranny, that those who supported it were as culpable as those who supported other totalitarian regimes of the time, and that fighting against it was necessary. The second, equally unquestionable, is that Stalinism operated powerfully and ruthlessly in certain sections of the Spanish Republican movement. The third, more debatable, adds up to a charge that this element in the movement "caused" the civil war, by a combination of provocative, insurrectionary activities and electoral corruption.

"Franco: A Historical Balance Sheet" begins with a telling chapter on the Chilean poet-hero of the left, Pablo Neruda, whose expressions of hatred against Franco were matched by his adulation of Stalin: "Stalinists. Let us be proud to bear the name. / Stalinists. The ruling class of our time."[39] The book goes on to discuss the background to the civil war in a way that many Spanish historians have dismissed as replicating what was said under the dictatorship itself, but that draws on admissions by Republican leaders such as Manuel Azaña. This usefully coun-

terbalances history written from the opposite point of view, but the problem is the same as with most Who Started It? arguments: the issue, though not quite counterfactual, is ultimately psychological and speculative. Besides, the fact that Moa's views are traditional matters less than the extent to which they depend on taking at face value quotations from Franco himself. (When Moa draws on some words of Franco's about the self-enclosedness of communism, its police terrorism, its denial of individual liberties, and the omnipresence of the state, the description, as the author himself points out, could be applied to Franco's own regime.)[40] Most readers will object more to Moa's shocking disregard for the social and economic causes of contemporary unrest: "Conservative thought, like religious thought, accepts the existence of injustice, need, and want as part of the human condition."[41] Many conservative thinkers, not to speak of many Christian ones, would demur, and this lack of nuance makes Moa's arguments dangerous as well as merely unintelligent.

Still, in writing about the civil war, while mainly dependent on the familiar but again ultimately fruitless exercise (equally favored by the left) of countering one set of questionable casualty figures with another, Moa also makes important concessions. Despite Nationalist claims to the contrary, for example, he admits that there wasn't a left-wing revolution in Spain.[42] As for the aftermath, he allows that the repression was "the blackest stain on Francoism" (thereby implicitly admitting that there were others), before lapsing into a new exercise in tit for tat: they were bad, but the other side had behaved much worse in 1936. Arguing from bad cases is a Moa specialty. Nationalist anti-Semitism? What about the neglect of Jewish refugees by the Western allies?[43] Dictatorship? The Russian dissident Solzhenitsyn said that contemporary Soviet citizens would have been astounded by the freedoms enjoyed by the Spanish. (It doesn't seem to bother Moa that Solzhenitsyn's remark was made in 1976, after Franco had died.)[44]

Moa is right, though, in another of his revisionist claims: that in some ways Spain flourished under the regime. Most people agree that the best characteristics of post-dictatorship Spain include strong democracy, social stability, and a degree of prosperity that, though now (along with that of much of the rest of Europe) clearly much weaker than it seemed, continues to give the poor a degree of security undreamed of

before the second half of the twentieth century. Many would go further and say that the foundations of all this were laid under Franco. In terms of sequence of events, in fact, this is undeniable, though it's problematic if you're thinking about cause and effect. Still, there's more common ground here between left and right than either side likes to admit, and Moa's view—which gives substance to what many ordinary people of his own generation have always said—has the advantage of providing a moral loophole. Those who have been living with the increasingly voluble reproaches of their children and grandchildren turn out to have some arguments on their side.

None of this is simple. Spain's increasing prosperity in the 1960s and '70s was part of a much broader Western phenomenon—one that Franco at first mishandled. The country also, like Portugal and Greece, benefited disproportionately from an offshoot of the newly spread wealth of northwest Europe: mass tourism. As for social stability, it was of course among the regime's main aims and came at great cost. Still, you don't have to be a Marxist to know that many processes in history, as in private life, work through reaction and counterreaction, and just as the regime's repressiveness was bound to encourage some of the resistance it sought to crush, so some members of the regime itself found themselves acknowledging and adapting to their opponents' aspirations, even at the risk of direct confrontation with Franco himself. This was particularly true after the mid-1950s, a period on which historians have by now done a lot of work and which they see as the first phase of what might be called the "long Transition."

ENEMIES WITHIN

Franco always faced internal as well as external opposition. He needed the traditionalist right, in the form of monarchists and the Falange as well as of the higher military, but feared their ambitions; and he was at odds with some rising factions in the Church. More and more was handled by his closest ally, Luis Carrero Blanco, and the two men placed an increasing amount of trust in members of Opus Dei, the relatively modern, and modernizing, Catholic organization founded in Spain but based in Rome, international in scope and contacts and character-

ized by two elements: that most of its members were laypeople who did ordinary jobs, some of them in positions of considerable power, and that they included ambitious, highly educated women. Opus Dei was well placed to help translate European and American concerns, especially about the economy, to the dictatorship in ways it could grasp and was willing to act on.

Outside government, while the regime enjoyed plenty of broad support, it was also under attack from various organizations that themselves had a range of interconnections as well as divergences. These included the Basque independence movement ETA, which eventually assassinated Carrero Blanco; the Communist Party of Spain and other outlawed political groups, mostly based abroad but also operating underground in Spain (see pp. 236–41 on Jorge Semprún); trade unions and other workers' organizations; prodemocratic student organizations; and groups within the Church motivated by concerns about social inequality and about the violence of repressive measures taken against activists with similar sympathies.[45]

A number of these elements of resistance and progress came together in 1956, the twentieth anniversary of the beginning of the civil war. "Coming together," in fact, was a conscious and crucial part of what they did by way of offering an alternative to Franco, who had always operated on a divide-and-rule basis, both within his own government and nationally.

Opposition of so many kinds and from so many quarters led to changes in how the dictatorship operated, some sporadic (periods of "openness" alternated with the opposite, much as they did in the Soviet Union), others steadier and more gradual, among them a dawning recognition that opposition and disagreement had intrinsic value. The transition to democracy, while not part of Franco's agenda, became inevitable given what was happening inside the country, itself in part a consequence of what was happening outside in an increasingly interconnected Western world. From this perspective, Pío Moa's autobiographical account of his experiences as a would-be revolutionary in the late 1960s and the 1970s—a time when other activists of his generation were either treating the regime as a subject for historical study or helping to build the new democracy, or both—makes richly ironic reading.[46] The Organización Marxista-Leninista Española (OMLE) that Moa

belonged to was frustrated by encountering little popular support. One of the reasons for this seemed to be that the regime was treating the trade unions with increasing tolerance. Another, of course, was prosperity. While most Spanish people were getting on with their work and their home lives and enjoying the noticeable benefits of what some have called pre-post-Francoism, a great deal of the activists' time was spent at international meetings in the course of which the nuances of difference between them were scrutinized and magnified. In 1971, Moa began his national service in the marines and found his fellow recruits as politically apathetic as the workers of the Madrid suburbs. Caught in possession of subversive literature, he spent some time in a military prison. Apparently undeterred, after returning to civilian life he became involved in a scheme to rob a bank as a way of raising funds for OMLE, an episode so drably related that its comic aspects strike the reader only afterward. Much the same is true of a mission to Bilbao, where he was supposed to form links with ETA but found its members strangely hard to get hold of. In situations like this, it would not have been surprising if there had been suspicion that he had become a police spy: a thought that, once it enters the reader's mind, is hard to shake off.

Moa says that his conversion to Francoism came between the events described and his describing them. One wonders why it took him so long to work out that many of the actions of OMLE and its more dynamically acronymed successor GRAPO (Grupos de Resistencia Antifascistas Primero de Octubre)—such as the killing of a bank guard in revenge for the death of an activist in Barcelona—resembled the kinds of behavior they objected to in the other side.[47] What's also missing from the text is a sense of personal process, of the unraveling of a puzzle. Anybody who seeks to explain his own time, one feels, ought to be able to make a better job of explaining himself. Did any element in Moa's eventual revision of his earlier beliefs begin during the years described? If so, when, how, and why? And if not, why not? His position, then as now, is all too often represented by two adjectives: *perseguido* and *excluido*.[48] Interestingly, this is the note struck, too, by the memory campaign.

The attitude to that campaign, meanwhile, of Transition-left historians such as Santos Juliá also has unexpected aspects. While many are supportive both of its grassroots origins and of its wish to expose, or at

least confirm, unsavory truths about Francoism, there's also some concern about the sentimental character of much of what's involved and the extent to which it has been exploited for political purposes. Juliá himself has submitted the latter to characteristically scrupulous analysis, finding its origins in the early 1990s in efforts by the long-governing but by then weakened and divided PSOE to discredit the increasingly electable PP by presenting it as the natural successor of Francoism.[49] From the point of view of most nonspecialist readers, one of the big questions is still not only what divides parties—and families, and individuals within themselves—but what unites them. If one mystery is how Spain came to fall upon itself, another is how it put itself back together again. The Transition is both an astonishing fact and a hopeful parable about human survival—one that lends itself as much to a writer of fiction as to a historian. The most powerful account we have of a key moment in the process is by a novelist, Javier Cercas.

YOU COULDN'T MAKE IT UP

Most of the second half of this book is about how fictional narratives, mainly novels and films, have been used to interpret and reinterpret events in Spain between the early 1930s and the establishment of democracy. Part of what writers have been doing, especially as time has passed since the events involved, is a meta-process, investigating the relations among documentary history, memory, and imagination. For general readers all over the world, Cercas's *Soldiers of Salamis* (*Soldados de Salamina*), first published in Spanish in 2001 and made into a film by David Trueba, is a key part of all this. The novel dramatizes, among other things, the connectedness of opposed sides in the civil war, and this notion is taken further by Cercas in an essentially nonfictional work, *The Anatomy of a Moment* (*Anatomía de un instante*, 2009), which also, and again like the earlier novel, explores the fictionality of history, the seeming artistry of events themselves. Here is a crucial passage:

> History fabricates strange figures, frequently resigns itself to sentimentalism and does not disdain the symmetries of fiction, as if it

wanted to endow itself with meaning that on its own it did not possess. Who could have predicted that the change from dictatorship to democracy in Spain would not be plotted by the democratic parties, but by the Falangists and the Communists, irreconcilable enemies of democracy and each other's irreconcilable enemies during three years of war and forty post-war years? Who would have predicted that the Secretary General of the Communist Party in exile would set himself up as the most faithful political ally of the last Secretary General of the Movimiento, the single fascist party? Who could have imagined that Santiago Carrillo would end up turning into an unconditional protector of Adolfo Suárez and into one of his last friends and confidants? No one did, but maybe it wasn't impossible to do: on the one hand, because only irreconcilable enemies could reconcile the irreconcilable Spain of Franco; on the other, because . . . Santiago Carrillo and Adolfo Suárez were profoundly similar in spite of their superficial differences.[50]

These thoughts are anchored in a particular moment in the Transition: the first crucial episode in Spanish history to have been broadcast live over the radio while simultaneously being filmed. This was an attempted military coup against the young democracy in February 1981, when armed civil guards burst into parliament just as a new, centrist prime minister was being sworn in. Shots were fired into the ceiling—the holes are still there—and everyone was ordered on to the floor, but three men disobeyed. The backgrounds of two of them might have been assumed to put them on the same side as the insurrectionists: the outgoing prime minister, Adolfo Suárez, was a former Francoist, as was his deputy, General Manuel Gutiérrez Mellado, who had fought with the Nationalists in the civil war and made his military career under the dictatorship. The other member of parliament who stayed put was the Communist leader Santiago Carrillo. Cercas explores the complex routes by which these three ultimately found themselves working together for parliamentary democracy against the rule of violence. The book is not a novel. An attempt by the writer to turn his material into fiction failed—failed, he came to believe, because "the reality of 23 February was of such magnitude that it was invincible. . . . none of what I could imagine about 23 February concerned me and excited

me as much or could be as complex and persuasive as the pure reality of 23 February."[51] The dichotomy is false, as much of the rest of the book makes clear, and Cercas's downplaying the role of imagination is itself a rhetorical device. Still, we know what he means, and much of the power of this remarkable work comes from the fact that what it relates actually happened in the ways described.

Paradoxically, the narrative takes a different trajectory from that of much contemporary historiography; it is confident, authoritative, "unitary," in a way that history writing has (itself in part under fiction's influence) become cautious of. It also lacks notes of the specific kinds that allow readers to check sources; you have to trust the teller as well as his tale. Such assurance rebukes those who claim that the past has been deliberately forgotten, erased. This, Cercas bluntly says, "is a lie." What happened was not only different but much more subtle and ethically wise. By shelving, not forgetting, the past, those who had been defeated in the civil war avoided "an ignominious settling of scores" and drew attention away from the fact that they were restoring, in more workable form, the system that had been defeated in 1939. It was as if they had all read Max Weber and thought, like him, that there was nothing more abject than to seek only to be right. Cercas roundly condemns those who "instead of being concerned with what the politician is interested in, the future and the responsibility towards that future, are concerned with politically sterile questions of past guilt."[52]

This is Cercas at his most essayistic as well as historiographical. Yet as he says, the elusive differences between fact and fiction, while they may be crucial aren't always so. What has been made of the Franco era by Spanish imaginative writers and filmmakers is, collectively, among the best ways available of accessing the truth.

Fiction's Memories [i]

First-Generation Novels of the Spanish War and Postwar

It's the night of July 17–18, 1936. The Republican prime minister sleeps uneasily. There have been warnings of a military coup, and his guard has been reinforced with new machine guns and extra troops; no one knows, though, whether the men are ready to fight. In the streets of Madrid, municipal workers clear rubbish while a couple of newspaper editors prepare for a long day's work. Communications with Morocco—at its closest, just ten miles from the peninsula, across the Strait of Gibraltar—have been cut since yesterday, but at government headquarters a call nevertheless comes through from Tetuán for General Pozas, in charge of the Guardia Civil. He's told that troops from the feared Spanish Legion, "El Tercio," have joined other regular soldiers in an uprising against the elected government. Pursing his lips, Pozas orders the Guardia to resist, but too late: the local commander has already been captured.

This is among the ways readers might expect a novel about the Spanish Civil War to begin, and Luis Romero obliges in *Tres días de julio* ("Three Days in July"), first published in 1967 in Barcelona and often reprinted. The prolific Catalan author lived through the period he describes—born in 1916, he began his literary career in the late 1940s—and often turned to it for material. The authenticity this implies is, of course, an artificial notion: like Picasso and Guernica, or the director

of the *DBE* and the *dictadura*, or Javier Cercas and the failed 1981 coup, Romero could "remember" the events involved in the sense people often use in ordinary speech, particularly when talking to those from a younger generation: he was alive at the time, cared about what was happening, heard people talking about it, followed the news. In any stricter understanding of the word, though, the memory is synthetic, a construct made from a range of information mixed with psychological—"imaginative"—responses to it. *Tres días* is a fluently written, vividly imagined historical novel in which various incidents and characters, and most of the dialogue, are invented but that supplies a strong, traditionally top-down outline of how the conflict started. It continues to give some Spanish readers a significant part of what they know about that time.

Like Shakespeare's Roman plays, the novel concentrates on the leading figures: within a few pages we encounter Francisco Franco and the family of José Antonio Primo de Rivera, as well as prime minister Azaña. Before long we are caught up in the battle for the strategically placed southern city Seville, soon to capitulate to a local coup led by General Queipo de Llano. Much is foreshortened and simplified: the book has some of its roots in journalism, an influence played with in the section headings: "Valencia Vacillates"; "Barcelona: Guardia Civil Attacks Hotel Colón"; "Franco Arrives in Morocco."[1] As in most historical novels, though, there are also threads involving representative figures caught up in, rather than directing, events. A wealthy family uses the pretext of a summer holiday to flee from Madrid by car, the trunk crammed with silver. Part of a cigarette smuggling operation between Holland and the Atlantic port of Vigo goes on under the nose of Falangist troops drinking in a café. Meanwhile, the claim to documentary authority is strengthened by photographs of individuals and events, and by a ten-page index of places and people.

Romero worked on the basis of interviews as well as newspaper reports, talking to and corresponding with a lot of people, among them exiles whom, he explains, he cannot safely identify—an acknowledgment bold in itself, even as late as 1967. He wrote the book for readers of all ages, including those born since the war, and he aimed for impartiality, which he took care to distinguish from centrism: "I've tried to position myself not in the middle ground, but at every point along the

line through which the events traveled."[2] Historical truth, he says in a long prologue, is often subjective, changeable, and multifaceted—even ideas such as loyalty and courage mean different things to different speakers.[3] For all that, this in many ways self-contradictory essay is keen to "correct" some claims with which Romero is unhappy, taking issue, for example, with Hugh Thomas's perfectly well-founded claim that foreign powers were involved in these earliest days of the war.[4] Again, there's a sense, in the paradoxical statement near the prologue's end—just when the novel proper is about to start, in July 1936—of wanting to please everyone: "What concerns us most about Spain is its future."[5] Still, Romero articulates debates that, almost half a century after his book appeared, have come to be regarded as daringly new. He lists some of those who died "for God and Spain" with a painstaking evenhandedness very unlike that shown by war memorials of the time. Generals Goded, Fanjul, and Núñez de Prado, key figures in the coup, were all shot—but so, too, he points out, were the president of Catalonia, Lluís Companys, and two generals who refused to take part in the uprising, Enrique Salcedo and Rogelio Caridad Pita.[6] Other prominent names from both sides are listed, and Romero is careful to say that there are many who aren't recorded—the location of whose graves, even, can't be established.[7]

Is there any justice, then? Contradicting the patriotic, religious claims of the dictatorship, Romero says no: by its nature, war dispenses with impartiality. Even those who by profession are members of the judiciary "take sides and, according to the side they're on, judge, condemn and execute." And there's no appeal against such judgments. "No one, as far as I know, has ever resurrected anyone after a war has ended."[8]

Campaigners against what they describe as Spain's cultural amnesia have themselves evidently forgotten that a bestselling writer published in Spain while Franco was still alive made so unforgetful a statement. The extent to which the dictatorship controlled what was written has been exaggerated in popular mythology, not only of itself but by comparison with liberties supposed to have been enjoyed in other parts of the world. While it's generally acknowledged that Spanish restrictions were eased somewhat in the 1960s, this tends to be attributed to the regime's wish to improve its reputation elsewhere: true

enough, but it's not as if conflicts over freedom of expression were un-known at the time in Britain or the United States. In Spain, meanwhile, in the same year as *Tres días*, another vivid novel of the civil war came out in which strong anti-Francoist opinions are voiced. Ángel María de Lera's *Las últimas banderas* (literally, "The Last Flags," 1967), which draws closely on the author's own experiences in the Republican army and as a political prisoner, is set in the war's final stages; the *banderas* are those of the side facing defeat. The mood is vengeful as well as em-bittered: one of the men who has been most articulate in defense of Republican values kills a Nationalist profiteer in cold blood. Madrid's long resistance to the siege is unmistakably depicted as heroic, but in these last months the Republican combatants are increasingly in disar-ray, bewildered by the factionalism of their own side, frightened of de-feat, and uncertain how the victors will behave. Emigration has its attractions, though one man who earlier fled the brutality of the Span-ish mines says that the reason he came back was that things were no better in Argentina. Another character is ridiculed for his optimism that, as a Republican intellectual, he may be needed by the victors to help with postwar reconstruction: "You suppose because you've put together a book on international chess out of press cuttings and bits plagiarized from other authors they're going to want your advice? . . . Franco will give you a call and say, 'I'm putting you in charge of foreign affairs.' Sure he will. Sure."[9]

Has the war been worth fighting? There are a thousand ways of looking at it, the protagonist Federico observes in what reads like an authorial comment, but any war is "tragic, deceitful, destructive and corrupting, because it enables hatred, falsehood, and betrayal to be seen as grand, heroic virtues."[10] This is sententious—de Lera is a moral-ist, an editor as much as a fiction writer—but some of the book's essayistic passages are still moving, for example when the subject is how overpopulated Spain has become, not with the living but the dead: perhaps graves should be dug vertically, to save space.[11] As for memory, another character asks himself what the good of that is. "We should gather up all this misery and set fire to it—all this use-less misery—because what will be left of it all anyway in a few years? Just other people's memories."[12]

CELA THE OUTSIDER

Some Spanish novels published during the regime, then, recorded the experiences of the 1930s in ways that were far removed from the Francoist myth of a glorious crusade. In doing so, they contributed to cultural memory while remaining skeptical about its usefulness. A particularly striking case is the winner of the 1989 Nobel Prize for Literature, Camilo José Cela, who had briefly served in the Nationalist army during the civil war and was wounded. He subsequently volunteered for a job in censorship, working in the department of "Investigación y Vigilancia." In 1957, at the height of anti-Francoist activity by radical intellectuals and students, he became the youngest member of the Spanish Royal Academy. This is not a résumé that readily ingratiates him with the more ideologically inflexible of Republican sympathizers, but another way of describing Cela is to say that he was an outsider, a troublesomely truthful artist whose sensitivity was partly protected by a shell of outrageous, often hilariously shocking rudeness. Born in 1916, the tubercular young man studied medicine in Madrid but spent most of his time attending lectures on contemporary literature and hanging out with writers, among them the radical playwright and novelist Max Aub (see pp. 165–71). Cela admired Joyce and other novelists who found inspiration in populous cities—especially, in Spain, Benito Pérez Galdós. He was attracted, too, by forms of art, such as surrealism, that shocked audiences: for the sake of that effect not only of itself (though he enjoyed it for itself) but because it asserted that much that we encounter in life does and should shock us, a view amply confirmed by the war. Working along parallel lines to Samuel Beckett and Albert Camus, Jean Genet and Michel Tournier, Cela began to write about life seen, as often as not, from the points of view of people impoverished financially, imaginatively, experientially; people, too, whose understanding of the world was more sexual than political. His bleak first novel, *La familia de Pascual Duarte* (*Pascual Duarte's Family*),[13] was published in 1942, the same year as Camus's *L'étranger* (*The Outsider*), and has some resemblances to it, particularly the unexplained violence and seeming amorality of its central figure. To many readers, these characteristics accurately reflect the brutal sociopolitical context from which the book emerged, in a way that counters the regime's idealiza-

tion of Spanish family values. As one critic has put it, the novel depicts "rape, matricide . . . premarital sex and pregnancy, abortion, prostitution, and adultery." In doing so, it represents "a lack of positive authority in all the spheres promoted by the regime: biological, political, and religious father figures are all abusive and inadequate, while neither biological mothers nor motherhood nurtures or provides for the sons and daughters. This is a novel which offers . . . a reconfiguration of the traumatized family of the nation with its bruised and battered children."[14]

From *Pascual Duarte*'s intense focus on one character, Cela turned to a cast of hundreds in *La colmena* (*The Hive*), different versions of which were rejected by the censors between 1946 and 1950, until Manuel Fraga, then secretary general of the Instituto de Cultura and later minister of the interior, prompted in part by the book's appearance in Argentina, intervened to let it through.[15] Set in Madrid in 1943—a time when some of its characters are beginning to fear that Hitler may not win the Second World War after all—the novel richly imagines the interlocking existences of people to most of whom politics and religion mean little or nothing, whereas the elusive and frankly depicted compulsions of appetite and, especially, sex are all-important.

Though less well known than *Pascual Duarte* or *The Hive*, another of Cela's most powerful books is *San Camilo, 1936*. It was published in Spain in 1969, while Franco was still in power, but did not appear in English until 1991, and then not from a commercial press.[16] The hectic, reiterative, sparsely punctuated, and unparagraphed narrative is set, like *Tres días de julio*, over the first days of the civil war, but is confined to Madrid. People who have come to dominate Spanish history books make occasional appearances: the socialist lieutenant José Castillo Sería, for example, murdered by Falangist gunmen, and the conservative parliamentarian José Calvo Sotelo, killed in turn by Castillo's fellow officers. But the focus is on ordinary people, both real and fictional, including several who are killed but whose deaths make no headlines: some prostitutes; a man running through the streets trying to find a midwife. Historical events, the narrator says, are always credited to a powerful individual rather than to "the people . . . perhaps more than twenty or thirty thousand men, each with his moving little novel stuck to his heart."[17] Most of the story is set in one or another of a range of brothels and "houses of assignation" in the center of Madrid,

including one known as the League of Nations, "because there they've got everything, Moors, Germans, Belgians, Frenchwomen, Portuguese, everything." The brothel is to *San Camilo* what the café is to *The Hive*, and like Cela's earlier novels, this one repeatedly insists on the coexistence of the trivial with the historically important: a fly in someone's coffee with Calvo Sotelo's assassination; the early days of conflict with what's happening in the Tour de France. Meanwhile, the text often broadens out in a philosophizing way. Cela laments the indiscriminacy of war and particularly its failure to change anything ("they kill priests, they kill Andalusian peasants or they kill schoolteachers, it depends on who's doing the killing, but finally . . . everything stays the same only with more people dead"). He points out the confusions that underlie war's simplistic polarities: the fact that a Republican may have conservative sympathies more in tune with the ideas of this or that individual among the internally divided fascists (Cela's word) than with the supposed position of the similarly faction-ridden government.

San Camilo, 1936 has been criticized for what has been seen as moral and political evasiveness. It's safe to ignore the more literal-minded of these attacks—one complained about the disproportionate amount of time Cela's characters seem to spend in brothels[18]—but it's true, and mattered more to readers during the dictatorship than it does today, that, as the exiled Spanish historian Tuñón de Lara pointed out, the novelist does not concern himself with the social-historical causes of the war, or with celebrating heroes. De Lara was a friend of Cela's but had been on the other side, was imprisoned by the Nazis, and, between 1946 and the end of Franco's life, wrote and taught in France. To him, the war was about clear-cut issues. Literary historians tend to forget, though, that the essay on Cela's novel in which De Lara made these criticisms was published by Cela himself, in a literary magazine he had founded in 1956 as a way of countering cultural officialdom and giving space to the ideas of Spanish writers living abroad.[19]

In the novel itself, the voices of what is presented as ideological brashness are answered by those of vacillation and muddle. A scene between a leftist turned reactionary named Cándido Modrego and his neighbor Olegario Murciego is typical, their words and actions sliding into one another's and simultaneously juxtaposed with large-scale events:

things are turning ugly Don Olegario, we must return to the Inquisition and torture of our ancestors, there's no other way, you see how people act up as soon as they get a little confidence, what we need here is an iron fist in the name of the cross and the sword, anything else is just the way to our downfall, yes maybe, I think you're wrong, I mean not a hundred percent right, but maybe you are right Modrego, who knows, I can't say, maybe they're all right and this really is going to be some mess, Cándido Modrego and Don Olegario smoke butts, there are lots of them in the bicarbonate boxes, there are at least three boxes full to overflowing. At 3 a.m. the president charges Martínez Barrio with the mission of forming a cabinet . . .

Above all, *San Camilo, 1936* grieves for Spain, gazing at a graveyard full of flowers of all colors, ignoring the shouts of "*¡Viva la república!*" and "*¡Viva España!*" because "it is no use being too enthusiastic when melancholy nests in the heart."[20]

The full title, *Vísperas, festividad y octava de San Camilo del año 1936 en Madrid* ("The Eve, Feast, and Octave of St. Camillus in the Year 1936 in Madrid"), provides its chronological frame (St. Camillus's Day was July 18; an octave is a period of commemoration lasting eight days[21]) while intimately linking author and subject. Camilo José Cela was named after St. Camillus, a sixteenth-century Italian soldier's son who had a difficult childhood and adolescence (he was a reckless gambler) and followed his father into the army but, in his mid-twenties, turned to work in a hospital for the incurably ill, what we would now call a hospice. Camillus was eventually put in charge there and founded, among other communities, a religious order of military nurses. The physical and moral world of the novel is superficially the polar opposite of what's suggested by the title, but they are joined by compassion. The civil war is as meaningless to Cela as the First World War was to the poets on both sides. His book is dedicated "To the conscripts of 1937, all of whom lost something: their life, their freedom, their dreams, their hope, their decency. And not to the adventurers from abroad, Fascists and Marxists, who had their fill of killing Spaniards like rabbits and whom no one had invited to take part in our funeral."

Among Cela's themes, as among those of de Lera in *Las últimas banderas*, is the fact that between memory and forgetting there is a real

choice. *Olvido* serves a psychological function. "No one knows whether it is better to remember or to forget," the text says at one point; "memory is sad and forgetting on the other hand usually repairs and heals."[22] A little later, the point is put more caustically: "the best thing is to go to the whorehouse and forget."[23] At one level such statements seem straightforward enough and in tune with Cela's concerns elsewhere with the immediate and the empirical. But as the violence mounts and some of the book's characters, in all their former immediacy, are killed, the vantage point shifts: "people don't usually attach much importance to memory and finally it crashes against a wall of impassive dead men, accusing dead men . . . people usually do not believe that memory acts as a ballast and keeps feeling on an even keel."[24] The whole book, in the end, is a puzzled, angry act of commemoration, or a collection of such acts. And its claims *not* to be that, its impulsive rejections of memory, are an intensifying trope, a mourner's refusal to mourn.

The complexities of this astonishing novel, its self-contradictions, its lurches between high intensity and moments of casual-seeming cynicism, are part of what makes it so powerful and true. "Historically true," one is tempted to say, if for no other reason than that *San Camilo, 1936* distills the experiences and feelings of someone who lived through the events described. But if we didn't independently know that Cela was a lifelong conservative, there would be no way of telling this from the book—any more than we can tell from Shakespeare's plays what his religious affiliation was, if any. *San Camilo, 1936* is a law of historical memory unto itself, strengthened rather than weakened by the interpretative demands it makes. And very close to the end, it delivers its own verdict on attempts to ameliorate what has already passed: "history is not a charitable form of knowledge but a heartless craft; it is useless to try to change it."[25]

SOME USES OF PROPAGANDA

Cela's position in world literature seems secure now, and a great deal has been written about him. Some comparisons help to clarify his individuality, whether by contrast or by unexpected resemblance. He began to write at a time when most, though not all, Spanish fiction set in

the recent past was split into two categories: novels blatantly opposed to the Republic, published in Spain itself, and those that began to appear abroad, written by men who had fought against Franco and were now in exile. At the time, relatively few "ordinary" readers within Spain had access to the latter, though the books were secretly circulated and read not only by those involved in, or just sympathetic to, the resistance but also by literary people who worked for the dictatorship in one way or another, especially those, like Cela, in censorship and political "vigilance." Writers, publishers, and critics tend to know one another pretty well, or at least about one another, they read each others' work, and the educated Spain of the mid-twentieth century was far from overpopulated. It also preserved a distinctive tradition of semi-public gatherings in cafés, the *tertulia*, in which simply by being in the same place at the same time, people could hear writers talking and reading from their work. Before the civil war, *tertulias*, although generally associated with particular authors and movements, often involved, indeed existed for, disagreement. The personal engagements of many imaginative people crossed party lines, and those lines were themselves much less clear than the simplifications of hindsight can make them look. To talk about Nationalists or Republicans, in this context, is to describe broad territories, themselves internally split into patterns as irregular as in a jigsaw puzzle. Some of the pieces could easily fit more than one place.

Still, there were novels that took a more propagandist line, especially while the civil war was being fought. Ramón J. Sender's autobiographical *The War in Spain*, for example, which appeared in Russian as well as English[26] before being published in Spain (as *Contraataque*) in 1938, and to which we'll return (see pp. 171–76), not only was explicitly sympathetic to communism but was adjusted by Sender in response to Soviet censorship. And around the same time two books came out that give as good an insight as anything into what the war felt like to those on the other side: the winning side, though in the period in which the novels are set, the outcome was far from certain.

The author of one of them, Wenceslao Fernández Flórez, in some ways identified himself with Franco. They were of roughly the same generation, came from the same region, and their families knew each other—the men's fathers had grown up together in the tightly knit

naval community of El Ferrol. Fernández Flórez's father died when Wenceslao was fifteen, and the boy was left to fend for himself, leaving school and making a career as a journalist and novelist. Franco, as we've seen, suffered a setback of his own when he found naval college closed to him, and in a break with family tradition, he joined the army. Resilient and determined, both young men were driven to succeed in unforeseen ways and became contemptuous of anything that threatened them. In one of the more memorable passages of *Una isla en el mar rojo* ("An Island in the Red Sea"), Fernández Flórez describes a Republican militia in terms for which the description "class hatred" might have been invented: "The small hours resounded with little trucks . . . carrying rowdy gangs of bricklayers, tarts, street performers, sewage workers, thieves, and lunatics into the Guadarramas, all exalted by the double ideal of ruling the universe and stealing a chicken . . ."[27] The novel was published in Madrid soon after the Nationalists declared victory in 1939, was often reprinted between then and the early 1950s,[28] and appeared in Italian translation in 1943 under Mussolini.[29]

Fernández Flórez was a prominent conservative journalist and novelist, as flagrantly elitist in his beliefs as his central male characters in *Una isla* yet sufficiently independent in some of his thinking—for example, in support of Galician separatism—to have been awarded a medal under the Second Republic.[30] When the military coup began, he had found himself stuck in loyalist Madrid and labeled an enemy of the ruling Republic and of most of what it stood for. This is the predicament, too, of Ricardo in the novel. In the opening chapter, set in the capital shortly before the coup, Ricardo and his fiancée are at a cinema watching the recent American film of *A Tale of Two Cities*.[31] They and their friends, talking about it immediately afterward, debate whether anything like the French Revolutionary scenes they've just watched could happen in Madrid. One of them argues that the film should be banned.[32] Very soon, militias of the Frente Popular are out on the streets: "a typically revolutionary mob," in Ricardo's description, composed of "filthy subhumans with murderous frowns and yelling, scruffy, hyena-like women."[33] We hear a lot more about such mobs, and also about their contemptible ideas. There are only a few explicitly political conversations in the book, and they generally consist of long

ultraconservative diatribes by Ricardo's brother-in-law Demetrio in reaction to some mild, and invariably very short, expression of a pro-Republican view. In the first such exchange, if it can be called that, a neighbor's young daughter, Irene—who, to Demetrio's disdain, describes herself as both a Communist and a Catholic—says that the people in a parade going by are workers. "Manual workers," Demetrio corrects her, and goes on to explain that to work with your hands in a mechanical age is a sign of inferiority, not its opposite.[34] The man we should admire most is the one who produces most. Besides, as a Catholic, she surely remembers that work is a curse from God. It must follow, then, that it's virtuous to work less, rather than more. Irene protests mildly that working people are the ones who suffer most, and are also the most numerous. Numbers are no argument, Demetrios says. Flies and ants are more numerous than humans, and in any case humanity is organized like a pyramid, with the masses at the bottom. He ignores the question of suffering, and when it's brought up again much later by Ricardo's fiancée's father, a member of the Republican government, it's sidestepped with similar dishonesty.

Nothing in the book overtly distances it from the views of Demetrios and Ricardo. Why should anyone now bother to read it? Precisely because it is so revealing about people like them, in that place at that time: cultural memory has no point if it recuperates only half the past. Fernández Flórez says in a foreword that the book is as much a memoir as a work of fiction, and much of what Ricardo experiences corresponds to his own story. A group of gunmen come for him, but he manages to get out of the house he's staying in by a back route. He spends a night in the streets before hiding in the garage of another friend. He's captured and imprisoned, witnessing some terrifying, ignominious scenes as people are taken away to be shot. Released after the intervention of Don Ramón, he spends more time hiding in the houses of his protector and other friends until he finds shelter in a foreign embassy and, six months later, an escape route to Valencia, from there by boat to northern Spain and on foot into France.

It might be a story of adventure, of courage, of idealism, albeit for a bad cause. Instead, Ricardo is frank about the fact that his predominant feeling, and that of most others in his predicament, is terror, combined with total inability to take action on his own behalf. He thinks of

no one but himself, and the idea that he might actually try to fight for his own side never crosses his mind. In the legation, the atmosphere among his thirty fellow fugitives is partly one of helplessness, partly of retreat into obsessive religiosity. No one even thinks of attempting a mass breakout or counterattack. The few who get away do so, like Ricardo, because the escape route has been organized from outside and they can afford to pay.

In all this, though, there's something that seems designed to resist our sympathy—indeed, to call up its opposite. "Why?" Ricardo asks when he learns that he's a target for assassination. "I've never been involved in politics, I've had nothing to do with the workers!"[35] Later, in the legation, while bombs and shells crash down on the city's outskirts, he thinks nostalgically of the Madrid of a few years earlier, the streetlights, the expensive cars, cafés, *tertulias*—of men leaving the casino with presents to appease their wives and of how they "protected those little bags of sweets against the pushing and shoving of the multitude."[36] Fernández Flórez was known as an ironist, and perhaps there is some satire at the expense of his fictional alter ego in his maudlin lament over the loss of good times: *"¡Oh, tan lejos, tan lejos!"*—"Oh, so long, long ago!" In these images of well-off men who've never troubled about their social inferiors except to keep their own trivial goodies out of the marauding hands of the mob, there's a novelist's clarity about the Spanish right, seventy-five years ago, that speaks about other cultures at other times, too.

Another anti-Republican novelist of the time has more to say about the blindness of his own class. Born in 1906, Agustín de Foxá was almost a generation younger than Wenceslao Fernández Flórez; belonged to a different world, that of the monarchist aristocracy; and saves most of his satire for it. Where Fernández describes the underclass getting out of hand, de Foxá's focus is on an upper class stuck in the wrong time. *Madrid de corte a checa* ("Madrid from Royal Court to Soviet Jail") was published in 1938, before *Una isla en el mar rojo*, but covers some of the same ground: the city under the Republic; well-off people being attacked by those who formerly worked for them; panic, executions, flight. De Foxá starts his story earlier, though, with the collapse of the Miguel Primo de Rivera dictatorship, the departure of King Alfonso XIII, and the election of the Second Republic in 1931.

Two elements characterize the whole work. One is the depiction of an enclosed, highly cultivated world in which not only every individual but every literary quotation is known to everyone. The other is the fact that it has scarcely changed over a century. To many of the main characters, the royal court of the title is a second home: one where they regularly play cards, drink, dance, gossip, and arrange their children's marriages. Outside, Republican students have barricaded the university against their opponents. Roof tiles rain down on policemen and on members of the Juventud Monárquica (Monarchist Youth Movement). Some are injured, and—here as everywhere in the book—it's assumed that their names will be recognized. Andrés Sáenz de Heredia, for example, who gets kicked in the stomach and staggers along corridors defaced with obscene graffiti, is a relative of the ex-dictator; his cousin José Antonio will soon found the Falange. This intimate social texture helps explain why *Madrid de corte a checa*, though successfully reissued in Spain in 1993—a time of electoral disappointment with the left—has never been translated into English.[37] The first two pages introduce the names of half a dozen real people, three places, and three organizations as well as the titles of two books and two periodicals, though *introduce* is scarcely the word for a process so lacking in background information. One is reminded—it's part of the point—that this world has functioned precisely by excluding those who don't have any bearings. Its doing so, though, is also what now makes it dysfunctional. At the theater on the evening of the riot, a government minister sits in his box and offers sweets to his guests, along with "nineteenth-century compliments." He assures everyone that what happened earlier was no more than an infantile squabble, "*una chiquillada*."

Childish maybe, but one of the students was killed, and what follows highlights a similar disconnection between how events are perceived and what their consequences will be. A meeting of the Monarchist Youth Movement is depicted as a quixotic affair in which boys fantasize about knightly quests, read chivalric romances with tears in their eyes, and tell competing stories about their great-grandfathers. The late arrival of one of them prompts a brief exchange of news about the new government, but this soon gives way to a discussion of the memoirs of a soldier in the reign of Ferdinand and Isabella. Here is part of the cultural context in which the king's departure into exile

leaves Madrid, according to the narrator, with "a strange sensation of having been orphaned."[38]

The story is poignant in that it offers no substitute for the anachronistic values it lightly satirizes. De Foxá has as little sympathy with the Republic as Fernández Flórez, though his distaste is as much aesthetic as political. The city's old culture is seen as having been thrown out in favor of Picasso's "anarchy of shapes and colors," and the jazz singing of Josephine Baker, with her "banana-leaf skirt" (*falda de plátanos*), in revolt against "the elegance of Viennese waltz."[39] The bookstalls, meanwhile, are filled with works about "sex and contraception, pseudoscientific pornography mixed up with Marxist pamphlets."[40] In social-historical terms, there are some half glimpses of fairness, as when it's acknowledged that the new regime has its origins in "centuries and centuries of slavery."[41] But how much self-criticism is there in this? A modern reader too easily forgets that to the courtiers of Alfonso XIII, slavery of one kind or another was part of the divine order. Natural "superiority" had come under attack, the book tells us, from "hunchbacks, the cross-eyed, the rickety, and loveless, flaccid-breasted tarts who've never known the pleasure of holding a young man's body in their arms." You need to read it in Spanish to hear the expectorant contempt: "*los jorobados, los bizcos, los raquíticos y las mujerzuelas . . .*"[42]

What might seem an all-too-programmatic contestation of opposites is again complicated, however, by its vividness. Agustín de Foxá was among the first members of the Falange and, like some others in that pre–civil war intake—Rafael Sánchez Mazas is now, thanks to Javier Cercas's *Soldiers of Salamis*, the best known of them outside Spain—a stylish writer: a poet; an admirer, for all his traditionalism, of the anarchic imagination of Ramón María del Valle-Inclán, whose avant-garde writing is mentioned on the novel's first page. *Madrid de corte a checa* has narrative flexibility as well as a keen eye for the absurdities of the world it elegizes. And in its main character, José Félix, one of "*los chicos 'bien'*"—boys from "good" families—de Foxá part-autobiographically delineates the confusions of a generation torn between social justice and the old order. The upper-class student radical is first seen on the roof of his university pelting monarchist fellow students. Thrown out of home by his father, he works for the liberal-progressive journal *El Sol* and is thrilled by the initial victory of the

Second Republic, "regime change without bloodshed."[43] Because his ideas are to do with youth and change, unsupported by any direct experience of politics or of social conditions outside his own world, he sees no contradiction, later, in supporting the charismatic José Antonio Primo de Rivera after first hearing him speak. José Antonio's, after all, is "a new language," one that speaks of a common, universal destiny and of the ability of poets to move ordinary people.[44] At last someone who offers idealism and grandeur instead of the prevailing bureaucratic vocabulary of representatives and commissions. "We belong in the fresh air," José Antonio proclaims, his rhetoric seductively indistinguishable from that of the left, "arm in arm under the stars."

CHOICE OR CHANCE?

Ideology, belief, reason, conscience—the abstractions associated with the civil war play next to no part in what for José Félix can scarcely even be called a decision. One of the themes that unite a number of otherwise disparate narratives set in this period is that for many characters in them, the side they were on was a result of factors almost as arbitrary as whether, a few years later, Europeans farther north happened to be British or German. This is among the concerns of Juan Iturralde in his novel *Días de llamas* ("Days of Flames"), written and rewritten between 1947 and 1973 but not published until after Spain had established its democratic constitution of 1978 (a document whose wording, as it happens, the novelist Cela, by then a senator, helped to polish).

Juan Iturralde was the pseudonym of a state attorney called José María Pérez Prat. During the civil war he was still at his Jesuit school in Madrid and he trained as a lawyer in the turbulent years immediately after the Nationalist victory. He later recalled this time as one of more or less permanent fear on his own part, and *Días de llamas* is an exploration both of that feeling and of the divided beliefs and loyalties of a group of men imprisoned in Republican Madrid. From the outset, the actualities of the narrator's predicament merge with his confused memories of the recent past: for example, of his father's burial, dressed in the mothballed uniform of an artillery colonel, especially of a

moment when the old conservative's cortege is saluted by men on a passing truck waving a red flag. Political change is shown as shifting how everything and everyone is seen, to the point where individual realities become deniable. One of the prisoners says he's seen newspaper references to not only "ex-General Fanjul" (one of the leaders of the coup, captured in Madrid and subsequently executed) but also "ex-philosopher Miguel de Unamuno," the Republican thinker who shocked his supporters by initially supporting the rebels. Yes, another jokes, "and also to 'ex-poet Pemán'"[45]—as if the latter's lifelong conservative monarchism now suddenly disqualifies him as an artist. (You have to imagine someone referring, say, to "ex-poet T. S. Eliot" after the British socialist victory of 1945.) Such changes of perception are accompanied by more concrete transformations. The narrator's brother, Miguel, a captain in the artillery, supported the Republicans at first, then changed sides, was captured, and was offered freedom if he changed back again, but refused. A similar deal is soon held out to the narrator himself: as a lawyer, will he participate in the new "People's Tribunals"? Although one of his colleagues refuses because the tribunals have no legal basis, the narrator believes that, whatever his politics and legal opinions, being involved will give him an opportunity to save some lives.

The judicial character of the story, as well as the fact that much of it takes place in prison, allows for an unhurried setting out of different points of view: about what's owed, or not, to the poor; about progress; about the balance of responsibility for atrocities. The book is not without physical drama (the bombing of Madrid, summary executions), but its biggest moments are those that occur during debates and interrogations: arguments in which tragedy is voiced and that themselves embody the terrible irresolubility of much of what's being discussed.

There's a similar but still more extended argumentativeness in a six-volume saga written in exile by someone who, before the war, was already among the most successful pro-Republican writers and public intellectuals: Max Aub. Born in 1903 in Paris to Jewish parents, his father German, his mother French, Aub grew up in Spain, joined the PSOE in his early twenties, was writer-manager of an avant-garde theater company in Valencia, published the first of his many novels in 1934, and, working as a cultural attaché for the Republican govern-

ment, was among those responsible for organizing the purchase and display of Picasso's *Guernica*. After the Republican defeat in 1939 he went into exile, first in France, where he was imprisoned as a Communist, and eventually in Mexico. There, between 1943 and 1967, he wrote and published his series of novels set in the civil war, later known as *El laberinto mágico* ("The Magic Labyrinth"). Aub was part of a whole school of Spanish writers in exile, among them Arturo Barea, who wrote and published in England and died there in 1957; Manuel Lamana in Argentina; Jorge Semprún, officially in Paris, though in fact he spent much of his time clandestinely in Spain; and Ramón Sender, at first in Mexico and, after 1942, mainly in the United States. The situations in which they wrote and the audiences for their work hardly overlapped with those of writers still in Spain, who are our main subject. But since they all in different ways suffered the same war, and their accounts of it have the benefits both of having been written in relative freedom and, in some cases, of having appeared first or been distributed most widely, they need to be seen as having helped create the historical memory of that time—through underground circulation, for their contemporaries in Spain, and also for subsequent generations.

THREE EARLY EXILES

1. Aub: Naming, Talking, Fantasizing

Aub has devoted readers in Spain, Germany, and, to a lesser extent, France, but only one of his novels has so far appeared in English: *Campo cerrado* (1943), the first volume in the Magic Labyrinth series, translated by Gerald Martin as *The Field of Honour*. In it, a self-educated young man is jostled between the gregarious, vociferous, anarchically overlapping intellectual and political groups and gangs in 1920s and '30s Barcelona: a world of many speechmakers and a few quiet idealists among whom he is led more by accident than choice, but via violence and revenge killing, into the Falange. The saga mixes real characters and fictional ones, historical and imaginary events; it is densely populated, garrulous, confusing, tender, funny. Antonio

Muñoz Molina has stressed the writer's debts to Galdós,[46] but he also owes something to Cela. Perhaps this is part of what Juan Goytisolo meant in calling Aub "the missing link in Spain's literary modernity." Gerald Martin's efforts to communicate in English Aub's own attempts, in the first volume, to render slangy Catalan dialogue in Castilian (Spanish) are a lesson in untranslatability. What comes through very strongly, though, here as in the rest of the sequence, is the psychology of an era in which fragile attempts to build new political economic structures couldn't withstand personal, emotional attachments. Aub understands idealism, but he knows its opposite at least as well, and finds more of it around. His third volume, for example, *Campo de sangre* ("Field of Blood"), opens memorably with an early morning scene in which a Republican judge and a doctor walk along in amiable philosophical conversation. They've just witnessed an execution. "Cruelty is a fundamental aspect of life," the judge observes. Denouncing your fellow human beings to the authorities is part of this: "People don't do it for the money: they enjoy ratting on each other."[47] Enjoyment is something his friend understands. Julián Templado, the doctor, became a socialist because he didn't like the other side, but his main interests are women and conversation. To him, "Under the microscope, there's not much to distinguish a fascist's saliva from mine."[48] Certainly social conscience isn't among his strengths, or not on a practical level. That night, forgetting that he has a date with an actress, he sits up talking to another friend, absorbed by his argument that civil war could have been avoided if the Republic hadn't been in such a hurry to introduce radical reforms, especially over land ownership. Teresa Guerrero isn't the only person Julián is neglecting here. In a cold corner of Barcelona a man waits most of the night for the doctor to attend to his sick son.[49] Having eventually eaten dinner with the actress, Julián shows up and quickly delivers his opinion: what the child needs is to eat.[50] Instantly he regrets his insensitivity, but not very much, and the narrative moves on: to a captain just back from the battle of Teruel; to a couple with five children, the mother embittered by their not having escaped to Argentina; to an air raid (Julián is in bed with a different woman); to the performance of a new play; and to yet another new character, Lola, a teenager in the Red Cross who becomes caught up in counterespionage.

Aub's affection for his characters is promiscuous. He loves to mix the real and the imagined, the living and the dead, and he loves to use their names. In exile, he fantasized about what Spain might have been like if the military coup had not succeeded, imagining, among other things, a version of the Real Academia Española (Spanish Royal Academy) in which the socialist poet Antonio Machado, instead of having died in 1939, in flight from National Catholicism, had been able to take the place to which he had been elected.[51] Max Aub, in turn, died in 1972 without seeing democracy restored to Spain, a fact movingly pondered still later by Antonio Muñoz Molina. Among the many things that link Spanish writers is a very Catholic notion of succession; while it's true that writers generally work in solitude, they also, whether they like it or not, form a body—some taking their place in an orderly procession, others arguing and competing. Aub's fantasy took the form of his imagined address on his imagined election to the academy in 1956, but it went further than that. He also wrote an imagined reply by an entirely imaginary fellow writer, and he appended a list of the names of the fantasy fellows, with their dates of election. Here, then, is Lorca, who in this fiction was not shot, and was elected in 1942; here are Rafael Alberti and Ramón Sender and Max Aub himself, none of whom went into exile. To a modern reader persuaded that there was an unbridgeable divide between the virtuous in exile and the compromised who stayed behind in Spain, it may seem surprising that Aub finds places for Cela and Miguel Delibes (of whom more later; see pp. 232–34) and odder still that both the latter were in truth elected to the academy in Franco's lifetime, though when he was writing, Aub couldn't have predicted this. The *discurso* plays with fiction's wonderful ability to remake the world as one would like it to be, and with the poetic power of names in themselves.

The latter is used by Aub differently in volume two of "The Magic Labyrinth," *Campo abierto*, where in addition to naming the chapters after individuals in the narrative, he gives ten pages of the text to a list of the names and, in most cases, a few key attributes of every barber in Madrid who volunteered for what became known as the Figaros' Battalion:

Juan Pajares, born in Argamesilla, aged twenty-four, bachelor and good-looking, dark-haired ... Juan Miguel González, born in Madrid,

aged thirty-six, married with three children . . . From the barber's in Peligros: Santiago Pérez, born in Guadalajara, as handsome as ever; Fernando Sánchez, born in Logroño, with his cold that no one can cure; Evaristo Alonso, born in Getafe, quiet, thinking about his family who wouldn't leave their village . . . From one in Hortaleza: two enemies, one a supporter of Madrid, the other of Athletic—Félix Amador, born in Cádiz, who left his wife behind with a fever and Faustino Romero, born in Madrid . . . Víctor Marco, a specialist in big moustaches who lives in la Prosperidad. Marcelo Salazar and Raúl Lexama, women's hairdressers from an elegant salon in calle del Carmen . . .

. . . and on to Pedro Hemosilla, who keeps asking everyone whether they know where his godfather is. *Campo abierto* was written in Mexico in 1948–50, published there in 1951, and appeared in Spain for the first time in 1978. How dare anyone talk about an amnesia deal?

If Aub conjures people to life simply by mentioning their names, he does so, too, by letting them talk. He's a dramatist-novelist with many registers, ranging from romantic sexuality to bleak descriptions of poverty and wartime violence, but what runs through his books and unites his enormous cast of characters is loquacity. Early in the saga, we're introduced to a "vegetarian pederast and sodomite" who for no evident reason captures his listeners' interest: "No one takes him seriously but they all listen with great attention. Ghosts, the dead, madness, strike them as important matters."[52] The six-hundred-page final volume, *Campo de los almendros* ("Almond Tree Field") is written almost entirely in dialogue. In this saga, the Spanish Civil War is many things, but one of them is a war of words through which it's possible to hear the garrulity of a man exiled from the country he grew up in, a man of the theater, of the book, of the *tertulia*, of an almost constitutional self-contradictoriness, writing down the characters and stories and relationships and betrayals of the years through which he lived and to which he knows there is no return.

It's apt, then, as well as funny, that among Aub's best pieces of fiction is a short story about a man who can't stand *vocingleros* ("people who talk too much"). Published in 1960, it has the, for the time, wonderfully optimistic title "The True Story of the Death of Francisco Franco."[53] A waiter called Nacho, born in 1918 in rural northern Mex-

ico, has worked in Guadalajara since the age of fifteen. In 1938 he moves to a bar in Mexico City. Nacho takes pride in his work, is good at it, and quickly becomes something of a local institution. The story describes the pleasure he takes in his physical surroundings, the deftness with which he pours coffee (the invention of espresso perturbs him). He takes his meals in the café, lives in a room nearby, and has no interests beyond his job. Most of his customers are regulars. He knows their habits, is used to their quiet conversations, the rhythms of the working day. Then, in the middle of 1939, everything changes with the arrival of Republican refugees from Franco's Spain.

They fill the café from morning to night. Though they have nothing else to do, they are vociferous in their demands for service. They talk loudly, ceaselessly, and obscenely. Nacho thinks of going back to Guadalajara, but his *patrón*, delighted by the increase in business, persuades him to stay. The Spanish newcomers, meanwhile, are as oblivious to the irritation they arouse in the descendants of their country's former colonial subjects as to the bewilderment caused by their rancorous, noisy factionalism. Much of their talk concerns the minutiae of exile etiquette: an anarchist of a certain kind may take coffee with a federalist but not with an anarchist from another grouping and certainly not with a Socialist, whatever his affiliation and whatever region he comes from. Meanwhile, to have served alongside someone in the army may be a reason for either friendship or enmity. Only one thing unites the refugees: intense soliloquizing about their individual pasts. In Nacho's increasingly tormented perception, every sentence begins "When I . . ." This goes on for weeks, months, years. Gradually, the original customers are driven out, with the exception of those who come for breakfast (the exiles not being early risers) and some local intellectuals, among them Octavio Paz. Equally gradually, a new phrase becomes audible, and finally dominant: "*Cuando caiga Franco . . .*"— "When Franco falls . . ."

In 1952 a new waiter from Puerto Rico joins the staff and befriends Nacho. He listens to his laments about the tone of the clientele and encourages him to widen his horizons. Nacho has some savings, portions of which he starts to lend out in the neighborhood at high interest. His thoughts of making a move are deferred by the rapid success of this new sideline. Meanwhile, he ponders the new waiter's reflections

on what their customers say. If they're so keen to get rid of Franco, why doesn't someone kill him? It's all talk. All talk!—precisely Nacho's objection. "*Cuando caiga Franco*"—the phrase takes over his dreams. If only Franco fell, the Spanish would go home, and order and peace would return to the café. Newly rich, newly resolute, Nacho decides to act. In twenty years, he hasn't taken a holiday. Now he talks first to his boss, then to the Puerto Rican. Spain doesn't recognize Mexico, so he needs a new passport. His friend has an American one; will he lend it to him? They change the photographs, Nacho gets a three-month visa to travel throughout western Europe and sets off for Madrid, arriving early in June. Making no plans, he nevertheless instinctively moves in the right way, befriending Mexicans working in the American embassy in Madrid and getting to know a Spanish army officer there. On the night of July 17, pretending that it's his birthday, Nacho entertains the soldier to a long, boozy supper, puts a narcotic in his drink, and, once he's asleep, steals his uniform and pistol. The day just dawning will see the annual parade commemorating the 1936 military uprising. Acting lieutenant Ignacio Jurado Martínez is ready for his own one-man revolution.

Protected by his uniform, he pushes officiously through the crowd, reaches the *generalísimo*'s dais, and, under cover of a noisy flyby, shoots him dead. Slipping away in the ensuing confusion, the unlikely assassin takes a taxi, returns to the hotel where his new friend is still asleep, swaps the uniform back for his own clothes, and sets off on holiday. Following an itinerary prepared for him earlier by a travel agent, he visits Barcelona, various parts of France and Italy, and, having plenty of time to spare, much of northern Europe. On September 17 he's back in Guadalajara and returns to work.

The action has been so absorbing, so rapid, so comically uncomplicated, that the reader hasn't considered what will follow. During Nacho's travels, the post-Franco Spain he brought about has been convulsed: an interim military government, a monarchy quickly proclaimed and as quickly overthrown, a Third Republic. Once again, those out of favor—especially, now, members of the Falange—have fled, many of them to Mexico. The bar he returns to is still full of vociferous Spanish refugees. The faces are new, but the noise is the same: "*Cuando yo . . .*"— "When I . . ." The storyteller enters the story. He was told all this by

Nacho, by then a deaf old man back in Guadalajara, a man who can't stop talking about how, for twenty years, he heard nothing but "*lo mismo y lo mismo y lo mismo*"—"the same and same again."[54] It's beautifully done, and Aub's new verbal economy makes its own point. The tale of a man who hated talk is best told in not too many words.

2. Sender: The Courage of Sympathy

Aub's collection named after this story, *La verdadera historia de la muerte de Francisco Franco y otros cuentos* ("The True Story of the Death of Francisco Franco and Other Tales"), was published in Mexico in 1960. By then he was halfway through the six volumes of "The Magic Labyrinth," and the exile school of Spanish writers was well established. The novelist and poet Ramón J. Sender is among the best known of them and for many reasons has a special place in the history of Spanish literature and Spanish exile. His work straddled the civil war and the dictatorship: as prolific as Aub, he, too, was well known on the left even before the Second Republic and he also wrote in a wide range of genres, including drama and essays. Unlike Aub, though, Sender had a substantial impact in the outside world while the civil war was still going on. This was partly because of what happened to him personally and the modest courage with which he described it.

When Sender's *The War in Spain* appeared in Britain in 1937, the possibility of official British support for the elected Republic was still alive in Parliament and among activists and voters, if not in the realpolitik of the intelligence services. The book had been translated—such are the vagaries of Anglo-Hispanic cultural history—by the recently retired head of the London Zoo and creator of the world's first open zoological park, Whipsnade, who had moved to Málaga just before civil war broke out. Sir Peter Chalmers Mitchell was a man of conscience, son of a Scottish Presbyterian minister, and had taken his first degree at Aberdeen in the 1880s. Author of a biography of the evolutionary biologist T. H. Huxley and of a book on human nature, and a prolific contributor to the great eleventh edition of the *Encyclopaedia Britannica*, he never stopped looking for new directions his life might take and in 1938 stood for Parliament.[55] In Spain, where he had a well-established reputation as a translator, he made many friends but none

he admired more than Sender, then still in his thirties. "He is," Chalmers Mitchell wrote with the confidence of his time,

> the most distinguished of living Spanish writers, and by many, including myself, is regarded as one of the most distinguished living authors of any country. He comes of a landholding, land-cultivating stock in Aragón, and was educated at a monastery school . . . At the age of eighteen he went to Madrid to study law, but like many young intellectuals of this century, his conscience was disturbed by the condition of the working-classes in town and country, and by the complacent belief of the holding classes that their interests were identical with those of the country, and that they were exercising a moral duty in defending them even by violence.[56]

Sender, as Chalmers Mitchell goes on to relate, had joined in student activities against the dictatorship of Miguel Primo de Rivera and had avoided prison only because his parents optimistically guaranteed to keep him under control. After military service in Morocco, which was to stand him and other Republican volunteers in good practical stead when civil war came, he worked as a writer and journalist in Madrid, and was active in leftist intellectual circles, meanwhile marrying and having two children. Then came the war, his heroic, naïve, and tragic experiences of which are related in the enthralling book that Chalmers Mitchell translated and Faber and Faber published: it's one of those unreprinted classics you can still pick up inexpensively in a first edition.

The War in Spain is worth reading for many reasons. The book is exceptionally alert to the feelings and views of people on the other side. Its descriptions of battle are as good as any: what it was like being bombed, or crawling forward under machine-gun fire; the rage, frustration, and suspicion against a distant high command that won't let you strike when you're in a perfect position to do so; the difficulty, for a brave, energetic, but inexperienced attacking group, of adapting to defense. The heroic aspects are matched by unheroic ones: an often all-consuming fear of spies; overwhelming confusion about what's going on, where; the volunteers who decide to devolunteer and the petty punitiveness of the others' response (in that case, you can leave your boots and trousers behind, as well as your gun . . .). Sender's own weak

points are valuably unedited, long passages of egalitarian rhetoric punctured, for example, when he's captured by his own side in Madrid and infuriated that no one believes he is who he says he is: "That sort of imbecility, I told them, would make us lose the war. They looked surprised . . ." All this is revealing and absorbing of itself, but nothing brings home the actuality of the conflict more powerfully than what's revealed in the closing pages—what's revealed, and how quietly, and the fact that it has hitherto been withheld.

Sender has more than once mentioned his house in the country, tantalizingly nearby during much of the action. It transpires that his wife and children were there, together with his pro-Nationalist sister and her husband, and a guest with children. When the Nationalist army under General Mola arrived, an elaborate plan was made to enable Sender's wife and their friend to escape across the mountains, leaving the children under the protection of the conservative adults and the latter under that of their politics. The local Falange prevented the evacuation, and the group soon learned that Sender's brother, a Republican who had been elected mayor of the family's home town in the northeast, had been shot. Sender's sister and her husband left, while his wife, friend, and the various children decided to take shelter in the wife's home town, Zamora, north of Salamanca. When they arrived, they learned that her brother, too, had been shot. She went to the local civil governor to try to get a passport for France.

This is one of those moments that only a novelist could manage—when the pressure of immediate emotion is partly balanced by an inability not to understand other people's feelings and their potential consequences:

> Not only had [my wife] never belonged to any political party, but her family had been regarded in the town as reputable people, liberal bourgeois. But the fact of asking for a passport after [her brother] had been murdered . . . was doubtless extremely suspicious. Besides, in every crime there is the seed of another crime, only waiting its opportunity to germinate. Terrorism terrorizes those who have practised it, more than any others. If my wife were to go to France, she could also go from there to loyal Spain and relate what she had seen . . . They arrested her in the Civil Governor's office itself. The children, thus left

derelict for the time, were at last recovered by persons whose hearts had not been contaminated. A month after her arrest, they brought a priest who confessed her, and then took her to the cemetery, where they shot her.[57]

Sender goes on to write an unmatchable coda, full of the bitterest paradoxes of war literature: that the narrator's most intimate story has had to be told in other people's words; that his own words are unutterable, nonexistent; that it takes cruelty and isolation to produce the highest courage and sense of commonality; that the person with most entitlement to act is the one who feels most disqualified:

These are the facts, without qualification . . . I have related them as they were told me, in the fewest possible words. The words I could use have not been spoken, and I wish to keep them in the realm of words that have not been created, in the recesses of the soul in which everyone keeps dead hopes. The crime binds me more closely in an unchanging and eternal way to my people and to the fecund passions of the working people. When I knew what had happened I went back to the front wondering if I had the right to go on fighting, in a war going on to its pitiless end, as an end had been made for me, perhaps for ever, of pity.

Sender's son and daughter were rescued by the Red Cross, and he was eventually reunited with them. His subsequent career was one of continuing passionate political commitment and occasional compromise and ambiguity. Its details are sometimes hard to be sure of, and even the outlines have become confused by too ready an identification between what happened and what he later turned into fiction. We know that he returned to action with the anarchists on the Aragón front line. It seems that he fell into dangerous disfavor as a result of internecine Communist maneuvers of the kind described by George Orwell in *Homage to Catalonia*. Whatever the details, the Republican government sent him on an American lecture tour to get him out of the way. Returning to France early in 1939, he found he was mistaken in expecting a welcome there but managed to get back to the States, where he survived the later antileft purges instigated by Senator Joseph

McCarthy and began a long-distance friendship with the novelist Carmen Laforet, who still lived in Spain (see pp. 184–87). None of this means that he always made the decisions he might have hoped to, or that his views underwent no changes.[58] He later made himself unpopular on the left by agreeing to sign an anticommunist statement—probably in order to protect a U.S. teaching job he needed to support his family, though, given what he knew by then about communism, it may not have cost him too much thought.

Among the best novels Sender wrote in exile is the imaginary life story of one of the Franco regime's official executioners. (The theme was to return in a still more powerful film by Luis García Berlanga; see pp. 208–10.) The 1952 *El verdugo afable* was translated two years later as *The Affable Hangman*,[59] but since the job in question is garrotting, *executioner* is the better noun. The book is a picturesque, believable tale, its frequent moments of charm fluttering dangerously over the moral swamp established in the opening pages, a bald narrative of four garrottings that yields nothing in grimness to Orwell's "A Hanging." What gives the novel much of its point is the straightforwardness with which the narrator, a respectable journalist on an upmarket newspaper, acknowledges his sense of affinity with his subject—his acceptance of the fact that it's often only luck that separates the lives of victor and victim.

This imaginative compulsion to cross political boundaries and delve into the emotional as well as moral difficulties they can create is the defining quality of the best known of Sender's works, the novella *Réquiem por un campesino español* (*Requiem for a Spanish Peasant*, 1953).[60] The story concerns a boy who, having been exposed to the extremes of rural poverty while accompanying the local priest on a pastoral visit, becomes a Socialist, is elected mayor, and in the early stages of the civil war is killed by members of the Falange. The tragedy, though, is not only Paco's but that of the priest, Mosén Millán, who, through a series of avoidable blunders, reveals where Paco is hiding. A year after Paco's murder, the priest is about to celebrate a Mass in his memory. As he prepares, his mind goes back through Paco's short life, in all the key moments of which Mosén was involved: baptism, education, marriage, death. It's a tragedy in the classical Greek sense: we know from early on that Paco has been killed, and all the action occurs

in a single place over a short time. Memory, in the sense both of recalling the past and of commemoration, is its main theme and determines its form; and while much of its operation is psychological, it also has a ritual aspect—not in the awaited Mass, which will occur outside the book's time scheme, but in a folk lament sung at intervals throughout the novella by an altar boy (a new version of Paco). This is Lorca-like, not only in style but in its impregnation of a secular poetry by religious feelings and associations. What the priest recalls, though, is more fully observed than anything in Lorca. He's a kind, conscientious man but, we come to see, a bit foolish in his innocence, and not without pride. It's his pretense—not exactly self-important but self-gratifying—that he knows Paco's hiding place that leads the young man's father to divulge it to him. Once Mosén knows the secret, he's too guileless to conceal the fact from Paco's enemies, and—in a context of actions of terrifying, arbitrary-seeming violence and, despite them, of his instinctive trust in people's goodness—he's easily persuaded that if he gets the pursuers to promise that they won't hurt Paco, he'll be doing more good than harm by giving him away.

3. Barea: Unhonored Prophet

Sender's tormented and self-tormenting priest has more than one thing in common with Arturo Barea, author and central character of *The Forging of a Rebel*. The film director Mario Camus has described the effect on him and his friends of secretly reading Barea in the 1950s, in copies of his trilogy found in clandestine bookshops: the revelations imparted by his truthfulness about matters that simply weren't talked about and also by his "abrupt, gruff, hard" style.[61] Yet Barea's work illustrates some of the problems encountered by many successful authors who leave their native country, adopt another culture, and are adopted by it. He had grown up poor in a working-class family in Madrid—his widowed mother was a laundress—and did military service in Morocco. Throughout much of the civil war, he ran the Republican press office in the besieged capital, where he was in charge of what journalists communicated to the outside world and knew his way around the facts, the rumors, and the propaganda better than anyone. He was the author of a collection of short stories published in 1938

that, although or because they are essentially propagandist, were among the very small number of works of fiction dealing with the civil war to appear under the Second Republic. Having escaped for England in 1938 and shaken off the crudest demands of party politics, he became one of the most audible of Spanish anti-Francoists, broadcasting and writing prolifically—in Spanish but also, with the help of his polyglot wife, Ilsa Kulcsar, in English translation—and increasingly making his mark among U.S. as well as British and Latin American audiences.

Inevitably his work was suppressed within Spain and attacked by Franco supporters abroad. (They called him Arturo Beria, in reference to Stalin's henchman.) Barea also attracted the envy of people on his own side, some of whom, under the faction-ridden and geographically divided Republican regime, had been rivals of him or his wife, or both. To understand this, one needs to remember how much the Anglophone literary market meant in terms of influence, prestige, and money to those whose work appeared only in Spanish. Through a combination of Cyril Connolly's magazine *Horizon*, the BBC's Latin American service, and publishers both in the United Kingdom and, soon, the United States, Barea reached immense audiences. At a time when many other Spanish intellectuals were struggling to survive in Paris and South America, he and his wife, while never rich, soon had more than one good, steady source of literary income and lived in a series of pleasant houses within easy reach of Oxford and London. Much of the material of his radio talks concerned the pleasures, the idiosyncrasies, and above all the freedoms of English life, and in 1948 he took British nationality. It's no surprise that some Spanish critics chose to point out stylistic flaws in his work, or to hint that it owed more than was acknowledged to his multilingual translator wife, or that, after his premature death and when longer-lived dissidents were returning to post-Franco Spain, the merits of other writers were more widely celebrated there.[62]

Those celebrations were mostly deserved, and Barea was among the people who had contributed to the reputations involved. The vulnerability of his own work to stylistic criticism, meanwhile, was heightened by the processes that brought him to a Spanish readership. Although he wrote in Spanish, he was immediately translated into English by his wife, with the help of Peter Chalmers Mitchell, and didn't keep his

original manuscripts. The version of the trilogy that first appeared in Spanish, *La forja de un rebelde*, published in Argentina in 1951, had been unsophisticatedly translated back from the English text. Barea was too busy to correct it and died a few years later.[63] Still, most of the raw power of the "original" survived, and this very roughness was part of its appeal and its originality. Barea hadn't been subjected to much formal literary education. He had seen—and heard and smelled—some of Spain's most powerful contemporary developments at close quarters. In his role as a censor he had dealt day by day with the output and professional criteria of Anglophone journalistic writers, Hemingway among them. He had an intelligent, forceful mentor in his Austrian wife. And under the extreme pressures of the siege of Madrid—the abandonment of the city by the Republican government, which moved to the relative safety of Valencia in November 1936; hunger, sleep deprivation; continual shelling and bombing; the savage intimacies of a routine in which people you had passed daily in the street were blown to pieces in front of your eyes—under all this, Barea suffered some kind of breakdown from which he never fully recovered, and that is felt in the harsh undertow of his work.

To his first readers, especially those who were living inside but in opposition to Franco's Spain and looking for examples to follow, the value of *The Forging of a Rebel* lay not only in its political idealism but also in its uncompromising frankness. To Barea as to Cela and Aub, this meant, among other things, honesty about sexuality: about how badly individuals—including the "I" of Barea's text—are capable of behaving in their relationships and also about how dominant those relationships can be; how much more compelling than, and how powerfully imbricated in, politics and work. Because Barea is so clear about and tough on himself, we trust the severity with which he judges others. This isn't just a matter of guilty Puritanism. Barea understands that most people have mixed motives, inconsistent beliefs; that they carry around their burdensome pasts at the same time they are trying to simplify their futures. The most obvious—and, to religious sympathizers with Republicanism, most liberating—example is his strong residual Christianity. In the third and climactic volume of the trilogy, which covers the civil war, he is unequivocal about the reasons for Republican atrocities against the Church: the collusion of so many priests

TOP: Republican mass grave in Málaga in the process of excavation, 2008 (courtesy of the author); ABOVE: The Nationalist memorial park Valle de los Caídos ("Valley of the Fallen"), which was built with the help of Republican prisoners in 1941–59 (© Patrimonio Nacional)

One of the military effigies in the basilica of the Valle de los Caídos (Luis Antonio Sanguino and Antonio Martín, © Patrimonio Nacional)

Byzantine-style wall painting in the parish church of Jánovas, built between
the twelfth and sixteenth centuries (courtesy of the author)

EXPOSICIÓN
NACIONAL
DE
BELLAS
ARTES

CATÁLOGO

BARCELONA · PALACIO NACIONAL · MAYO, MCMLX

From the catalogue of the 1960 Exposición Nacional de Bellas Artes: title page (*top left*), and illustrations of *Obreros* by Francisco Vila Rufas (*top right*) and *Hotel en Torre-Valentina* by José Antonio Coderch de Sentmenat (*above*) (Biblioteca Nacional de España)

Antonio Saura's *Portrait imaginaire de Brigitte Bardot* (1958, oil on canvas, 100 ³/₈ x 76 ³/₄ in.) (Museo de Arte Abstracto Español, Fundación Juan March, Cuenca; © Succession Antonio Saura/www.antoniosaura.org, VEGAP/DACS, 201x; photograph by Santiago Toralba)

TOP: Eduardo Chillida's *Wind Combs*, first planned in 1952 and installed at a beach in San Sebastían in 1977; ABOVE: The insignia of the Spanish Legion cut into a hillside near Sanabria (both images courtesy of the author)

TOP: The mayor (José Isbert) dreams of being a U.S. sheriff in Luis García Berlanga's *¡Bienvenido, Mister Marshall!* (*Welcome, Mr. Marshall!*, 1952); ABOVE: Ana (Ana Torrent) and the fugitive (Juan Margallo) in Víctor Erice's *The Spirit of the Beehive* (*El espíritu de la colmena*, 1973) (both images courtesy of Egeda)

The reluctant executioner (Nino Manfredi) being dragged to work in Luis García Berlanga's *El verdugo* (*The Executioner*, 1963) (courtesy of Egeda)

with the exploitative class; the use of religious buildings as munitions stores and military emplacements. Still, Barea had been educated by priests and monks—educated within some of the ecclesiastical buildings in Madrid that he now saw being looted and set on fire. (He watched as one of his teacher priests, now a harmless octogenarian, was carried away on a stretcher.) The destruction of Madrid was the destruction of his childhood. Besides, all violence, whether anticlerical or antifascist, repelled him—in part because of what he saw as its necessity, a paradox he expressed in religious terms. One passage, in particular, needs to be quoted at length:

> Everything round me was destruction, loathsome as the crushing of a spider underfoot; and it was the barbaric destruction of people herded together and lashed by hunger, ignorance, and the fear of being finally, totally, crushed.
>
> I was choked by the feeling of personal impotence in face of the tragedy. It was bitter to think that I loved peace, and bitter to think of the word pacifism. I had to be a belligerent. I could not shut my eyes and cross my arms while my country was being wantonly assassinated so that a few could seize power and enslave the survivors. I knew that there existed Fascists who had good faith, admirers of the "better" past, or dreamers of bygone empires and conquerors, who saw themselves as crusaders; but they were the cannon fodder of Fascism. There were the others, the heirs of the corrupt ruling caste of Spain, the same people who had manoeuvred the Moroccan war with its stupendous corruption and humiliating retreats to their own greater glory. We had to fight them. It was not a question of political theories. It was life against death. We had to fight against the death-bringers, the Francos, the Sanjurjos, the Molas, the Millán Astrays . . .
>
> We had to fight them. This meant we would have to shell or bomb Burgos and its towers. Cordova and its flowered courtyards, Seville and its gardens. We would have to kill so as to purchase the right to live.
>
> I wanted to scream.
>
> A shell had killed the street vendor outside the Telefónica. There was her little daughter, a small, brown, little girl who had been hopping round between the tables in the Miami Bar and the Gran Vía café like a sparrow . . .

No, I could not think in political terms, in terms of party or revolution. I had to think of the crime it was to send shells against human flesh and of the need for me, the pacifist, the lover of Saint Francis, to help in the task of finishing with the breed of Cain . . . The other thing—to forgive—was Christ's alone. Saint Peter took to the sword.[64]

There were other paradoxes. Barea's way of fighting was to run the Republican censorship office in Madrid, an activity dependent on the assumption that it was necessary to suppress some truths—for example, about Republican defeats. Yet at the same time as he was preventing others from publishing or broadcasting what they knew to be the case, in his own writing he was moving away from propaganda and toward a plainness, stylistic as much as factual, that would enable him "to shape and express the life of my own people."[65] In doing that, he ultimately had to remove himself physically from the battleground and recover some kind of equanimity: a decision he was able to reach only when the person who pressed it on him was a priest, Father Lobo, who "of all those I met in our war . . . command[ed] my deepest respect and love."[66]

Barea makes his readers, too, love Father Lobo. The intensity with which the lapsed Catholic, divorced from the mother of his children, living "in sin" with an unbeliever, draws in his desperation on the creed he believes himself to have renounced, finds its mirror image in an overtly Christian narrative first published a few years after *The Clash* but, unlike Barea's work, in Spanish and within Spain. Among the ways in which José María Gironella's *The Cypresses Believe in God* (*Los cipreses creen en Dios*, 1953), itself the first volume in a trilogy, forms a counterpart to *The Forging of a Rebel* are, once again, its efforts to see what's good about the other side or sides.

THREE VIEWS FROM INSIDE

1. Gironella: A Thousand Ways of Life

Echoes of James Joyce are heard in Gironella: not of the experimental stylist but of the Irishman trying to express his nation, another country at war with itself, another site both of religious struggle and of

battles between insular mythmaking and cosmopolitan innovation. No Anglophone reader can follow the experiences of Gironella's independent-minded central character, Ignacio, in the seminary without being reminded of Stephen Dedalus. Gironella's criticisms of the Church—or rather, of individual Catholics—are friendlier than Joyce's, but what seems remarkable, in a book published in Spain at this early date, is that they are linked to views often openly hostile to Francoism. Subsequent volumes of the trilogy are less evenhanded, a shift that is among several aspects of the author's work that have undermined his reputation inside Spain and abroad. Critics who, with varying degrees of discrimination, hailed partisan literature coming from the left as "engaged" were markedly less keen on engagements they themselves disagreed with, and Gironella has been castigated for the pro-Nationalist sympathies increasingly evident in the trilogy's second and third volumes, *Un millón de muertos* ("A Million Dead," 1961) and *Ha estallado la paz* ("Peace Has Broken Out," 1966).[67] His persistence in depicting admirable aspects of the left, on the other hand—the courage Republicans showed in the defense of Madrid, for example—was inevitably attacked by conservative critics. Meanwhile, when, as throughout most of *The Cypresses Believe in God*, he steers fluidly and fairly between the ideological positions of many of the different parties involved, he is accused of being schematic. If these all-party assaults weren't enough, he also fell afoul of a trend in Spanish criticism that, following Ortega y Gasset in his 1925 essay "La deshumanización del arte" ("The Dehumanization of Art"), held that history and fiction were irreconcilable. Finally, everyone seems to agree that in persisting with a naturalistic, "sociological," stylistically unintrusive kind of narrative that is assumed, against all the evidence, to have died out with the nineteenth century, he fails to live up to the challenges of modernity.

In Gironella's defense it needs to be said, first, that a persistent vein of social realism is found in a great deal of the best writing of his time, as also of our own, and indeed is one of the strongest characteristics of mid-twentieth-century war literature in general, whether Spanish, American, English, Italian, or Russian. Yes, literary modernism was a triumph—one that, as far as fiction concerning Spain's mid-century is concerned, had its main impact on Cela and, as we'll see, the younger Juan Benet—but in no artistic form did it oust earlier methods and

modes. Many artists believed, and some overtly argued, that the facts of war should humble the imaginative artist; that there's something narcissistic about "experimenting" with such material. During the Second World War the American poet Wallace Stevens wrote that "In the presence of the violent reality of war, consciousness takes the place of the imagination."[68] Still more provocatively, though more figuratively than tends to be assumed, the critic Theodor Adorno famously proclaimed in 1949 that Auschwitz had made poetry impossible.[69] A more modest adherence to the merits of traditional (and therefore, to its readers, unintrusive) narrative as a mode appropriate to writing about war isn't "correct" or universal, but lies behind some great work in many languages.

If Gironella's view of Catholicism has Joycean aspects, his technical approach as a novelist is better compared to that of Vasily Grossman in his epic of wartime Stalingrad, *Life and Fate*—in scale, in passion, in patriotism, above all in its determination to maintain one of the fundamental doctrines of the biggest novels of the past: that every individual possesses "an equivalent centre of self."[70] A consequence of this idea, for Gironella as for Grossman, is that the ideas and beliefs of individual characters must be expressed, and respected. Marxism, Christianity, fascism—for the novelist as for the historian, the task is to show what any of these and other ideologies mean in practice, why individuals believe in them, and what the effects of belief are on them. Adopting one side or another may be satisfying, it may even be morally right, and it's certainly less difficult, but it doesn't take the reader anywhere new.

Gironella came from a working-class background, and despite having spent most of the civil war as a volunteer in a Nationalist mountain regiment, he subsequently found little work. While he was writing his first books he depended on his wife's earnings—in itself a break with the orthodoxy of the time. (It's said that the only present he could afford to give her when they married in 1946 was a copy of Carmen Laforet's *Nada*: a bleak choice; see pp. 184–87.) They lived in Paris for some years, Magda Gironella working as a babysitter in luxury hotels, and their physical separateness from Spain may have helped reinforce the political balance Gironella aimed at in *Los cipreses creen en Dios*. He was concerned with the diversity of people's personalities and opinions—with the fact that while war forces people onto one of two

sides, in everyday life there are many parties to choose from, and although you can't be in all of them, you may try. He took pains to articulate this view when his book first came out in the United States:

> Even writers of high order succumb to the temptation . . . to treat our [Spanish people's] customs and our psychology as though everything about them were of a piece . . .
>
> I defend the complexity of Spain. If this book attempts to demonstrate anything it is this: that there are in this land thousands of possible ways of life . . .
>
> A Spanish Freemason is not an international Freemason. A Spanish Communist is not even an orthodox Communist. In every instance what is characteristic is a tendency toward the instinctive, toward the individualistic, and toward the anarchic. Spaniards follow men better than they follow ideas, which are judged not by their content, but by the men who embody them. This accounts for the inclemency of personal relationships, the small respect for laws; this, too, is what causes our periodic civil wars.[71]

It's a strong manifesto, though incomplete as an account of what the author actually does. Many kinds of behavior and belief are depicted in the trilogy. Gironella shares with others the observation that Spanish people are not only interested in ideas but like to articulate them and to argue about them—and can be influenced by them. (Along with Aub and Iturralde, later Javier Marías, Javier Cercas, and others, he owed some of his passion for debate to the status of philosophy in the Spanish school curriculum.) But while different readers of *The Cypresses Believe in God* will be attracted to the arguments of different characters, the novel shares with *Life and Fate* (and with *War and Peace*, on which both are modeled) and *A Portrait of the Artist* an emphasis on what happens to one person in particular. Ignacio Alvear steers his own course. He is a Christian but far from a saintly one; he has strong socialist sympathies but isn't a dogmatist. Several people in the book change, but Ignacio more than anyone: from a boy reluctantly cast as a future priest to an adolescent caught up in a love affair with a prostitute; from a friend and pupil of Socialists to a bank clerk training as a lawyer. The novel doesn't rely on Ignacio's perceptions: it

speaks on its own account of the benefits the Republic brings to the poor, and of the damage it causes to the Church. But many of its perplexities are faced personally by him. In any lawsuit, he learns, "the defense of one side implied attacking the other," and it's the prevalence of oppositional modes of thinking and behavior that gives the book its unifying tension.

While Gironella is a philosophical novelist, he is above everything else a novelist. His characters live and breathe and contradict themselves—as the business impresarios the Corta brothers do by supporting Izquierda Republicana, the Republican left. In his work, people's experiences are as tactile as they are mental: the schoolboys going to the dormitory, "sliding their hand against the grain of the banister"; a billiard player "sticking out his tongue and lifting his right leg when he missed a shot." Going against the grain, experiencing failure—these are common experiences in Gironella's world. The spoiled, snobbish priest Mosén Alberto, with his cushy job superintending the diocesan museum, has come from a modest background, but when people of his own kind find themselves in prison, although he tries to communicate with them, he can't. The conservative victors in the 1933 general election, meanwhile, are similarly incapable of responding to what's all around them. They have fought against a democratic Republican-Socialist regime without ever considering what it was that had brought it to power. "The winners . . . showed no sense of urgency. Portfolio deals, displays of strength, banquets. And meanwhile growing unemployment, famine areas in the country, plans for educational reform at a standstill." Critics have been too quick to dismiss Gironella. He has plenty to say to today's readers, and not just in Spain.

2. Laforet: Postwar Trauma

From today's distance, one of the absorbing aspects of the time is the extent to which national romanticism could transcend party political differences. This is less the case in the work of those who, unlike Sender and Gironella, wrote in the harsh Spain of the 1940s and '50s. Among the most moving records of that time—among our prime imaginative sources for understanding it—are two other novels of exceptional power written and published in Franco's Spain: *Nada*, "Nothing," a

spare, harsh text written by a woman in her early twenties, Carmen Laforet; and *El Jarama*, by Rafael Sánchez Ferlosio, also in his twenties and the son of a powerful Falangist.

Laforet's narrator, Andrea, arrives as a student in Barcelona, where she will stay with her grandmother, aunt, and uncles, once comfortably off but now impoverished grotesques in a gothic setting:

> In front of me was a foyer illuminated by a single weak light bulb in one of the arms of the magnificent lamp, dirty with cobwebs, that hung from the ceiling. A dark background of articles of furniture piled one on top of the other as if the household were in the middle of moving. And in the foreground the black-white blotch of a decrepit little old woman in a nightgown, a shawl thrown around her shoulders . . . Through one of the doors came a tall, skinny man in pyjamas who took charge of the situation. This was Juan, one of my uncles . . . [The] heat was suffocating.[72]

Mario Vargas Llosa has written vividly about Carmen Laforet's prose, "both exalted and icy," and how it communicates the predicament of "a girl imprisoned in a hungry, half-crazed family on the Calle de Aribau," a family "calcified in good manners and visceral putrefaction," impressions so strong that from today's vantage point we may not notice the precise historical circumstances.[73] What is it that has brought the family to such a situation? Vargas Llosa says, "there is not the slightest political allusion except, perhaps, a passing reference to churches burned during the Civil War," but that all the same "politics weighs on the entire story like an ominous silence, like a spreading cancer that devours and destroys everything." He's right about the nature of the disease but not about the absence of symptoms or etiology. As a young man, Andrea's uncle Juan served in the Spanish Legion in Morocco (Franco's army) but subsequently became a painter and a Republican. His brother Román, on the other hand, tried to persuade him to join the Nationalists, for whom Román himself spied against the Republicans. At some point, Román was denounced, imprisoned, and tortured. All this and more we learn from the intense, self-serving, in some respects mendacious conversations of Juan's wife, Gloria, with her mother-in-law: about how the maid, Antonia, is in love with

Román, has accused Gloria of being his denouncer, and threatened to slit her stomach open; about how a Republican militia came to search the house and how, when they mocked the grandmother for showing them her religious statues, the grandmother told them she must be more of a Republican than they because "I don't care what other people think; I believe in freedom of ideas"; about how Gloria gave birth to her son during the Nationalist bombing and capture of Barcelona in January 1939. Very specifically, then, as well as in mood, this is a novel of the war's long, bitter aftermath.

Carmen Laforet was at university in both Barcelona and Madrid during those years. She tried philosophy first, then law, but abandoned her formal studies in favor of marriage in 1942, when she was twenty-one. Her husband, Manuel Cerezales González, was twelve years older, had spent the civil war in one of the ultratraditionalist Carlist regiments, and, when Franco came to power, quickly established himself as a literary critic and editor on papers that, despite the censorship, maintained a strong liberal-conservative critique of the regime's restrictions on intellectual freedom. Two of their five children, Cristina Cerezales Laforet and Agustín Cerezales, are today professional writers. Their shy, insecure mother chafed under the values of a domestic and literary regime in which she was always being asked which she cared about more, her children or her books. She also suffered the frustration of many artists whose success comes early, at being most famous for what she came to regard as an immature book. The couple separated in 1970. Both lived on into the new millennium, she sinking into a social isolation eventually compounded by Alzheimer's, he into deep, irremediable deafness.[74] They could have been characters in *Nada*. Whatever the novel's predictive power, it is, with Cela's *The Hive*, among the works that defined the moral misery of the time for subsequent generations.[75] Trauma, here, is passed between relatives and between generations like an infection, and a bitter consciousness of this fact permeates Andrea's departure at the novel's end.

However transmissible trauma may be, the deposits it leaves in high culture are more vulnerable. In terms of its availability in Spain, *Nada* was fortunate for a number of reasons—most important, that a male-dominated censorship apparatus could easily approve of its ending, which, read in the simplest way, has Andrea leaving behind a

self-destructive household in favor of marriage to a respectable older businessman. The novel won the Eugenio Nadal Prize and was often reprinted. A collected edition of Laforet's work appeared in 1967. But *Nada* wasn't read simply, least of all by women, many of whom found the depiction of its alert, autonomous protagonist complex, unorthodox, powerfully unresolved, and true to their own experiences. As far as an international audience was concerned, while it was translated into German in the early 1950s and Italian in the 1960s, Anglophone readers had to wait more than sixty years.[76]

3. Sánchez Ferlosio: Postwar Amnesia

El Jarama was quicker to appear in English. First published in Spanish in 1955 and set at that time, the book came out in an American version, *The One Day of the Week*, in 1962. Rafael Sánchez Ferlosio's elusive, enthralling novel is set on a hot Sunday in the countryside twelve miles south of Madrid, close to a bridge over the River Jarama, not far from where Barajas Airport is now; its construction is a background element. A party of a dozen young people have come out to swim, picnic, laze around, and flirt. They mainly drift between the riverbank and the garden of a local bar, where they buy their drinks along with various regulars from the neighborhood: a barber; a shepherd; the owner of the bar and his wife and daughter; and a mordant, solitary man in his early sixties called Lucio, who spends all day sitting in a corner. Most of the story is told through conversations. Most of it in fact *is* those conversations, since not much "happens" in the book's first three quarters, though we learn a little about these people and their relationships while also becoming more and more conscious of what we don't know. Some of what's said is inconsequential, some of it quite the opposite, and there's a constant, quiet setting up of expectations, not all unfulfilled. We learn, for example, that the young were here before, last year, and that one of them, Miguel, sang on that occasion. We guess that he may sing again before this day ends, and so he does.

In an introduction by a recent English-language translator, Margaret Jull Costa, the text is seen as imitating the flow of the omnipresent Jarama:

Like the river "plaiting and unplaiting currents," the different conversations amongst the different groups—the young people by the river and later up at the *merendero*, the bar-cum-picnic-spot; the bar's regulars from the local villages; the family from Madrid—flow in and out, picking up the same themes, for example, the importance or unimportance of appearances; or living for the moment versus planning ahead. And this narrative flow back and forth between the groups of young and old allows for a seamless juxtaposition of tragedy, absurdity, banality, even joy, which is both realistic and poetic.[77]

The River, accordingly, is what Jull Costa's version is called, which is better than *The One Day of the Week*, yet in both titles a crucial aspect of what the book is about is cut off. Almost twenty years before the action of the novel, when the young characters were babies or unborn, the Jarama gave its name to one of the worst battles of the civil war.

The river, which flows through Spain from north to south and, by the time it passes Madrid, is wide and full flowing, formed a natural boundary to the east and south of the Republican-held city. In February 1937 the Nationalists, who had failed to take the capital from the north and west the previous autumn, mounted a huge new attack from the other side. Previous failure was one element in the intensity of the rebel onslaught. Still more important was the fact that, at the height of the Battle of Madrid, the Republicans had massacred about a thousand Nationalist prisoners near Paracuellos del Jarama, an atrocity kept alive in the memory of Spanish conservatives today, though not much mentioned by the other side. The new attack began near Paracuellos. Earlier, the Republican government had moved to Valencia for safety, and one of the rebels' aims in crossing the river was to capture the main road between the two cities, cutting them off from each other. The Republican defense of Madrid, meanwhile, if anything gained strength from people's perception of having been abandoned by their elected rulers.

On February 6, after weeks of very bad weather, rebel troops in great strength advanced on the river, quickly reaching Ciempozuelos, which stands between it and the main southward road out of Madrid, and, a few miles farther north, taking the hill at La Marañosa.[78] These feats were achieved by about 25,000 infantry with the help of German

troops, tanks, artillery, and aircraft, and including Moroccan regulars. For their part, the Republicans had an initially superior Soviet presence in the air, and their troops included the redoubtable Eleventh International Brigade. Within two days, the Republicans lost 2,000 men and a large number were pinned down on what British volunteers—225 out of 600 of whom died there—called Suicide Hill. In the weeks that followed, bogged down in mud, half-starved because the fighting had delayed food supplies, both sides having made suicidal attacks or defended indefensible positions on the orders of stubborn, quarrelsome, and competitive generals, tens of thousands of troops found themselves in a stalemate. A new, ill-advised Nationalist armored thrust, mainly by Italians, on March 8 was countered by the Republican army, in which Russian soldiers and tanks distinguished themselves, as did a machine-gun company led by a Spanish woman, Encarnación Fernández Luna. The Nationalists were held back—albeit on what had until then been the Republican side of the Jarama—and Madrid was not to be taken for another two years. On each side, thousands, perhaps tens of thousands, had been killed.

To call a book *El Jarama*, then, is like calling one *The Somme*. And if what goes on in it seems to have nothing whatever to do with war or a battle, all the more reason not to change a title that brings those matters into the room as surely as the dead Banquo is conjured up by his empty place at the Macbeths' table. For, at one level, even as early as 1955, this is a novel about amnesia: the young getting on with their lives and their love affairs, almost but not quite oblivious to what has happened in this place—though, as onlookers, we can't be, any more than was the author, who is one of the sons of the Falangist leader Rafael Sánchez Mazas. From the first pages, everything that happens here, however trivial, every conversation, however banal, is haunted:

> The rectangle of sunlight had broadened slightly; it was reflected on the ceiling now. Flies buzzed in the glimmering dust and light. Lucio shifted in his seat and said:
>
> "There'll be plenty of people coming to the river today."
>
> "Even more than last Sunday, if that's possible. Especially considering how hot it's been all week . . ."
>
> "Yes, there'll be a lot of people coming today, I reckon."[79]

There's a direct hint when Lucio speaks up from his corner. The owner has asked his young barman, Demetrio, if he can work that evening. Demetrio has other plans and suggests that Lucio might help out—"he never does anything." Lucio says:

> "I did quite enough when I was your age."
> "Oh, yes? Like what?"
> "Lots of things, more than you've done."
> "Give me an example . . ."
> "More than you've done."[80]

The banter goes nowhere, and we never, in fact, find out what it is that Lucio did, but the idea that a generation gap is also an experience gap (and for these generations, on a large scale) is left hanging so that we are particularly alert to Lucio and to what he sees but doesn't comment on: the freedoms of these kids, their motorbikes, the girls in trousers, the plenty on offer that they take for granted, "wine, lemonade, orangeade, coca-cola, pineapple juice?"[81]

In four hundred pages, the war is mentioned explicitly on only two occasions. In the bar, a man briefly mentions that his father was killed in 1935, that he himself was conscripted in 1937, and the consequences for his family. Earlier, there's a brief conversation about it between some of the young sitting by the river, the topic quickly joked about and then brushed aside:

> "A lot of people died in this river during the war."
> "Yes, further up, in Paracuellos del Jarama, that was where the fighting was worst, but the whole river was on the front line, as far as Titulcia."
> "Titulcia?"
> "Haven't you heard of it? An uncle of mine, my mother's brother, he died in the offensive, in Titulcia itself, that's why I know about it. I'll never forget. We heard the news while we were having supper."
> "Fancy this being the front line," said Mely, "and all those people dying here."
> "I know, and here we are happily swimming about in it."

"Just as if nothing had happened; you could be stepping in a place
    where a corpse used to be."
Luci interrupted them.
"Stop it! You're just imagining things now."
The other three were back. Miguel said:
"What are you talking about?"
"Oh, nothing, Luci doesn't like stories about dead people."
"What dead people?"
"The ones from the war. I was just telling them that there were quite a
    few people killed here, including my uncle."
"Five to twelve."
"Right, then, you girls could be thinking about getting changed."[82]

But death and the past are not that easy to shake off. There's a graveyard nearby, for example, and Mely is surprised that it's on such low
ground: you would think the bodies would get washed away.[83] In the
bar, as the day wears on, Lucio grumbles unspecifically about wanting
"them" to give him back the life he feels has been stolen from him.
Even the behavior of the young has some of its origins in militarism:
Mely's boyfriend, Zacarias, smokes marijuana, a pleasure he learned
on national service in Morocco.[84] These distant associations swirl and
mingle, and Miguel begins to sing, and Federico and Lolita dance while
the others clap—and, unknown to them, Luci, the girl who doesn't like
stories about dead people, has gone for a swim, is caught up in the current, and drowns.

Nothing here lends itself to summary: the difficulty of saying what
it "means" is part of its meaning. As Harold Pinter wrote not long afterward to a friend who wanted an answer to the questions posed by
Waiting for Godot:

is it Beckett's business to answer questions he himself poses? I do not
see that . . . If the question was answered explicitly, the question would
cease to exist, it would be consumed in the answer. There would be no
impulse, no work, no play . . . Both in [Beckett] and Kafka, surely, you
get all the questions and any answer you want, off any shelf, in any
permutation, according to your taste and disposition . . . I prefer . . .
a most stern and ruthless activity without question or answer . . . a

necessity. The necessity to what? The necessity to *say*. To say what? Whatever's to be said . . . some people say it better than others.[85]

Everyone has heard of Beckett's *Godot*; few people outside Spain of Ferlosio's *El Jarama*. The reasons include the Franco effect: work published in Spain at this time was tainted by association, and readers looked elsewhere.

El Jarama is a novel of Spain's 1950s yet it's already a novel of transition; to its careless younger generation, the civil war is a secondhand memory. Just as Spain's transition began earlier than is often suggested, it involved kinds of opening up that went beyond economic liberalization and democratic elections. Before turning to ways in which new fictions expressed these developments, it's useful to consider film, and both to fast-forward and then reverse for a while.

8

Franco's Films

I'll never forget coming out of the Amaya cinema in Madrid one afternoon when I was in my teens after seeing *El espíritu de la colmena*; or
the racket that rose from the stalls not long afterward, when *La prima
Angélica* and *Furtivos* were shown. What was happening in the cinema was what we were living through, the tedious Franco years and
our rage at so much injustice, and our longing for freedom—the trem-
bling sense of already experiencing it even before we had got it.

This is the novelist Antonio Muñoz Molina, writing in his fifties
about the multidirectionality of imaginative time.[1] The movies he
mentions came out between 1973 and 1975, the last years of the Franco
era. No one then had videos or DVDs, and the Internet didn't exist.
Old films were reshown as one-offs on television or in cinema clubs,
but seeing a film still felt like an evanescent experience, almost comparable to live performance in that there was no certainty of repetition.
This is one of those facts about technological change that contribute to
the mentalities of different generations. Yet there was never a *pacto de
olvido* in Spanish moviemaking, and as the ability of audiences to
watch films has become independent of cinemas and their distribution
arrangements, the power of movies to influence historical understanding has grown. A consequence is that historically based criticism has

also become more important. It can really matter whether what is depicted is "true," and in what senses.

As with prose fiction, the underlying issues change as the distances grow between the "now" of the work, when it was made, and when it is seen. Often this process of change, including the operation of memory itself, plays a part of its own—even becomes the main story, which is one of the ways in which a film made in the twenty-first century can find its own truth about the events of the past. In the pursuit of novelty by filmmakers, by their audiences, and (helping to drive both) by commercial enterprises, the past can also of course get lost: we're too busy catching up with the latest film to watch an older one about the same situation. This chapter will mainly be about films made during the dictatorship. But again, like fiction (which has often provided its stories), Spanish cinema powerfully reflects the country's absorption in and anxiety about memory and forgetting in themselves.

RECENT PREOCCUPATIONS: MEMORY VERSUS MOVING ON; HISTORY VERSUS MYTH; WHAT THE CHILDREN SAW

Of all today's filmmakers, Pedro Almodóvar is the one who has made the most out of the combined parallels and differences between life and performance, what lasts and what, as soon as it arrives, is lost. It's an old trope, of course, both of theater and of other arts, but cinema, TV, and the Internet have all given it new turns, and Almodóvar is fabulously alert to where the new and the disappearing meet: city and country; movie actresses aging in life but not on the screen; new media and old habits. *Volver* (2006) is a good example. At one point, Raimunda, played by Penélope Cruz, sings the old Argentinian song that gives the film its title, about a woman's return to the town of her youth, about memories of first love twenty years earlier, about aging and how life is just a breath (*"un soplo"*). "I'm afraid of meeting the past which is about to confront my life," she sings, "but a traveler who runs away sooner or later stops in her tracks. And although the *olvido* which destroys everything may have killed most of my old dreams, I still keep in my heart a modest hope which is all the fortune I have."[2]

The movie is about many things, generational recurrence among

them, but while it broods on different ways in which the past can haunt the present and dictate the future, it represents a new turn in the director's work by celebrating decisive action, "moving on." The story itself is a new version of one embedded in an earlier film, *La flor de mi secreto* (*The Flower of My Secret*, 1995), but with a different emphasis. As the critic Daniel Mendelsohn put it in a review at the time, not only does *Volver* embody "a series of subtle, complicated, intense yet finally manageable feelings among female characters, emotions that . . . really do constitute a kaleidoscopic vision of what 'True Love' is but at various points it suggests that getting on with the present, in all its difficulty, may be more important than dwelling on how it came about—compelling though that is."[3]

In Almodóvar's case this is, it should be stressed, just one development. What seem to be the positions taken by works of art are generally provisional, experimental. There's no question of Almodóvar's being "against" memory, whatever that would mean for a narrative artist, and indeed he has spoken in favor of a firmer application of the Spanish memory law, "because otherwise fantasy memories are going to pervert and corrupt [history]." He has also talked about basing a film on the life of the poet Marcos Ana, who fought for the Republic as a boy, was arrested in 1941, and spent twenty years in Nationalist prisons before being released after a campaign by Amnesty International. To date, though, among the many distinctive aspects of this director's work is that while it's generally agreed to embody pretty well everything that Francoism was against, it does so with scarcely any explicit reference to the dictatorship under which he grew up. Almodóvar was born in 1949 and educated at a Catholic boarding school. Many of his films satirize and subvert religious ideas and practices, but even his story of the victim of an abusive priest schoolmaster, *Bad Education* (*La mala educación,* 2004; the title could also be translated "Bad Upbringing"), is tender about same-sex adult-child romance as distinct from physical exploitation, and Almodóvar has in any case firmly denied suggestions that the latter aspect is autobiographical: he himself suffered no such abuse. There are "remembered" childhood scenes in *Bad Education*—priests and boys playing soccer; a boy singing an innocent song of religious love to the corrupted Father Manolo—that complicate the otherwise condemnatory, vengeful present-day narrative.

The moral and historical diagrams drawn by recent films and TV series have not all been so subtle. Folktales don't have a lot of shading—we like them for the boldness of their patterning, the ease with which messages can be taken from them—and many Spanish films about the civil war and its aftermath depend as much on simple paradigms of good (Republican) and evil (Nationalist), as do their Anglo-American Second World War counterparts in depicting the Western Allies versus the Nazis. The most obvious example is a movie made not by a Spanish director but by the Mexican Guillermo del Toro, which had as big a success in Spain as everywhere else and, for good or ill, has played its part in shaping how people think about the period. Narratives based on particular historical periods tend, the further separated they are from those times, to take one of two routes: either toward ever more painstaking "authenticity," or toward myth—but sometimes both happen at once. The differences and also the connections are familiar to Anglophone viewers from, on the one hand, the Omaha Beach sequence of Steven Spielberg's *Saving Private Ryan*, and on the other, Anthony Minghella's version of Michael Ondaatje's novel *The English Patient*. Del Toro's *Pan's Labyrinth* (*El laberinto del fauno*, 2006) illustrates in an extreme form the mythologizing, in every sense, of Spain's mid-century history. A fantasy movie in which the forces of good and evil operate below- as well as aboveground, it juxtaposes classically based myth, literary allusion, and romanticized history, and its broad-brush polarities include those between a brave, innocent, but independent girl and her sadistic stepfather, who is a Francoist military officer; an unborn child and that same evil soldier; fauns and fairy-eating ogres; Republican resistance fighters and Nationalist oppressors; the starving and the grotesquely feasting. Somewhere in the mix, along with a mandrake and the guidance of an ancient book, is a radically new version of *Hamlet* in which a daughter called Ofelia unhesitatingly pursues vengeance on behalf of her dead, supplanted father and all is resolved in a Disneyesque fairyland.

Yet a myth of a different kind is also involved: the in some ways more seductive one of heightened and simplified "realism." (Another foreign-made example of this tendency is the socialist British director Ken Loach's preposterous 1995 film about the civil war, *Land and Freedom*.) In the "real-life" dimension of *Pan's Labyrinth*, we're prepared

for the vile manipulativeness of members of the dictatorial class by the fact that they not only wear tightly fitting black leather gloves but can light their cigarettes and adjust their wristwatches without taking those gloves off. And of course the film is full of action and suspense and is absolutely thrilling. Among its borrowings are elements from half a dozen Spanish movies, especially one that made an impact on Muñoz Molina: Víctor Erice's *The Spirit of the Beehive* (*El espíritu de la colmena*, 1973).

In some ways, *The Spirit of the Beehive* does for 1940s Spain what *Empire of the Sun* does for Japan in the same period. Like Ballard's novel, Erice's script begins with a child watching a movie: here, James Whale's classic version of *Frankenstein*, which is being shown in a Spanish village hall in 1940. And, again as in Ballard, the child character, while deeply affected by recent and current events, also transcends them through a self-reliance that is a matter partly of practicality, partly of being absorbed in her own imaginative world. Thanks to the Francoist censorship, the *Frankenstein* screening begins with an introduction in which the audience is told that while only God can create life, the story to come is a fable carrying important moral messages. To little Ana in the audience, what matters more is her sense of identification with Maria, the monster's unintended victim.

Ana and her sister, Isabel, live in a rambling mansion with their loveless parents. Their melancholy father, Fernando (played by Fernando Fernán Gómez), occupies himself with various activities, among them the beekeeping that gives the film its title. His beautiful younger wife, Teresa, is in correspondence with a former lover from whom she has been divided by the war, and who may or may not be the fugitive Republican who arrives on their land. One of the film's subtleties lies in the lack of communication between Teresa and Fernando, done not with any Pinteresque portentousness but simply as an absence. It's possible not to notice that although they are often in the same scene, they never speak to each other. Their younger daughter, Ana, meanwhile, lives in an isolation of her own, but like Maria with Frankenstein's monster, she finds companionship in the fugitive hiding in a nearby barn, to whom she takes food and clothing. He is shot by the police, the news spreads, Ana's mother burns some letters, and Ana runs away and has a dream that replicates the scene between Maria and the

monster in *Frankenstein*. While a limited rapprochement is achieved by her parents, Ana is bereft, and the film ends with her traumatized loneliness—a condition associated with the parental civil war generation, though we now realize it is handed on and may deepen.

Unlike *Pan's Labyrinth*, *The Spirit of the Beehive* scarcely mentions the war or the ensuing regime and shows no violence. The early 1940s are present here, in the shabbiness of the big house and its wide, almost empty landscape; cumbersome police, watchful villagers, children in a schoolroom scene of memorable authenticity and innocence, a man jumping off a train. With the exception of Ana's questions to her sister, people's thoughts and feelings find no overt expression. The killing of the fugitive is a scattering of gun flashes at night around the barn he hides in and a few bloodstains found afterward by Ana. No one screams or makes speeches. There are moments of real tension: Isabella teases her younger sister by pretending to be dead in an episode that begins to make us as scared as Ana. And there are more riddles than answers, about Teresa (including her relationship with the family doctor) and about Fernando. This unforgettable film is "about growing up" and "about loneliness" and "about postwar trauma," but the vivid elements are its mood—Bergman-like except in its lightness of touch—and its unforgettability: the memorable here is not what is said or done but the emotional haze in which everything is apprehended.

War and postwar, in other parts of Europe as well as in Spain, intensified childhood in all kinds of ways, among the most intimate of which was a sense that adults knew things that children couldn't understand or be part of. Any childhood is like this to some degree of course, so stories set against a background of war can, in this respect as in others, speak for all of life. War, Clausewitz taught, is a natural condition. In simpler, practical terms, people made films (and wrote novels) about children's experience of the period because that was what they and many people in their audience knew about. Víctor Erice, whose first film was *The Spirit of the Beehive*, grew up in the 1940s in the Basque region, where the civil war was complicated even further by the region's long tensions and where "nationalism" meant the opposite of what it meant to Spanish conservatives. He shares this background with Antonio Mercero, director of *La guerra de papá* (*Daddy's War*), based on Miguel Delibes's *El príncipe destronado* ("The Dethroned Prince";

see p. 232). An equally important part of the world of these and other directors, though, were the films they had seen and heard about, among the first of which was conceived by the caudillo himself, and starts with a version of his own childhood.

RAZA

Franco's novel *Raza* was his second book—the first, the diary of a military flag in Morocco (*Diario de una bandera*), was published in 1922 and reissued in 1939 to celebrate his victory in the civil war. Not so much written as orally composed, *Raza* was dictated to a couple of ghostwriters, who finished it early in 1941. Almost immediately, plans were made to turn it into a film. The director was José Luis Sáenz de Heredia, a cousin of José Antonio Primo de Rivera.

Franco loved the cinema. He enjoyed it in the ways everyone does— between 1946 and his death, private screenings were held more than once a week on average for the dictator, his family, and friends in the former royal theater of the palace he had taken over, El Pardo.[4] Because of the censorship his own regime imposed, some of the films he watched, *Casablanca* among them, were not generally available in Spain. Like other dictators, though, Franco saw the medium as a means of shaping the minds of the people he ruled and, partly the same thing, of aggrandizing himself. In these ambitions he was both successful and unsuccessful.

The successes were obvious. Under Franco, the subsidized industry poured out films that celebrated Spanish national and imperial greatness, depicted in terms of Spain's folk traditions, or of the union between Church and state embodied by the reign of Ferdinand and Isabella, or of what were presented as the country's noble crusades against Islam, Judaism, South American paganism, Freemasonry, and communism.[5] Franco saw himself, and ensured that he was seen by others, as a continuation of the crusader story. Many films made after 1940 glorified the civil war as Spain's heroic victory over infidels of various kinds. The dictator both played the conquering part in life and wrote his own fictionalized version of it.

The word *raza* means "race" and also "breed"—Franco was more

than usually infatuated with Nazism at this time,[6] and Sáenz de Heredia's high-budget film follows the novel in presenting an ideal version of Spanishness in the form of a devout naval family, a romanticization of the author's own background. We are told by a voice-over at the beginning that we're about to experience "scenes from the life of a generation, unmatched episodes from the Spanish Crusade, spurred on by the nobility and spirituality characteristic of our race." Then there's a prelude: the father's return from sea. The first thing he does is go to Mass with his family. Afterward, he tells his children stories about Spanish naval history, discovery, and colonization, while their mother sits sewing and rocking a cradle that has a cross at its head. Duty, in the form of Spain's disastrous 1898 war with the United States over Cuba and the Philippines, soon calls him back. He dies in battle, kissing the cross his wife gave him when he left, and now the story proper begins. The children have grown up—José, the Franco figure, into a dashing, opinionated, brave young man. Early in the civil war, José is wounded— "It's nothing," he says; "*No es nada*"—captured by the Republicans, tried on the pretext of being a spy, and sentenced to death. Facing the firing squad, he refuses to be blindfolded and shouts "*¡Arriba España!*"—"Up with Spain!" His body is taken home, but he proves to be still alive, a miracle juxtaposed with episodes in which priests and monks try to defend Christian buildings and their contents against desecration by the mob. José's younger brother, Jaime, a priest, is himself killed by Republicans. José, meanwhile, having made a good recovery, travels to the front, where he encounters fellow volunteers of all kinds, ranging from spirited flamenco guitarists to an old man whose sons have been killed by Republicans and who is desperate for revenge. No Moroccans, Germans, or Italians are in evidence; in general, the film plays down a number of historical elements that might have alienated even sympathetic viewers. While a crusader motif runs through the story, more modern gestures such as the Nazi fascist salute, as well as some racist and xenophobic speeches, were quietly suppressed in a 1950 version of the 1942 original, *El espíritu de una raza* ("The Spirit of a Race").

The essence of *Raza* is to justify the military uprising of 1936. It was the first film to appear that did this, thanks in part to the censors' helpful suppression of a potential rival, *El crucero Baleares* ("The Cruiser

Baleares"), made by a Mexican actor and director, Enrique del Campo.[7] Sáenz de Heredia went on to enjoy a triumphant career as the regime's cinematic semi-laureate, this aspect of his work culminating in *Franco, ese hombre* ("That Man Franco"), produced to coincide with the twenty-fifth anniversary of the dictatorship in 1964. In some respects, *Raza* is more sophisticated than a brief summary suggests. Franco had a brother who for a time supported the Republic, and although this embarrassing fact is represented in the narrative in a way that shows no sympathy for the brother—called "Insurrectionist! Freemason!" by the precocious José in a childhood fight—it must have comforted the many Nationalists whose families were similarly divided. (Franco, who watched the film often in his private cinema, is said to have wept profusely at the first viewing.[8]) In the film, this brother undergoes a politico-religious conversion and he, too, faces a Republican firing squad, an experience that unlike José, he doesn't survive. And there is a love interest. As a whole, though, the project, right down (or up) to the aristocratic authorial pseudonym Jaime de Andrade adopted by Franco, has been fairly described by the Spanish critic Román Gubern as exemplifying the caudillo's "irresistible vocation for social climbing, for self-aggrandisement."[9] The noble life and death of José's father are in sharp contrast, Gubern points out, with the hard-drinking, womanizing, domestically absenteeist career of the real-life Nicolás Franco, and José's own trajectory doesn't include any setback analogous to Franco's rejection as a possible candidate for the conservative Acción Popular in Cuenca in 1933.[10]

SOCIAL REALISM, SURREALISM, AND *VIRIDIANA*

At the same time as works such as Sáenz de Heredia's were appearing, however, the messages they conveyed were being turned inside out and upside down. Spanish filmmakers were more cosmopolitan than most of their compatriots, and their links with the Italian industry were particularly liberating, not least because of the strength of communism in postwar Italy. Social realism, often hard to distinguish in this period from socialist realism, had long been an element in Spanish films as well as novels and, despite the Francoist censorship, was encouraged

by the Italian connection—especially after 1951, when a week was devoted to screenings of current Italian films in Madrid. The future director Carlos Saura, then still in his teens, was to describe the shock of realizing "that you could make films in the street and put ordinary people into them."[11] Meanwhile, some of those who worked in Spanish cinema in the 1950s and '60s were themselves Italian, among them Marco Ferreri, director of a number of social satires that got past the censors.[12] Spain's problems, though, were visible not only to those on the left. José Antonio Nieves Conde, who had joined the Falange and fought with the Nationalists in the civil war, found himself on the wrong side of ecclesiastical criticism with his exposure of poverty, corruption, and rural depopulation in his celebrated 1951 film, *Surcos* ("Furrows").

In 1955 a series of discussions on the state of Spanish cinema was mounted in Salamanca, the capital city of National Catholicism. A famous concluding statement was delivered by the director Juan Antonio Bardem, then in his early thirties. Spanish film, he proclaimed, was "politically ineffective, socially false, intellectually inferior, aesthetically null, industrially enfeebled."[13] Bardem was one of those who tried to ensure that, as time went by, such criticisms became less valid. But matters were still further complicated by the strong vein of anarchism in Spanish culture, especially in the form of surrealism. In the first decades of Franco's rule the name of Buñuel, who, having spied on behalf of the Republic in 1936–37, emigrated to France and then New York—he got a job at MoMA but was fired, largely because his old friend Dalí denounced him as a Communist—and finally Mexico, was banned from Spanish reference books. But it isn't reference books that artists draw on for their material, and his influence remained powerful.[14] He provides an interesting example of some of the difficulties faced by attempts at state control of the arts, both interpretative and practical.

Most of Buñuel's career was spent outside Spain among exiles—exiles from Hollywood's anticommunism as well as from the Spanish dictatorship. In 1961, however, a time when the Franco regime, partly under foreign pressure, was relaxing some of its controls, he was persuaded by Carlos Saura to come home. The first film he made in Spain since his 1932 documentary on rural poverty in northern Extremadura, *Tierra sin pan* (*Land Without Bread*), was *Viridiana*, a kind of

social-realist morality play. The young Viridiana is about to take her vows as a nun when she is reluctantly persuaded to visit her widowed uncle Jaime, who has supported her financially. Jaime lives in a state of religiose permanent mourning in a dilapidated country mansion: a figure for Spanish traditionalism. His niece by marriage closely resembles his wife, who died on their wedding night, and in a series of fetishistic episodes, Jaime persuades her to put on her aunt's wedding dress, drugs her, molests her in her sleep, and subsequently pretends that he has had sex with her in order, he hopes, to force her to marry him. Viridiana refuses and, after she has set off back to the convent, he hangs himself. Her journey is interrupted by the police, a force of stability and authority throughout the film, who take her back to the mansion, which she now inherits a share of.

The second half of the film shows two conflicting versions of how the place might be organized. On the one hand, Viridiana's co-heir, Jorge, Jaime's illegitimate son, wants to run it in an efficient, modern way, installing electricity and replanting the neglected estates. In this he resembles the new "technocratic" element in the Spanish government embodied by Opus Dei. On the other hand, Viridiana, standing now for traditional lay Catholicism, tries to put her vocation into practice by providing a home for local beggars. Both schemes start out well. While it's clear that the beggars are hypocritical in their respect for her, Viridiana persuades them to work and pray, and there are glimpses of a possible utopia. Soon, though, she and Jorge go away from the estate on business and the beggars, thinking they have a night to themselves, take over the main house, help themselves to food and drink, and, in a scene that overtly turns the Last Supper into an orgy of misrule, start to break the place up. When the owners return unexpectedly, it looks as though some of the chief beneficiaries of Viridiana's good work will rape her and murder Jorge, but they are outwitted by a combination of Jorge's cunning and the common sense of Ramona, the permanent housekeeper, who in the film combines the practical Martha and the sexual Mary Magdalene of the Gospels. It's Ramona who fetches the police.

The regime at first not only licensed the film but also endorsed it as Spain's entry in the 1961 Cannes Film Festival, where it won the Palme d'Or. In moral terms it can be seen as essentially conservative: look

after what you own, don't behave in extreme ways, be charitable but not gullibly so. Meanwhile, the religious beliefs of Viridiana are evidently sincere, as is Ramona's secular loyalty to the house. There's also, though, a strong thread of satire against Catholic authoritarianism, and an element of (in itself far from original) sexual and fetishistic treatment of the nun—repeatedly spied on as she undresses, and invaded in her bedroom—and of Christian objects such as a penknife that doubles as a crucifix. So it was to the regime's embarrassment and the delight of its opponents that *Viridiana* was denounced by the Vatican newspaper, *L'Osservatore Romano*, and, partly in consequence, became an international hit. The official who had let the project through was forced to resign, every print of the film remaining in Spain was destroyed, and all the director's work was once again blacklisted.[15] *Viridiana* wasn't shown in the country again until 1977.

THE CENSORSHIP TIGHTROPE: GARCÍA BERLANGA

Government control of the film industry wasn't a Nationalist initiative—nor, of course, was it confined to Spain.[16] Besides, the Francoist censorship of the arts had frequently offered challenges of kinds that proved imaginatively stimulating. Is a film that satirizes hypocritical or overauthoritarian behavior by Catholics a subversive attack on the Church or a piece of sound Christian doctrine? Does a comedy about a collision between small-town naïveté and the hopes raised by international aid present the country in a bad light, or is it capricious foreigners who are being criticized? If one of the ways we define the goodness of good art is its openness to a range of interpretations, it follows that the best work will cause censors the most difficulties. Much has rightly been made, particularly outside Spain, of the so-called *estética franquista*, Francoist aesthetic, by means of which several excellent, unorthodox films were released there in the 1950s and '60s, but from today's perspective the methods it used—irony, symbolism, above all ambiguity—are not all that different from those to be found in the cinematic repertoires of other, less heavily censored cultures. Besides, few films made (or novels written) even in democratic regimes are all that good, and many of the best have been done in the teeth of difficulties of

one kind or another, whether political or economic. It shouldn't surprise us that the *dictadura* challenged the best talents to produce their strongest work. Luis García Berlanga is a case in point.

Politically, Berlanga had learned early on how to walk a tightrope. Educated in Valencia by Jesuits, at the age of twenty he joined the División Azul, the "Blue Division" sent by Franco to support the Nazi invasion of the Soviet Union in 1941. Berlanga's aim in doing so, he later said, was to give some protection to his father, a liberal leftist who had been imprisoned by the Nationalists, but there's some evidence that his enthusiasm for the Falange was genuine enough at the time.[17] If so, he was far from alone in this among his contemporaries. Any consideration of films made by him and other Spanish directors, whether during or in some way about the dictatorship, or both, needs also to take account of one of the many unintended consequences of Francoism: the extent to which it helped these directors acquire and disseminate their subversive skills. Berlanga, like his subsequent collaborator Juan Antonio Bardem and most of the other key figures in mid-twentieth-century Spanish cinema—Saura, Erice, José Luis Borau, Basilio Martín Patino, Mario Camus, Manuel Gutiérrez Aragón—studied and taught at what later, and in the circumstances somewhat ironically, became known as the Escuela Oficial de Cine (Official Film School) in Madrid, founded by the government in 1947.[18]

Berlanga's comic masterpiece, *¡Bienvenido, Mister Marshall!* (*Welcome, Mr. Marshall!*), which was screened for Franco himself in El Pardo on February 10, 1952,[19] has a simple plot. Villar del Río, a dusty village in the middle of nowhere, is visited by two sets of outsiders: a flamenco dancer and her impresario manager; and an official party of men in suits from the capital. The high-handed delegation tells the town's bewildered, deaf old mayor that a party of American benefactors is expected. He should put on a fiesta for them. The villagers have heard a lot about the Marshall Plan, the post–Second World War European recovery program that between 1947 and 1952 disbursed some $12 billion to aid reconstruction and economic growth in western Europe. Marshall aid went to many countries, among them France, Italy, and Czechoslovakia, but Spain did not qualify, partly because as a neutral country it had suffered relatively little in the Second World War, partly because the Western democracies, having sat on their

hands during the civil war, now claimed to disapprove of the ensuing dictatorship. Besides, Marshall aid was intended to counter Communist influence, and this, thanks to Franco, was no longer much of a threat in Spain. To poor people, though, "Mr. Marshall" remained a figure of fantasy. In the film, urgent but inconclusive discussions take place between the mayor, the priest, an impoverished local aristocrat, and others. Eventually the mayor accepts the impresario's help, and the town is theatrically transformed into a tourist agent's notion of somewhere in Andalucía. The residents, meanwhile, are encouraged to rehearse the requests they will be asked to make, while also learning to dance flamenco and practicing a reception parade for the American visitors. A long, particularly funny section of the story takes place at night, when each member of the organizing committee has his own dream—or, in the case of the anti-American priest, nightmare—about what will happen.

In the event, the American party is no more than glimpsed in a cavalcade of cars that tears through the village without stopping. The welcome party is dispersed without singing its absurdist set-piece song in praise of "los americanos" ("The Yankees have come . . . with a thousand gifts . . . Americans come to Spain . . . *olé* Virginia and Michigan and *viva* Texas . . . *olé* my mother, *olé* my mother-in-law and *olé* my aunt . . ."), the scenery is taken down, U.S. flags float away in the gutter, and a poor but peaceful normality is resumed.

Blending Gogol's classic comedy of gullible provincial expectations, *The Government Inspector*; Thornton Wilder's 1930s *Our Town*; and, in terms of the symbolic nonarrival of a long-awaited savior, Samuel Beckett's 1952 *Waiting for Godot*, *¡Bienvenido, Mister Marshall!* is among the funniest and, from one point of view, most innocent and charming films ever made. Every moment carries some quiet, half-hidden joke: the bull's head on a shield in the re-themed village bar, for example, which turns out to belong, for economy's sake, to a live bull, the rest of which is stamping on the other side of the wall. And there's light but genuine pathos in the villagers' humble hopes: for a clarinet, a bicycle, a pair of cows. Much more than this is going on, though. The two busy deputations in their black limousines—menacingly officious Spanish authorities; invisible American "benefactors"—are indistinguishable from each other in their re-

moteness from and uselessness to the people whose lives they throw into turmoil. And the disturbances they create involve some sharply satirical cameos: the ignorant priest who denounces America and later has a nightmare of being dragged away by a Ku Klux Klan group with its own jazz band, to be tried by a Dalíesque blend of the Inquisition and the House Un-American Activities Committee; or the aristocrat Don Luis, who in his dream is a conquistador boiled in oil by Indians, a fantasy enacted as a creaking stage play within the gimcrack pageant the village itself is putting on. And what about that pageant? Structurally, we could be in something by Lorca, an allusion so undesirable to the authorities that they can't have realized it existed. To Spanish cinema audiences, the film hilariously spoofed at least one key aspect of Francoism's impact in Spain. *"Españolada,"* presenting Spanishness through idealized stereotypes, was intended to help create a united Spanish identity, as against the regional customs that underpinned the country's strong tendency toward devolution. In practice, although Franco would have hated to be told this, the results were more in keeping with foreign versions of the country—especially those of Bizet and Mérimée—than anything more authentic. The dressing-up of Villar del Río in *¡Bienvenido, Mister Marshall!* parodies all this, and the ease, even relief, with which the villagers abandon the project reinforces the idea, very strong in liberal Spanish philosophy as in everyday Spanish life, that individuals not only should but naturally do resist homogenization.

While all this makes fun of Francoism, the film's message is, again, essentially conservative, and there's a similar ambivalence in its attitude to American influence. The population of the United States, the village priest warns, consists of forty-nine million Protestants, numerous Chinese, five million Jews, thirteen million blacks, and countless divorcees—therefore, far from having anything good to offer to the village, America is in need of conversion. Exactly who and what is being sent up here? Some U.S. viewers took the film as an attack on their country: Edward G. Robinson made a big fuss when it was shown at the Cannes Film Festival, where he was on the jury.[20] Yet in a characteristically casual-seeming touch, the film offers a glimpse of a poster for a movie being shown in the village, a Western. This hint that the people of Villar del Río aren't at all averse to American cultural

imperialism is reinforced by the mayor's dream of being a sheriff, a hilarious sequence that works in counterpoint to one in which the flamenco singer Carmen Vargas, played by the teenage Lolita Sevilla, performs classically and beautifully to an utterly indifferent local audience. Again, the priest's comic anti-Americanism (and racism and bigotry) has more to say about National Catholicism than about the United States. Berlanga's success, then, in terms not only of his ability to get his work past the censors but also of the lasting quality of *¡Bienvenido, Mister Marshall!* is partly to do with the number of targets he hits, as well as his sheer comic fertility. This is true, too, of his much darker film, *El verdugo* (*The Executioner*).

Made at the beginning of the 1960s, *El verdugo*—the word also means "murderer"—is a satirical sitcom that owes something to Sender's novel *El verdugo afable* (see p. 175). The film opens with the predicament of an official executioner in Madrid, Amadeo, who has a daughter, Carmen, but no sons. The shrewd, opportunistic old garrottist—played by José Isbert, the mayor in *Mister Marshall*—is about to retire. If he's to hang on to the accommodation that goes with the job, he needs a male relative to pass it on to, so he sets up the attractive if no longer young Carmen with an amiable young undertaker called José Luis, soon catching them not in flagrante (this is Franco's Spain) but pretty obviously *post flagrantem*. José Luis dutifully marries the pregnant Carmen and is eventually but much more reluctantly inveigled into going into his father-in-law's trade. Time passes, and his first garrotting job comes up. It's in Palma de Mallorca, and Carmen is keen to go there on holiday with their young son and her father. So the reluctant José Luis, wearing a little summer hat, finds himself trying to get out of what, mainly in the pursuit of a decent place for his child to grow up in, he has signed on to do.

At one level, *El verdugo* is simply a satire on capital punishment. The death penalty had been abandoned in Italy after the Second World War but was still in use in Spain, where, in the year the film was released, Franco caused an international outcry by having three alleged terrorists executed, two of them by garrotting. Again, this fact needs to be seen in a comparative light. The debate to which the film contributed was going on in liberal democracies as well as dictatorships: judicial hanging was not abolished in the United Kingdom until 1969, and

the last British execution happened a year after *El verdugo*'s triumph at the Venice Film Festival. The movie is also, though, a critique of other aspects of the Franco regime, among them nepotism and bureaucratic and ecclesiastical corruption, and of the ways ordinary people were persuaded to connive in these practices through traditionalism, through passivity, perhaps above all through the modest aspirations of family life, that keystone of conservative Catholicism. It's a wide-reaching as well as tragic commentary on the moral compromises almost everyone ends up making in life.

The long climax begins when José Luis, played by the Italian comic actor Nino Manfredi, is taken by a deferential police escort to carry out the execution. Increasingly, his behavior is that of a condemned victim. He keeps trying to find a way out, both literally and metaphorically. The prison warders and priest try to reassure him; the governor gives him a glass of champagne. Begging to be let off his task, José Luis, in a wonderful touch of believable irrelevancy, shows everyone the family pictures he has in his wallet. (The other men dutifully pass them around, explaining to each other, "The executioner's wife and son.") We glimpse the (real) condemned man being led calmly to the place of execution; he has made his confession, the governor says, had no last requests, and mustn't be kept waiting. José Luis, by contrast, has to be physically dragged across the prison yard. His white hat, straight out of a Marx Brothers movie, falls off in the struggle, he briefly breaks away, is recaptured, and, in a brilliantly lit diagonal shot, we see him disappear through a door in a wall into darkness, while a guard walks hastily back to retrieve the hat.

El verdugo caused a commotion. The Spanish authorities were torn between denouncing it and using it as evidence of a new liberalism on their part. When it was shown at the Venice Film Festival, the Spanish ambassador in Italy described it as libelous, false, caricatural, an illustration of the shabby, talentless depths to which attacks on the Spanish regime had sunk. Franco himself guilefully pronounced that although Berlanga was not a Communist, he was something even worse: a bad Spaniard. Berlanga later said that various cuts were made in the version distributed in Spain; for example, the sinister rattling of the garrotting equipment in the executioner's bag was removed from the soundtrack, as was a whole scene in which prison staff assemble the

machine. It is among the most powerful works in the Spanish cinematic canon. Like *Mister Marshall*, it owes much of its success to comic social realism—the sheer believability of the way José Luis becomes entrapped, the tragic ordinariness of all the main characters' motivations. There are moments of pure technical brio but they aren't ostentatious, just as the elements of symbolism are never allowed too much weight.

This can't be said of more self-consciously "European" Spanish films of this period, such as those of Berlanga's friend and earlier collaborator Juan Antonio Bardem, however brave the latter was in exposing injustices and irresponsibilities in Spanish life. In the opening scene of Bardem's overcelebrated 1955 *Muerte de un ciclista* (*Death of a Cyclist*), a car driven by the well-off María José hits and kills a cyclist. Apart from her lover, Juan, a philandering but conscience-wracked academic who is the main character, there are no witnesses, so they simply drive away, but Juan's guilty subsequent attempts to find out about the dead man take him into a world of poverty that contrasts all too obviously with the privileges he has been enjoying with María José. The schematism is at its baldest in the film's climax, when, to prevent Juan from confessing their crime, María José drives her car over him, too. To praise the film as a representation of the ways in which the ruling class denies its guilt and protects the status quo is to underestimate the audience's critical intelligence. Still, in a subplot from Juan's professional life, *Muerte de un ciclista* does something new in showing the beginnings of increasingly widespread student protests that, coinciding with industrial activism, were to have much more radical outcomes in Spain than their counterparts in other parts of the world. This episode, too, though, was removed by the censors from the version distributed in Spain.[21]

Muerte de un ciclista is Bardem's most famous movie and attracted the censors' attentions in ways that he increasingly refused to compromise with, while seeing his work obstructed to the point where it often became impossible to complete. Yet it would be hard to say that the lifting of censorship after Franco's death benefited either Bardem or Berlanga. The works Bardem made under democracy, such as *El Puente* (*Foul Play*) and a TV series about Lorca, are ideologically predictable, while Berlanga's became soft, their jaunty, aren't-we-Spanish-

funny? elements taking on a complacent, formulaic air. The younger Carlos Saura, by contrast, continued to grow through a series of ambitious changes.

THE UNPREDICTABLE SAURA

Urban poverty was among the issues that perturbed and divided the regime, and Saura, like some of those closest to Franco himself, found his own way of drawing attention to it. Outside Spain, Saura's *La caza* (*The Hunt*, 1966) is the best known of his films from the Franco era, but his first full-length work was a bleak piece of social realism, *Los golfos* (*The Delinquents*, 1960), developed in collaboration with his former student Mario Camus. In many ways, *Los golfos*, though harder to get hold of, has more to offer today's audiences than *La caza*. The setting is an urban Spain of poor high-rise blocks surrounded by wasteland shantytowns. Work is hard to find; theft, especially from the old and vulnerable, endemic as a means of survival: the pre-credits sequence shows a blind old woman, a lottery ticket seller, being robbed. One of the most dreamed-of means of escape for a young man in this milieu is to become a bullfighter, and the film follows one such attempt, counterpointed and in the end thwarted by an endless cycle of crime and punishment, violence and revenge. *Los golfos* was shot in various poor areas of Madrid, used nonprofessional actors, and was to a large extent improvised. Though it was an international success at film festivals in 1960 and '61—Cannes, London, Punta del Este (Uruguay), New York, Melbourne—the nerves it touched most painfully were domestic, and thanks to a hostile censorship rating, it wasn't shown in Madrid until 1962.

In the spring of the previous year, during an official tour of Andalucía, Franco had been taken to see some of the shantytowns that had sprung up around Seville, like most other Spanish cities. He seems to have been genuinely shocked, but as so often, his response was to sit on the laurels of a by now aging military success and call on its beneficiaries, the region's landed and business classes, to "collaborate in a Christian spirit in the creation of social justice."[22] It's the consequences of this pass-the-buck approach to social responsibility that *Los golfos*

depicts, and a final still of the sightless eye of a bull killed not only pointlessly but—what matters more from a Spanish point of view— messily carries with it all the symbolic associations between bulls and Spain itself.

The *generalísimo*, meanwhile, spent increasing amounts of time enjoying the rewards of success and late middle age, particularly fishing and shooting in the Andalusian Sierra de Cazorla, where he made long hunting trips every autumn. Field sports, the pursuit and killing of wild creatures, provided Spanish novels and films with a ready metaphorical language in which to direct covert attention to the dictatorship's raw mechanisms of power and some of its more blatant forms of injustice. *La caza* is the best in the genre.

All Saura's work is characterized by the calm attentiveness of its photography, and he was to turn more and more to films that not only were but were *about* works of art. His earlier productions, by comparison, tend to look outside themselves, at a society that operates in ways cruelly at odds with this visual aesthetic. *La caza* can seem today to manipulate such contrasts a little too hard. An effort is needed to re-imagine their bite during the lifetime of the caudillo, and the film has been the subject of a small library of explication. Its main sources of power, though, need little analysis, consisting as they do of a series of bold antitheses: for example, between the shinily precise weapons deployed on the shoot and the psychologically inefficient middle-aged men using them, a contrast made almost tactile when a close-up slides from the smooth barrels of a shotgun to the rumpled old corduroy of one of the men's trousers. These ex-Falangists with their myths of entitlement, we see, are just as vulnerable as, and a lot less nimble than, the rabbits they massacre. Their essential unfitness, for all their belief in the survival of the fittest and their nostalgia for wartime values, is evident in the confusions of their present lives: one is an alcoholic, another deep in marital breakdown and debt. To Spanish audiences, the impact of these personal disintegrations was sharpened by the casting: Paco, in particular, an arrogant, selfish old man, is played by Alfredo Mayo, who had made a career playing Nationalist heroes, above all, José Churruca, the Franco character in *Raza*.[23] But any viewer will see that all three older men are oblivious to the wrongness of the divisions between their world—which brings pop music, girlie magazines, and

elegantly boxed glasses and decanters into a harsh desert landscape—
and that of the skilled but impoverished lame countryman, Juan, who
is working for them. Many of these elements were to be developed by
one of Saura's early collaborators, Mario Camus, in his later, still grimmer *Los santos inocentes* ("The Holy Innocents"), but crucial to *La caza*
is the unselfconscious and, by the older men, unnoticed ease and
beauty with which Juan's adolescent daughter performs her practical
tasks, in contrast with the misapplied, disproportionate power with
which the men not only blast away at the landscape but accidentally set
fire to half of it.

A social-political point of a different sort is driven home by the
ending, in which the senior members of the group end up dead or dying while Enrique, representing a postwar generation both fascinated
and repelled by the recent past, runs off. It's not the case, though, that
the old are shown as more dutiful. In one sequence, the landowner José
shows Paco a cave in which someone was killed in the civil war. The
corpse is still there. "Why don't you bury him properly?" Paco asks.
"What would be the point?" José replies. Today the exchange has a new
reverberation.

Another film made by Saura under the dictatorship, though more
artificial, is also more interesting and original. Made while Franco was
still alive, in 1973, a prizewinner at Cannes, and nominated for an
Oscar, *La prima Angélica* ("Cousin Angélica") anticipates many of the
concerns of early twenty-first-century Spain. An unmarried middle-
aged businessman called Luis moves between the 1970s present and
his civil war childhood, which he spent with Falangist members of his
family while his father was fighting for the Republicans. In the present,
Luis has his mother's remains exhumed from a Barcelona graveyard
and takes them back to her family's crypt in Segovia. Memory and exhumation, then, are literally as well as symbolically linked, but while
the war and its political divisions are part of this, more important is
Luis's childhood relationship with the now-married, regretful Angélica.

A technique crucial to *La prima Angélica* is that the ten-year-old
Luis is played by his middle-aged self while the characters he's remembering appear as he remembers them having been at the time. (The
same device had been used by Bergman in *Wild Strawberries*.) At its
simplest, this prevents us from forgetting that what we're seeing is

what he recalls, but it also produces a persistent series of small shocks. Luis doesn't recognize the priest of his childhood but the priest recognizes him. How? On the other hand, when Angélica recites back to him a poem she believes he wrote for her, he confesses that it is by Machado. So while we're being invited to think about the lastingness of personal identity, we're also forced to ask how this can make sense: What responsibility can today's Luis be said to have for a long-ago deception? And, by extension, how far should we blame anyone for the past? Is the past to blame for *being* the past? Questions such as these, in all their unanswerability, are underpinned by some surreal imagery: Luis's blue-shirted Falangist uncle, his arm held up by a plaster cast in a permanent fascist salute; a nun with her lips padlocked—images of fixity and of the incommunicable that reinforce Luis's bewilderment and Angélica's plight, her silenced hopes. In a different way, though, and almost in defiance of José Luis López Vázquez's much-praised but extravagantly lugubrious and self-conscious performance as Luis, the film simultaneously communicates an optimistic sense of permanency through the double casting of other key actors. María Clara Fernández de Loaysa, for example, plays both Angélica as a child and, once Angélica has grown up and married, her daughter at the same age. So the brief rekindling and quenching of Angélica and Luis's romance gains hope as well as poignancy, and an element of complication, from the continuing presence of young Angélica in physical as well as psychological form. Again, in Luis's mind the frustrating, sometimes punitive interventions of the girl's father when they were children, and the obstacles presented now by her marriage, are embodied by the actor Fernando Delgado, who plays both father and husband.

"Spain . . . is the real subject of the film," wrote Vincent Canby when it was released in the United States in 1977,[24] and it certainly depicts conservative male authority in the combined forms of family, Church, and Falange with a comic disrespect that prompted noisy outbursts among its first audiences. The fascist salute episode caused particular outrage. During the 1974 Cannes festival, neo-Nationalist protestors in Madrid broke into a projection booth and stole two reels of *La prima Angélica*, perhaps under the delusion that only one copy existed. Though the film was never actually banned in Spain, when it was shown in Barcelona the cinema was conveniently firebombed,

with the result that there were no more screenings. In the short term, of course, all this simply added to international curiosity: the movie became Saura's first big commercial success. From today's point of view, more to the point is its portrayal not only of the sadnesses of aging but of the problems involved in treating memory as any kind of criterion, whether of faithfulness, continuity, or personal/social identity.

DOCUMENTARY PATINO

The necessity to communicate history both "as it was" and as it seems now to those remembering was a main concern of Spanish filmmakers during Franco's life and throughout the exhilarating, perilous transition to democracy. From 1968, when the dictator was in his mid-seventies, reports that he seemed to be losing his grip were confirmed by his increasingly weak public appearances, including on television. The student agitation common throughout the West had particular momentum in Spain despite the violence of the regime's repressive measures, and labor unrest also became widespread. The Basque separatist movement ETA made the most of a new atmosphere—one in which, wherever people stood politically, they knew that Franco wouldn't be there much longer. In 1969 a state of emergency was declared, and then lifted. Since the early 1960s, different approaches to censorship had been tried out, first by the moderate Manuel Fraga Iribarne, who introduced written criteria in an attempt to avoid absolute subjectivism, then by the more conservative Alfredo Sánchez Bella, on whose watch the government adopted a more pragmatic approach by not paying subsidies to work that didn't support its policies. Increasingly, however, "information" was seen as related to tourism, the latter being encouraged by reducing restrictions on the former. Yet despite this slow *apertura*, it was in clandestine conditions that Basilio Martín Patino, then in his early forties, made two documentaries during 1971 that were not released until five years later. Each provided an alternative version of the past to the one given in *Raza*.

As it happened, the long last throes of dictatorship in Spain coincided with a period of intense reexamination by German historians of their own national past: a questioning in particular of the idea that

Nazism was a minority phenomenon rather than, as more people were now beginning to accept, one that had been widespread and deeply rooted in German cultural history. It was in Berlin, at the city's International Film Festival in the summer of 1977, that Patino's film *Caudillo* made its initial impact. A rising young Spanish critic, Ángel Sánchez Harguindey, reported that the audience gave it "one of the longest ovations in the Festival so far, dispelling the myth that films on national issues can only be appreciated in their country of origin" and called on the Spanish government to respond with official approval. *Caudillo* was the director's second attempt at understanding his country's recent past: a project he saw in personal terms as fulfilling a promise to himself "never to submit."[25] The first, *Canciones para después de una guerra* ("Songs for After a War"), made in 1971 but not released in Spain until 1976, is also a collage of documentary footage, little of it seen before, though there's an enjoyable irony in the fact that some of the clips (for example, of the Nationalist victory parade) also appear in *Raza*. The film's art has as much to do with juxtaposition as with selection: Nationalist victory celebrations intercut with shots of ruined buildings and people in tears running for their lives; a sequence showing Republican road signs being removed followed by one of the ceremonial reburial of Nationalist corpses. Unlike in *Caudillo*, there's no running commentary, but as its title suggests, *Canciones* offers its own comments through music: Falangist songs and commercial jingles, for example, accompanying, and timed to fit the action of, scenes of despoliation, in a kind of grim ballet.

The fact that *Canciones para después de una guerra* was released immediately after Franco's death gives a special meaning to the phrase "after a war," as if the *guerra* had been not just the military one but the entire thirty-four-year dictatorship. Indeed, the history covered extends well into the 1950s. Perhaps inevitably, tension is sacrificed: the rhythm of contrasts established early on comes to lack variety; too many social-historical as well as political developments are touched on. A risk of a different kind is involved in the sheer cheerfulness of much of the footage, and of the soundtrack. What starts out as a shocking, poignant series of dislocations between event and tone becomes casual-seeming. When Patino shows Spanish people dancing in counterpoint with shots of the bombing of Hiroshima and the Nuremberg

Trials, does he intend a satire on Spanish isolation from the rest of the world's concerns, or is the aim merely, as before, to intensify the effect by a form of emotional denial? Either way, he has already used the technique too often for it to achieve much. Still, *Canciones* provides a vivid, breakneck tour of Spanish culture over two decades. Among its unmistakable messages is one that more narrowly focused dramas have difficulty communicating: the sheer numbers of those whose lives were affected; crowds in the city centers; lines waiting for food handouts; piles of corpses; powerless, desperate multitudes for whom at one point the film provides a complexly effective metaphor in the elaborate machinery used by the national lottery. Speaking as the image does of ungraspable numerousness, magnitude, and chance, and of the arbitrary bestowal of rewards, it makes a strong contrast with shots of the rich and powerful, always seen in privilegedly small numbers: well-dressed couples dancing or driving new cars; individuals in grand uniforms raised on daises above the crowd. The post-Franco world has come nowhere near solving the issues on which *Canciones* places its emphases, but at least, thanks in part to Patino, it began to remember that they existed.

Caudillo is more focused. Again, it achieves a lot through contrast: propaganda portraits of Franco in heroic poses; corpses in the street. While the film is neither doctrinaire nor excessively linear, it makes good use of the intrinsic narrative strength both of Franco's career and of Spain's social and political history between the 1920s and 1939—where, give or take some glimpses of related later developments, the story ends. Historically, the main distortion lies in the film's reticence about Republican atrocities, especially against the Church. Although Patino has been careful to acknowledge the conservatism of his background—both his brothers had ecclesiastical careers—he himself became an anarchist, and there is little sympathy for Catholicism in his work. In other respects, pathos is heightened rather than diminished in *Caudillo* by a degree of balance that comes across as generous-minded rather than just journalistically correct.

There's a particularly telling sequence in which Franco, bronzed and relaxed, speaks directly to his audience, just after we've watched the elderly, stiff, myopic Republican Largo Caballero, prime minister in 1936 and '37, addressing the Cortes from behind a thick script held

directly in front of his face. Franco, it's plain to see, could be very attractive. The camera liked his brown eyes, his shy, ready smile, in a way that made this fat little man seem likably confidence-inspiring. Patino's is an art of unsettlement, though: he rarely leaves us with a simple point. A little later, just after a painful episode showing the bombing of Guernica, Franco is seen in a propaganda clip with his wife and their daughter Carmen, the latter then about eleven years old. Her beaming father asks if she would like to say something to the children watching. "What shall I say?" she asks. "Whatever you like!" he answers. Carmen says she hopes children in the rest of the world won't experience what the children of her country's enemies are going through. (Or does she say her father's enemies? Is it *patria* or *padre*?) Sitting in her white dress, she wishes them God's blessing, sends them a kiss, and flings up her slender white right arm: "*¡Viva España!*" The speech has clearly been rehearsed; if we were in any doubt about this, we're given a glimpse of the dictator behind his daughter, lips moving slightly ahead of hers like those of an incompetent ventriloquist. As he realizes what he's doing, he produces a fixed grin, and the camera cuts away. Almost immediately, Patino brings in shots of refugees, many of them children, and of bodies, some of them children's bodies—children of Carmen's father's enemies perhaps, but how were the bombers to tell? There's much more: Neruda's inflamed poems; Moorish cavalry in Salamanca's Plaza Mayor; Queipo de Llano in full, frightening, contemptuous rhetorical flow; protesting speeches by Koestler and Einstein; horrifyingly immediate footage of battles seen from both sides. Above all what we see are people grieving—more and more of every degree and kind of grief.

Patino went on using his work as a way of contemplating Spanish history and culture. In his 1977 *Queridísimos verdugos* ("Dearest Executioners"), for example, he undertook a documentary investigation of the profession explored journalistically in Sender's *El verdugo afable* and fictionally in Berlanga's *El verdugo*, interviewing a number of retired professional executioners in their domestic surroundings: respectable, phlegmatic men surrounded by their families, recalling the crimes of those they dispatched and explaining the special merits of the garrotte. And in his later *Los paraísos perdidos* (*The Lost Paradise*,

1985), he adopts a more poetic approach to what is communicated as not so much the necessity of memory—a topic that was by then becoming a cultural obsession—as the tragedy of its simultaneous compulsiveness and inadequacy. Here as in several other films of the time, such as Víctor Erice's *El Sur* ("The South," 1983), a representative of the postwar generation—in *Paraísos* the daughter of a Republican who has died in exile—in one way or another returns to the past to sort out its literal and metaphorical legacy. Patino's central character, Berta, whose mother dies early in the film and who has recently separated from her German husband, is left with her father's books and papers, which she hopes will form the basis of a public collection, and also with a big, old, empty house. She reestablishes contact with her extended family and with old friends, including a former lover, now married, and in doing so tries to adjust to the strange cultural schizophrenia of early 1980s Spain: slow-moving old people in traditional dress; a fast-talking man of her own generation, now running the town's new democracy; medieval walls sheltering a cinema advertising porn movies. As a pastime, she works on a translation of Hölderlin's late eighteenth-century philosophical novel *Hyperion*, whose brooding central character searches, particularly in classical literature and art, for a solution to questions about, and conflicts in, the nature of personal identity, and finds a fragile, interim answer in the shape of a life as recaptured by memory.

Los paraísos perdidos is subtle and multilayered, and although some of its ironies can seem a bit ready-made for critical interpretation, others are telling. Interviewed on a slick radio talk show about her return, the woman is seen to become moved: but of course it's we who see her, not her fictional listeners, who are less attentive; a couple in bed switches off to go to sleep. The protagonist joins in a cheerful cod-historical festival—*españolada* for the democratic era—but her life is still without any real coherence. The idea that her father's library will interest anyone is, she finds, a fantasy. As in *La prima Angélica* but from a different angle, while someone may not be able to help mourning the past, doing so achieves nothing. It's in Hölderlin that Berta finds consistency: a modern woman seeking meaning in an old work about a then-modern man seeking meaning in . . .

TRANSITIONAL TOPICS: RURAL LIFE,
GENERATIONAL CHANGE

Such searches were replicated in many ways in Spanish films of the post-Franco decades. There was a sustained effort, for example, to make use of the literature of Spain's own past, including work by the controversial Cela. Long before the novelist won the Nobel Prize, both *Pascual Duarte* and *La colmena* were adapted as films that spoke clearly to new contexts: the first in 1976, against every frustration the censors could put in its way, and by a director of the postwar generation still in his twenties, Ricardo Franco. *La colmena* was made a few years later, by Mario Camus. Saura, meanwhile, directed a film version of Lorca's play *Bodas de sangre* (*Blood Wedding*), widely known outside Spain but suppressed there under the dictatorship. A psychological novel of the civil war, Max Aub's *Las buenas intenciones* ("Good Intentions," 1954) was the basis for *Soldados* (*Soldiers*), made in the late 1970s by Alfonso Ungría, who, like Ricardo Franco, was born after the events it concerns took place. In terms of new scripts, the 1970s saw a number of films set in rural Spain, portraying social poverty and feudal exploitation and glamorizing forms of social and/or political resistance. Among them are *Furtivos* (*Poachers*, 1975), another of the movies that had an impact on Antonio Muñoz Molina; *El corazón del bosque* (*Heart of the Forest*, 1979); and Mario Camus's *Los santos inocentes* ("The Holy Innocents," 1981).

The first of these, directed by José Luis Borau with a script he co-wrote with the young Manuel Gutiérrez Aragón, isn't about political resistance in any literal sense but explores the interactions of three individuals, each a rebel. Ángel, a poacher, makes a living by outwitting the local gamekeepers while trying to withstand his ferociously possessive mother, Martina. A young girl, Milagros, who picks him up, has escaped from a reformatory but is also in love with a criminal, himself on the run. Milagros embodies, too, the powers and freedoms of an emancipated new generation of women, while the film swarms ominously with figures of old-style masculine authority: police, gamekeepers, and the members of a shooting party. One of the latter—Ángel's "milk-brother," wet-nursed by Martina when he was a baby—is the provincial governor, and the film ends with the reinforcement of

conservative male power. The mother (played by the redoubtable Lola Gaos) kills Milagros. Ángel kills her in turn, after first ensuring that she has made her confession to a priest. Ángel, meanwhile, with help from the governor, has literally turned from poacher to gamekeeper. The unmistakable force of the story comes, then, not from any overtly radical message but—as with Lorca's *Blood Wedding*—from its enactment of psychological, sexual, and mythological energies: sex, family, survival, nature tooth and claw; blood in every sense of the word.

The slightly later *El corazón del bosque*, directed as well as written by Manuel Gutiérrez Aragón, is similarly intense: a visually powerful though, in terms of motivation and plot, far-fetched meditation on what's presented as the collapse of Republican resistance. Here, the main rebel character, El Andarín, has been part of an active guerrilla group in the post–civil war Pyrenees. In 1952 the movement disbands and one of its members, Juan, is sent to find El Andarín and bring him back. The task is complicated by the uncertain loyalties of local people, many of whom have begun to compromise with their new circumstances. In El Andarín's words, everyone is at bottom a traitor, and among the pragmatists is Juan's sister Amparo (played by Ángela Molina), once in love with the brigand but now engaged to a genial local shoemaker, Suso, who has friends in the Guardia Civil. The fact that times have changed is indicated early, at a local fiesta, where Suso is playing saxophone. The song, "Solamente una vez" ("Only Once"), is from the 1930s, but the style and instrument are new in Spain, and it's to this tune that Juan finds himself dancing with Amparo. Juan, though, has his errand to carry out, and in the course of it he brings war back to the woodland. Followed by the Guardia, who are after El Andarín, Juan is rescued and hidden by a former guerrilla living peaceably in the mountains with his wife and daughter. The story from now on becomes complicated, drawn out, and heavily emotional: pretty well every male character in the film breaks down and sobs at least once. But the main outlines are clear enough: Juan's protector is arrested and killed by the Guardia; as a fugitive, Juan himself becomes steadily more feral and ends up killing El Andarín. Amparo and Suso, meanwhile, get married. From the perspective of the late 1970s transition to democracy, then, while what Gutiérrez seems to have intended is a tragedy of lost idealism and of fierce, pointless heroism ("Only

once in my life has hope lit up my garden"), what comes across, as in *Furtivos*, is ultimately a conservative message: better to adapt. Nothing wrong with that, but the processes of adaptation, the nuances of alignment and realignment in the village community that Amparo and Suso are part of, are precisely what the story ignores. The camera dwells long and often on Ángela Molina as if in mute apology for the underwriting of her role.

Intergenerational relations were a potent theme in themselves. The sins of the fathers come under the children's scrutiny in *La guerra de papá* (*Daddy's War*, 1977), based on Miguel Delibes's novel *El príncipe destronado*; *Arriba Hazaña* (*Hail Hazana*, 1978) and *Demonios en el jardín* ("Devils in the Garden," 1982). The Church had become a subject of newly uninhibited scrutiny, and here, too, young directors played a part. It's not easy for people who have always lived with freedom of expression—whatever the limitations of that concept in practice—to imagine how thrilling all this was. The Vatican's index of prohibited books, the *Librorum Prohibitorum*, had been abandoned in 1966 under Pope Paul VI, but although the change had some effect in Spain, both the political and the ecclesiastical arms of the regime were hostile to what they saw as excessive tolerance on the Vatican's part, and the cultural atmosphere had remained inhibited. De-censorship wasn't an unequivocally good thing: you don't have to be a dictator to think that a free-for-all of pornography isn't a high point in any civilization. Nor is it the case, as we've seen, that Spanish cinema under Franco had been unable to engage with social, political, and historical realities. But the 1970s and early '80s provided a climate in which topics could be addressed that until then had either been taboo or were treated in oblique ways. Many of the resulting films still, though, raise questions of historical accuracy, fairness, truth—in short, of what time does to the past. In doing so, they illustrate, sometimes apparently unwittingly, the processes of simplification, fictionalization, even falsification that, on the surface, at least, they set out to remedy. Audience reception was an element in this process, both when filmmakers' oversimplifications were the result of commercial dumbing down and when viewers' knowledge of a director's career led them to glamorize his work.

Gutiérrez Aragón illustrates all this. His devotion to political-historical themes from the beginning of his career in the 1970s won

him a degree of respect that grew when his *Camada negra* ("Black Brood," or *Black Litter*) appeared in 1977. The film is about a violent Falangist gang fighting against democracy and was initially banned by the post-Franco censors. After winning a minor award at Cannes, it was shown in Madrid despite right-wing demonstrations. No serious critic has ever made much of a claim for it, and it is now almost unobtainable, yet it added to Gutiérrez Aragón's reputation in a way that contributed to the exaggerated success of *Demonios en el jardín*. This latter film won top prize at San Sebastián in 1986 despite the heavy-handed symbolism of an opening episode, in which a rural wedding party is interrupted by an escaped bull that gets into the church. The scene anticipates the main element of the plot: the prosperous bride-groom's troublesome younger brother, Juan, a member of the Falange, impregnates a pretty maid, Ángela, and disappears. Most of what follows is the story of the upbringing and disillusionment of Ángela's illegitimate son, Juanito. Having caught a glimpse of his father in Franco's company in a piece of newsreel, Juanito believes him to be important. Sometime afterward, Franco comes to the region on a fishing trip with a fantastic retinue of Moorish outriders and white-jacketed Spanish servants, among them the father, who turns out to be a waiter. The story compounds its own clichés with an affair between Juan and his brother's wife, Ana; Ángela's imprisonment for a theft actually committed by Ana; an attempt at a forced marriage between Ángela and Juan; and an inevitable shooting.

Demonios en el jardín isn't exceptional in its creakiness. Over-output in the post-Franco Spanish film industry, combined with a high degree of overlap between cinema and TV, encouraged an element of automatism that had already crept in with the new tolerance. Anything went, so almost everything went. Some work of the time was enjoyable enough. In 1985 the increasingly populist Berlanga made a comedy about an attempt by civil war Republican troops to penetrate a Nationalist festival and steal a bull (*La vaquilla*). In Vicente Aranda's *Libertarias* (*Freedomfighters*, 1996), a glamorous nun escaping from a Republican mob finds herself taking refuge in a brothel, where she is about to be put to work—her first client is a fat bishop—when business is interrupted by the arrival of a group of zealous Republican women who, with cries of "*¡Vivan las mujeres libres!*" ("Long live free women!"),

persuade all the hookers to join the militias. A religious conclusion introduces what could, in different hands, have complicated the whole story; no Spanish Xavier Beauvois, though, has yet turned up to direct a national version of *Des hommes et des dieux* (*Of Gods and Men*); there's a genuine opportunity, here.

Work by a few great filmmakers has continued to rise above such cheerful, opportunistic nonsense. In 1998, Carlos Saura brought out an enthralling work that, while clearly belonging to a phase focusing on other art forms—painting (*Goya in Bordeaux*); music (*Carmen*; *Fados*; *Io, Don Giovanni*); above all, Spanish dance—involves, indeed ties together, the themes of his generation. *Tango: No me dejes nunca* ("Tango: Never Leave Me," 1998) is a simultaneously joyous celebration of tango as a form and a social practice, and a dark, self-reflexive film about aging: especially about someone such as Carlos Saura, who is making a work of art about a kind of dancing that is about life and sex and betrayal and death. In all this, it has absorbing things to say both about the memory movement and about how the arts can affect our lives.

The film is set in Argentina, where tango began, and only gradually brings attention to the country's resemblances with Spain. Many exiles from the Spanish dictatorship moved to the relatively benign Argentina of the Peróns, only to find themselves caught up in a succession of military coups. Mario, the Saura character, who has spent many years in Europe in voluntary exile, was taught in Argentina by a Spaniard, who began every lesson with the words "*¡Viva la República!*" He is a melancholy, driven, self-absorbed man—there's an element of satire in Saura's self-portrayal—creating a musical that will be partly about his own predicament, partly about the beauty of the dance. In his view of himself, that predicament is to do with personal freedom and especially the freedom to pursue the kind of work he wants: ideals soon put to the test when the musical's main backer, a mafioso called Angelo, asks him to audition his twenty-three-year-old girlfriend, Elena. Mario does so, becomes infatuated with Elena, and gives her a leading role. Escaping the bodyguards Angelo surrounds her with, Elena becomes Mario's lover, and while the relationship echoes the crossgenerational freedoms of tango itself—the film is full of old men dancing wonderfully, and of children learning the movements—the couple's perilous situation reminds Mario of his own country's past brutality.

He decides to incorporate this into his work, devising a ballet set against backdrops from Goya's *Disasters of War*. In this sequence, soldiers kill civilians and throw them into mass graves; people are tortured, face a firing squad; refugees trudge toward what they hope will be safety. In rehearsal, the new element has a mixed reception from Mario's backers: the audience will be confused, some of them say; fear doesn't belong in a musical; besides, why bring up things that have been forgotten? Mario has been prepared for this by Elena's reaction, when he talks to her in bed about his dead friends: "Why think about all that? Ugly things are best forgotten." Hitherto, Mario has been established as somewhat corny in his thinking, and his answer to her is suitably messagey: "Who we are, how we live, the little we are, if we forget all that, what identity will we have?" By the time he's confronted by the backers, though, his response has become more complicated. He paraphrases the Argentinian writer Borges: "The past is indestructible. Sooner or later things turn up again. One of the things that turn up is a plan to destroy the past."

How the conflict between director and backers will be resolved is left hanging. Angelo, the mafioso, hasn't given his opinion but does make a threat against Elena. At the next rehearsal, during the new political-historical sequence, while she's dancing with one of the refugees, a man who has been lurking in the wings breaks in on the couple and stabs her. Angelo jumps to his feet and shouts, "No"; Mario rushes onstage and holds Elena—but it has all been part of the act. Angelo asks whether he got the timing right. He's bothered about this; he doesn't want to spoil the show. Can he have an extra rehearsal tomorrow?

This is where the film ends. Saura has resolved his big themes of historical memory and the uses of art but without prejudicing the celebration of dance that is *Tango*'s raison d'être: there have been ten full numbers, ranging from duos to big pieces of choreography, all danced and played with a virtuosity that embodies the film's arguments and is characteristically unclichéd and no less characteristically art-centered. The past is indestructible and tragically recurrent, points made on the authority of Argentina's greatest writer and with the backing of one of Spain's greatest painters. Yet art can and does help. Angelo's becoming directly involved as a performer in the work he has financed acts as a

harmless outlet for his obsession with Elena. The mafioso has said no to violence.

Saura's work has had a strong influence on that of Almodóvar. The directors compete on level terms with the world's best cinematic artists, in part because their handling of distinctively Spanish themes is so unprovincial yet so uncompromising. The results in each case are unlike films by anyone else. The same is true of early Berlanga as well as Erice and Patino, so it's hard to explain why their films of the 1950s and '60s are so little known outside Spain except as another consequence of the Franco effect: their eclipse by their Latin American contemporaries was a consequence of the politics of taste. Surely nothing good could have come out of the *dictadura*.

Fiction's Memories (ii)

Moving On

One way of defining the Spanish transition is to say that it began with Franco's death toward the end of 1975 and ended with the establishment of a new democratic constitution in 1978. But the process was more gradual, starting with various political adjustments as early as the 1950s and continuing well into the 1980s, even the 2010s. Transitions don't simply move in one direction; as I write, new forms of conservative nationalism, xenophobia, and isolationism are on the rise throughout Europe, and there are signs of a revival of socialist ideals in opposition to them. Behind these changes lies the fact that the economic comforts and political liberalizations that two generations in the West, including in Spain, took to be permanent are unraveling. For related reasons, to distinguish key turning points in the arts at this time can also be hazardous. New circumstances may make what seemed to be archaic phenomena freshly relevant, while new styles, and new artists, may not be as important as they appeared. To be of use in discussing Spanish writing, the idea of transition is best thought about less as a chronological marker than as a set of criteria that includes stylistic and thematic innovation and an ability to see Spain's history in the context of wider international concerns, but not necessarily all these at once.

In fiction as in cinema, there's no clear pattern in terms of what has

and hasn't made an impact abroad. Stylistically the most interesting Spanish writer between the late 1960s and the 1980s is Juan Benet, whose work has not appeared in English.[1] Miguel Delibes, too, is little known outside the Hispanic world, though not for reasons of style. His concern with innocence of various kinds is matched by a narrative simplicity through which he communicates themes that were to become increasingly prominent: how the children of those who fought on one side or the other responded to what they knew or suspected about their parents; and whether there is an underlying permanence in the phenomena associated with Francoism. Three other writers are particularly relevant. Luis Martín-Santos's bleak social-realist *Tiempo de silencio* (*Time of Silence*, 1962) soon became canonical, both under Franco, albeit in censored form, and afterward. It appeared rapidly in English translation and was rightly taken by foreign readers as evidence of what was happening in Spain. The transitional character of Jorge Semprún's work, on the other hand, is the result of personal circumstances that led to his becoming a key figure in the political transition itself and that were also distinctively European, more than Spanish. Circumstantial difficulties in the transmission of texts were nothing compared with the nightmares, literal as well as metaphorical, endured by Semprún in surviving, let alone communicating, his own experiences of the civil war and dictatorship. His story—the story of his life and the story of the stories he based on it—is among the most thrilling of his century. It's also, in dreadful but also inspiring ways, a deeply European narrative, one that, while crossing and recrossing geographical borders, asks questions about their meaning and that, in these and other respects, belongs to a transitional historical phase and mentality. Semprún experienced what Delibes and Benet intuited, that "Spanish exceptionalism" didn't exist and that the evils Spain suffered were commonplaces—banalities, in Hannah Arendt's sense—that affected the whole continent. Antonio Muñoz Molina, meanwhile, was a teenager in the mid-1970s, when the others were in their forties or fifties, but his 2001 novel *Sefarad* synthesizes and augments what they achieved, offering a cosmopolitan twenty-first-century perspective on older Spanish griefs.

The earliest of these writers is Martín-Santos. *Time of Silence* is set mainly in the shantytown world of Saura's film *Los golfos*, an environment of hopeless urban poverty and crime familiar to readers of Spanish fiction since Galdós, one that never entirely went away and that is now on the rise again. There's current resonance, too, in the novel's other main strand: its persuasive depiction of the stunting of Spanish scientific research by a compound of national insularity and poverty. The two forms of deprivation, private and public, are linked through the characters of Amador, a lab assistant, and Pedro, a young medical researcher working on genetic inheritance in forms of cancer. Mice carrying the relevant strain have been acquired from an American research laboratory but there's no money for replacements. Amador knows that an enterprising villain in the barrio, Muecas, who supplies dogs for research, stole some of the laboratory mice earlier and, with his daughters' help, has been breeding them in the expectation of being able to sell them back at a rate that undercuts the U.S. supplier. It transpires that the daughters have been bitten by the cancerous mice while incubating them in their underwear. Pedro, who dreams of winning a Nobel Prize, speculates excitedly about the possibilities of using human subjects for his research.

Here the scientific strand of the story becomes caught up with Martín-Santos's exposure of some of the grimmer aspects of this family's life. Muecas is a violent, sexually abusive husband and father. When Florita, one of his daughters, becomes pregnant by him, he tries to carry out an abortion. It fails, and he seeks help from Amador, who enlists Pedro. Pedro not only has no gynecological experience but also isn't yet medically qualified, and is drunk. It's not his fault that Florita dies while he's trying to treat her, but he runs away in panic, and those left behind, the victim's boyfriend among them, claim that he killed her. Pedro takes refuge in a brothel and is picked up there by the police, who assume that it was he who got Florita pregnant as well as carried out the botched termination.

Time of Silence is one of those books whose impact derives partly from their making earlier stylistic innovations palatable to a wide readership. The novel's use of firmly separated streams of consciousness, its combination of cool, essayistic, authorial commentary with giddying hallucinatory passages at times when characters are under stress—these

are skillfully done, though in 1962 they weren't as original as some critics have claimed. More unusual is the detailed scientific background, which Martín-Santos knew plenty about. Trained as a doctor, in the late 1940s he worked at the Consejo Superior de Investigaciones Científicas in Madrid, while in his spare time hanging out with writers, among them Rafael Sánchez Ferlosio and Juan Benet. He went on to train in Germany as a psychiatrist and practiced in San Sebastián, where he was also politically active, getting into trouble with the police for involving himself in propaganda on behalf of the outlawed PSOE and more than once spending time in prison.

For today's readers the book's realistic depiction of poverty is the main source of its power—that and a strong, tense plot whose elements (especially the determination of the keeper of the boardinghouse where Pedro lives to marry off her daughter to him) are conventional enough but that turns unpredictably. From the point of view of Spain's twentieth-century history, the book is interesting because of just how much it shows, and how uncompromisingly. Pedro is driven in part by national pride—he wants his research to reveal something unknown outside Spain. But his narrative is, from the book's first pages, full of his frustration with the lack of Spanish resources and his frequent desire to move to America, or at least to the place he romanticizes America as being. Madrid, he thinks,

> is so stunted, so lacking in historical substance, treated in such an offhand way by arbitrary rulers, capriciously built in a desert . . . far from the sea or any river, ostentatious in the display of its shabby poverty . . . bereft of an authentic nobility, peopled by its slumdwellers who can be so heroic on occasion . . . [2]

These words come early on, in a passage about a man wandering through the city he lives in, caught up in a love-hate relationship with it, finding in it "not only his justification, his reason for being, but also the stumbling-blocks as well as the invincible obstacles" that prevent him from becoming himself.[3] This mix of romantic self-abandonment and simple curiosity dominates Pedro's feelings when he goes to visit Muecas and his family in their shack, first crossing the vast garbage heap that separates the shantytown from the city. The place is, he real-

izes, at least as rich in material for anthropological study as any "primitive" remote settlement, a discovery he expresses in terms that parody the self-vaunting isolationism, and the racism, of Franco's Spain:

> Why pursue the study of human customs in far-off Tasmania . . . ? Is not the solution of eternal human problems achieved with greater originality here by our own people? Is not the taboo of incest more daringly violated in these primitive bridal chambers than in the grass huts of any paradise island? As though the primary institutions of these groups were not more noteworthy and more complex than those of peoples who have not yet succeeded in progressing beyond the tribal stage . . . As though it were not known that the average age of loss of virginity is lower in these huts than among the tribes of Central Africa which have the advantage of such complicated and grotesque initiation rites. As though the steatopygic fat of the Hottentots were not perfectly counterbalanced by the progressive lipodystrophy of our Mediterranean females. As though belief in a Supreme Being is not matched here by a more reverential fear of the equally omnipotent forces of public order.[4]

". . . *un temor reverencial más positivo ante las fuerzas del orden público igualmente omnipotentes*"—the censors can't have supposed that Martín-Santos was paying the regime a compliment.[5] Yet all they cut was the first brothel scene, leaving intact the second, in which, among other things, the arresting policeman suddenly has to use the lavatory despite his fears of catching a disease in it. It's worth looking at what the book didn't leave out, even in the form in which it was first published: poverty at the level of state as well as individual; incest and abortion and prostitution; drug addiction (Pedro's friend Matías discusses his case with a lawyer in a bar where everyone is smoking dope); police cruelty (in a gripping episode, Pedro is held incommunicado for seventy-two hours in a tiny cell without being charged; this, it's made clear, is routine); and arbitrary dismissal (even when acquitted, he loses his research grant). Favorite policies of the regime are lightly mocked in the interstices of all this, *espanõlada* in particular: "If the illustrious foreign visitor insists on being shown *majas* and bullfighters . . . there must be a reason for this. We shall have to . . . accept

the fact that the Spain of tambourines is going to attract more and more visitors."[6] Martín-Santos experienced the country in his own way and succeeded in bringing attention to what he saw. *Tiempo de silencio* was translated into sixteen languages, and after Franco's death it became a set text in Spanish schools and colleges.

Social reality of different kinds, some middle-class, some rural and feudal, is Miguel Delibes's theme, too. Intergenerational strains will be a main topic of the next chapter, on recent Spanish fiction, but Delibes is among the first writers to have explored them in relation to Spain's civil war. *El príncipe destronado* ("The Dethroned Prince"), which was also a hit as the film *La guerra de papá* (*Daddy's War*), though written in the early 1960s, did not come out until 1973. It vividly depicts the *posguerra* world of a small boy in a large family, newly displaced by the arrival of a baby sister. Domestic regime change here affects father as well as child. The former Francoist soldier discovers that the assumptions of traditional Spanish husbands are no longer shared by their wives. As one of the novel's Spanish critics has put it, Pablo's

> sole achievement in life is to have fought on the winning side in the civil war and to have killed "a hundred bad people" in the course of it, on which account he sees himself as being in possession of the truth, and his ideas as being irrefutable. For the same reason, his offspring are required to hold the same beliefs . . . which they have received from him as part of their genetic inheritance.[7]

With his wife, Pablo is aggressive and domineering. The couple's unhappiness is as palpable as the fact that, for them as for all respectable Catholics at the time, divorce is out of the question.

Delibes later returned to writing from a child's perspective in *Madera de héroe* (*The Stuff of Heroes*, 1987), a part magic-realist bildungsroman set in the 1920s and '30s about a boy, Gervasio, whose hair literally stands on end in situations he associates with heroism. It happens first when he plays military music on a phonograph that belonged to his grandfather, a Carlist—a hint that valuably puts "the" civil war into a historical context in which, as tends to be forgotten, Spain was always a divided nation and had seen three wars of succession in the previous century. Gervasio would have preferred to achieve

heroic status without dying or being hurt, a caution heightened by his growing realization that national loyalties come about more through accident of birth than through reason. What people are stuck with as human beings, and the tolerance this should encourage in them, is a wider concern to the boy as he begins to understand that one of his uncles is homosexual, yet that homosexuality is somehow disapproved of—just as his Catholic teachers disapprove of Republicanism, yet many of his family have Republican sympathies. The Second Republic, when it came, banned the Jesuit movement, but Gervasio's uncle Felipe Neri hid a Jesuit in his house. Against this ambiguous upbringing, Gervasio tries to make sense of a war in the early days of which, while he's still too young to fight, relatives on both sides are murdered and a school-friend is killed fighting for the rebel Nationalists by whom Gervasio's father is imprisoned in the local bullring. Gervasio eventually enlists in the Nationalist navy; suffers from seasickness; goes to sleep while on watch; fails to have any fun with a prostitute; takes part (shades of *The Naked and the Dead*) in the capture of a small undefended island; and is then involved in more serious military action, finding to his bewilderment that a man he has admired is spying for the enemy, while what seemed at the time the chaotic behavior of the crew as a whole, himself included, is afterward treated as having contributed to a heroic victory.

There are many literary, not to say historical, precedents for the moral topsy-turvyness of *The Stuff of Heroes*, but Delibes himself, for all the complexities he depicts, was no relativist. His most famous novel is the earlier *Los santos inocentes* ("The Holy Innocents," 1981), still untranslated into English but made into a powerful film by Mario Camus. The innocents of the title are a disabled child and her simple-minded old uncle Azarías, both of them expendable in any society based on the survival of the fittest but protected by the values of Christianity and—the novel implies but does not need to say—of liberal democracy. The book is set on a feudal country estate, and other vulnerable creatures are involved here, especially the birds shot for sport by the aristocratic owners. Azarías keeps a pet bird that, along with his care for it, is disdained by his *señorito* Iván.[8] And his aging brother-in-law, Paco, on whose skills as a gamekeeper Iván depends, breaks a leg just before an important shoot. Iván's ruthlessness—"This isn't a rest home," he tells Paco at one point ("*El mío no es un asilo*")[9]—shades into sadism,

but he hasn't reckoned with the family loyalty, cunning, and sheer strength of Azarías, the symbolic nature of whose revenge isn't allowed to interfere with its narrative plausibility and power. Similarly, although there's very little in the text that explicitly connects this remote rural world with the dictatorship, Azarías's touching way of explaining what happened to his brother in the civil war says it all: "*Se murió, Franco lo mandó al cielo*"—"He died, Franco sent him to heaven."[10]

Delibes knew intimately the worlds he wrote about. He was a country lover and a keen shot. Like the central character of *The Stuff of Heroes*, he had served in the Nationalist navy in his teens, an affiliation that didn't protect his writing from censorship, though he was also awarded several important literary prizes during the *dictadura*.[11] With his narrative fluency and his instinct for his readers' preoccupations, it is easy to see why his work was and still is popular. The strangest thing about his younger contemporary Juan Benet, by contrast, is how strange readers found his first novel when it appeared in 1967. It's true that its title, *Volverás a Región*, sounds as odd in Spanish as it does in English: "You'll Return to Region." From the opening sentence, we're introduced in the most specific terms to the place—a desolate mountainous area split by a road and a river—which Benet has called by this semiabstract name, as if he had called a character Man and then given him a highly distinctive appearance and personality. The area between Galicia, Asturias, and Castilla corresponds to how Región is described, just as the bleak existences of the three main characters—a doctor escaping his past, a woman recovering from hers, and an adolescent boy vegetating into his future—together with the local events of the war that has recently ended, are recognizable enough. Yet even the most admiring of early reviewers found the book "difficult," "obtuse," "confused"—and these descriptions have stuck.[12]

Like Cela—to whose politics he was opposed but who influenced his work—Benet admired Beckett. He was also inspired by Faulkner. What these antecedents have in common is a view that life is painful and inelegant and that communicating it truthfully entails a refusal both of charm, whether in style or characterization, and of any artificial gratifications of plot. Little that happens or has happened in Región is entirely clear, whether in terms of time or sequence or cause, but life can be like that. And what we understand as readers is more than suf-

ficient. We know, for example, that the woman's father was a company commander on the Nationalist side, that she was forcibly seduced (the ambiguity is hers) as an act of revenge for what his side did, and that she sees this as in some deep sense fair enough, while not disguising, either from herself or from the doctor she confides in, what the civil war has meant for her: that "within one week I suffered everything it brought to me: a father dead, a lover disappeared, an education turned to shreds."[13] A tragedy, then—but not quite of the kind it seems. Among the worst aspects, she says, is being treated as a martyr, so that she can't admit to having been in love with her enemy.

The personal agonies, confusions, and ironies of the civil war in Región are seen in a large context, both geophysical—those vast, torn rock formations, like a Tàpies painting—and of human history. There's an implicit comment on both Nationalist and Republican mythopoeia, and on what happens more broadly in memory, in Benet's account of "illusions which grow with distance and time until they transform into grandeur and honour things that in their day weren't short of arrogance and destruction, poverty and fear."[14] If this is a truism about warfare, to Benet it's a condition of life in general: the landscape remains while buildings (and families) collapse and feats of modern technology (motorcars, for example) break down. Juan Benet, we remember, was an engineer, a dam builder. Pitting his wits against water, rocks, and gravity was his moral education as well as his job. " 'Every household is a struggle for permanence,' the doctor reflects, 'and every change in it anticipates its decomposition.' "[15] War, in this worldview, is just one element in a destructive pattern against which law, order, and a sense of decency find their meaning only in failure. The Carlists fought in these five thousand hectares of wild mountains, the doctor says at another point; there are as many valleys here as days in a year, and they contain Celtic forts, and relics of ancient Roman religious practices that survived long into the Islamic occupation.[16] Amid these reflections, a particular scene keeps recurring, like the one in *Catch-22* where Yossarian tries helplessly to nurse the dying Snowden; in Benet's version, a girl in the back of a truck with a man vomiting blood all over her.

None of this is obscure, except insofar as the novel doesn't pretend to tell us what it all "means." The difficulty, as with Cela, lies in accepting art on these harsh terms—and art not only in the sense of invention.

Benet later wrote a short factual history of the civil war in which although his sympathies remain with the Republic, his emphases are absorbingly unorthodox.[17] Again, he presents the conflict as part of a long process he traces back to the beginning of the nineteenth century. He also insists on its role in world events—not just because of the International Brigades but also because, in his view, it was the beginning of the Second World War. Without the Nationalist victory, he argues, even after his unopposed seizure of Czechoslovakia, Hitler might have been more cautious. Benet treats the events of 1936–46 as the last flurry—he calls it a fireworks display[18]—of two and a half centuries of European power. He argues, too, that the origins of the civil war lie with both sets of combatants: while the right rose against the constitutional government, the Marxist-anarchist left was no less opposed to what he describes as "the reformist, democratic-capitalist regime of 1931–36"; and extremism and acts of terror characterized both sides. For all these reasons, he sees *Republican* as an adjective no less tendentious than *Nationalist* and denies that a victory for the former side would have brought political freedom to Spain.

Before Benet was ten, his father, a barrister, was killed by Republicans, but anyone who grew up during those years, whatever their family circumstances, became, as he wrote, obsessed by it. The war wasn't his only theme but he kept coming back to it—most exhaustively in the three volumes of *Herrumbrosas lanzas* ("Rusty Lances," 1983–86). By his own account, writing was a way of occupying himself during long evenings in the remote places where he did his engineering work on behalf of the dictatorship in the 1950s and '60s. It's strange and moving to think of him on those long-term construction sites in the mountains of Ponferrada and Oviedo, picking over his imaginings, finding the right words for them—strange and moving both in itself and in juxtaposition with other projects that were going on in Spain then: the art exhibitions in Madrid and Barcelona; the early films of Berlanga and Saura; a generation of future artists and intellectuals such as Pedro Almodóvar and Santos Juliá at their Catholic schools; the tunneling of the Valle de los Caídos; and the differently subterranean activities of anti-Francoist activists, among them Jorge Semprún.

Semprún was a contemporary of Martín-Santos, a few years younger than Delibes, a few years older than Benet. Unlike the others, he grew

up in a cosmopolitan political family, initially in Madrid. His maternal grandfather, the cultivated Antonio Maura, had been prime minister of Spain five times; his father was a diplomat and politician who spent most of the civil war as Spain's ambassador to The Hague, and when the Netherlands recognized the Franco government, he moved with his family to Paris. The clever eldest son, Jorge, then sixteen, was at the Lycée Henri IV at the time of the German invasion and went on to the Sorbonne. He has written vividly about his and his schoolfriends' first encounters with anti-Semitism—one day in a dangerous but at the time lighthearted act of solidarity with a Jewish classmate, they all decided to wear yellow stars—and about the many paradoxes of being a Spanish Republican in Nazi France. With the passionate, brave logic that marked all his actions, he joined the Resistance. The Gestapo caught him in 1943, and he was sent to Buchenwald. Helped by the fact that he wasn't Jewish and by a prison culture that produced one of the few groups in the camps that managed to arm themselves and actively prepare for liberation, Semprún survived and, after the Allied victory, became a key figure in the Spanish Communist Party both in Paris and, between 1953 and 1962, in Spain itself, where he worked clandestinely under various pseudonyms, chiefly Federico Sánchez. He writes about this period in the first volume of his autobiography,[19] an invigoratingly idiosyncratic narrative addressed by Semprún to his alter ego, Sánchez, in which a good number of Spanish radical taboos are broken. He not only has revisionist things to say about heroes and heroines of the left—La Pasionaria, Santiago Carrillo (whose own accounts of the period he ruthlessly demolishes),[20] Fidel Castro, Louis Althusser—but is generally impatient with what he describes as "the nostalgic, victory-shall-be-ours platitudes of exile; the beatific murmurs of meetings completely out of touch with any form of social reality; the manipulation of a ritualistic Marxist language, as though the essential task were to keep a prayer wheel turning."[21] There's more than a whiff of score settling here, but the book is deftly, vividly, tensely, sometimes almost comically constructed, racing from anecdote to reflection to satirical self-depiction—Semprún is particularly severe on his own Communist poetry—to shocking event and back, within an overall structure in which we're made to wait from the first page to the last for what La Pasionaria is going to say to him in 1959, from her lofty

Moscow position in the party that will eventually expel him. The so-phistication of the narrative shows up Pío Moa's later memoirs of the underground opposition as amateurishly self-serving. Semprún's most vivid, moving, and at the same time experimental writing, though, is to be found in the first of his several accounts of Buchenwald, *Le grand voyage* (1963, written in French and translated into English by Richard Seaver as *The Long Voyage*, 1964, later retitled *The Cattle Truck*), which appeared in Spanish in Peru in 1969 but in Spain itself not until after Franco's death.[22] Semprún began working on it in 1960, during a pe-riod when, after a big police raid on his organization in Madrid, he and others had to lie low, severing all their contacts.[23]

The frame of the part-fictionalized narrative is the train journey from Auxerre to Buchenwald, but the story itself (related in the first person by a man called Gérard) slides backward and forward, encom-passing his early life, his later difficulties in communicating his experi-ences of the camp, and everything between. Part of this involves the return journey to France in 1945 and Gérard's ironic view of the na-tional border it crosses, a boundary that he sees as fictitious in itself. Even literally interpreted, the voyage of the book's title is one between arbitrarily divided regions: when his returning companions are excited to cross from Germany into France, the narrator observes, "I looked up at the trees, and the trees hadn't given me any warning. If I were to be-lieve these shouts, a while back the trees were German and here the trees were French . . . I looked at the leaves on the trees. They were the same green as before."[24] Of course the journey is also metaphorical, but its literal aspects are more than usually important, partly because of the sheer physicality of the prisoners' experiences—the squalor of the carriage, the length of the route, the ironic beauty and productivity of the Moselle vineyards through which they pass—but also because of Gérard's insistence that the only way of understanding anything is by taking it literally and that this must start as an empirical, sensory process.

Over and over in this extraordinary text people protect themselves from the truth by refusing to see it: the citizens of Compiègne, for ex-ample, who avert their eyes from the wretched column of prisoners being marched past them. Boundaries are useful because they indicate what needn't be looked beyond. When the burghers of Weimar go for

their traditional Sunday walk in the beech wood, the camp named after it is invisible to them, as it is also to a woman whose house on a hill overlooks its blazing chimneys. Gérard later forces this woman to see what's in front of her eyes, just as he forces the French girls visiting the abandoned camp to look at the torture chambers and the ovens: "It's essential for them to see," he explains.[25] Looking truth in the face is, for Gérard, the beginning of responsibility and, with that, of freedom—the freedom that, as he movingly tells his guard in a German transit camp, he himself possesses even in prison, because he chose his way of life in full knowledge of the possible consequences.

Experience in the novel, though, is also a matter of imagination, and literature is an important part of it—one experience among others as well as a means of communicating them. At the Lycée, he says, he learned almost everything from his precocious reading. On the journey, he distracts himself by remembering as much as he can of the first volume of Proust's *À la recherche du temps perdu*, and in the camp itself he struggles to recall Valéry's poem "Le cimetière marin" ("The Graveyard by the Sea") with its mixed messages of despair and courage—"The wind is rising! . . . We must try to live!"—like those of the "Ulysses" canto of Dante's *Inferno*, which, around the same time, Primo Levi was trying to recite to a friend in Auschwitz. Goethe, too, acquired a special importance to Semprún: the tree under which the poet used to sit and that had been a place of pilgrimage in the nineteenth century was enclosed by the concentration camp fence and eventually burned to a cinder in an Allied air raid.

The importance and the difficulty of remembering are dominant motifs, along with melancholy acceptance of the fact that a time will come "when there will no longer be any real memory of this, only the memory of memories related by those who will never really know . . . what all this really was."[26] Memory, to Semprún, is always a frail resource, and forgetting has its own value, as does invention. In a much later book, *L'écriture ou la vie* (*Literature or Life?*, 1994), he wrote more analytically about both processes, quoting some words of the anti-Nazi French philosopher Maurice Blanchot: "Whoever wishes to remember must trust to oblivion, to the risk entailed in forgetting absolutely, and to this wonderful accident that memory then becomes."[27] Blanchot was drawing on a famous idea of Nietzsche's about "active forgetting,"

which also influenced Freud's theory that forgetting, like dreaming, plays an indispensable role in emotional stability. A moving passage in *Literature or Life?* describes Buchenwald after it has been abandoned by the guards, and a pile of bodies there in which one man, not yet dead, is singing Kaddish. But is this true? Even in the darkest corners of Semprún's reflections there's something mischievous: he tells us that he inserted fictional characters and episodes into *The Long Voyage* to make it "work," and in *Literature or Life?* he wonders if Jesus would have been able to chant the Jewish prayer for the dead.[28] Almost anything, as he illustrates, can be seen from a new angle, described in a new tone. Because the camp latrines were so filthy that the SS and *kapos* wouldn't go into them, they became a convivial place for the prisoners, a combined club and marketplace. The point, at such moments, does not lie just in the obvious paradox. Semprún's subject is the difficulty of communicating what he has experienced: the difficulty, first, of fully recalling it, when in order to survive psychologically he had first to forget it—"the cure of silence and studied amnesia"[29]; then of separating out what he himself experienced from what he has read or been told or invented; and finally, of "Telling a story well, [which] means: so as to be understood. You can't manage it without a bit of artifice. Enough artifice to make it art!"[30] Behind all this lies the existential question of communication, the question that is asked in the book's title and echoed in its quotation from the Peruvian poet César Vallejo: "*no poseo para expresar mi vida, sino mi muerte*"—"My death is the only way I have of expressing my life."

Le grand voyage is a French book by a Spanish author about a set of events that began in Germany, ended in Japan, and were hideously international at all points in between: there were Russian prisoners in Buchenwald, just as there were Spanish volunteers in the German army that invaded Russia, and the Jews in the camp—children among them—came from all over Europe. A Danish inmate who has managed to acquire a trumpet plays a tune written by an American of Scottish origin, "Stardust," made famous in the 1930s by, among others, a black American, the grandson of slaves, who added the words "oh memory, oh memory."[31] After the camp is liberated, Semprún enjoys Camel cigarettes given to him by a soldier from New Mexico. What, except in this cosmopolitan sense, does any of this have to do with

Spain? A great deal, in fact. In the first place, Gérard (despite his name) is consistently treated as Spanish, a *Rotspanier*,[32] not least when he's disqualified from the repatriation bonus given to French survivors on their return. The fact that he's, in some people's eyes, an outsider in this conflict makes him a perfect insider: as strange to it all, and as intimate with it, as any Jew; as international as any Communist; and as alert to the bitter ironies of "nationalism" as only a Spaniard of this time could be. Why were the Spanish Nationalists so called, he asks, "when they fought the [civil] war using Moroccan troops, the Foreign Legion, German planes and the Littorio divisions?"[33]

Internationalism was a socialist aspiration, but its most effective implements have been capitalism and, especially by means of the Holocaust, Nazism. Semprún's work is evidence of the paradox by which the attempted extermination of the Jews resulted in their becoming emblematic of every kind of oppression, and the object of every kind of self-identification. The Nazi project had plenty of precursors, among them the Spanish campaign of ethnic cleansing begun by Ferdinand and Isabella. In the broad sense of Transition I've been using, the work of transitional Spanish writers has been marked, among other things, by their attempts to put twentieth-century national events into a longer and wider frame. Recently, as we'll see, there has been a return to specifically Iberian topics of the mid-twentieth century, though one that for obvious reasons has developed the intergenerational concerns of Miguel Delibes. One writer in particular, however, has followed Benet and Semprún in working together literary and historical sources with human stories in a way that treats Spanish fiction as a global enterprise.

Antonio Muñoz Molina is among the heavyweights of Spanish intellectual life today: a critic, a columnist, a productive novelist, and a cultural figure of world standing. His most ambitious book to date is called *Sefarad*, the Hebrew name for Spain, and acts as a *One Thousand and One Nights* of stories that link episodes from the author's autobiography to a general modern sense of dislocation and specifically to the stories of individual Jews, most of them Holocaust victims, many Spanish (Sephardic) in family origin. Given the familiarity of some of its contents—the individual stories as well as the somewhat pietistic tone—*Sefarad* (2001)[34] is a hazardous enterprise, and an ambitious one. It may be that the biographies of Franz Kafka and Milena

Jesenská, Primo Levi and Jean Améry, have been less invoked in Spanish writing than elsewhere in the West. Holocaust studies apart, anyone familiar with the work of W. G. Sebald will recognize the tone in which *Sefarad* broods on narratives such as these; and Vasily Grossman's *Life and Fate* long ago made it commonplace to link such episodes with ones from the gulag. Several elements, though, help the book to be more distinctive than this may suggest. First is a mixture of anxiety and consolation in its handling of forgetfulness: "the greatest hells on Earth are erased after one or two generations."[35] Then there are the troubles specific to Sephardim, or at least to those who come into these pages, especially Señor Isaac Salama, whose exiled family was long resident in Hungary and most of whom were killed in the camps, though his father escaped to Tangiers, where he thrived while becoming increasingly Orthodox. Salama not only doesn't want to take over his father's business, but also relishes escaping from Morocco to Spain—relishes escaping every memory, every aspect of his inheritance:

> you can't imagine the weight that was lifted from my shoulders—free of father and his shop and his mourning and all the Jews killed by Hitler, all the lists of names in the synagogue and in the Jewish publications my father subscribed to, and the ads in the Israeli newspapers where you asked for information about missing people. I was alone now. I began and ended in me alone. Someone nearby on the deck was listening to one of the American songs that were popular then. It seemed to me that the song was filled with the same kind of promise the trip held for me. I have never had a more intensely physical sense of happiness than I felt when the boat began to move . . . [36]

Economically scattered through the book are the humdrum recollections of someone like Muñoz Molina himself, the clever, dutiful child of a provincial Catholic family, his eyes opened by an exhibition in Madrid about exiled Spanish Republicans in Mexico and, above all, by his reading and, once he becomes a celebrated writer, his travels. In a German tea shop full of comfortable elderly people, this slightly disheveled, dark-haired man suddenly feels (though he isn't) Jewish. And the book's densely orchestrated rhythms and movements come to a

climax in a displacement within a displacement. The writer and his wife, about to return to Spain after a period in Manhattan, visit that perfect relic of reversed colonization, a fossil of museology itself in what is now mainly a Spanish-speaking Caribbean area of Harlem— the Hispanic Society of America on West 155th Street, a crumbling fin de siècle palace housing the immense collection of Spanish treasures made by a young railroad heir, one of the Huntington family, at the historical moment when Spain made one of its more quixotic attempts to reassert a lost dignity: going to war with the United States over Cuba.

• •

Fiction's Memories (iii)

The Children's and Grandchildren's Stories

Sefarad illustrates that nothing in recent Spanish culture is more caught up with the twentieth-century past than its fiction. As with the campaign for historical memory, the intensity of imaginative engagement is roughly proportionate to the degree of generational separation and is reinforced by an awareness that those who witnessed the civil war are fast dying off. With the novelists, it's more than usually relevant to know what personal and, especially, paternal histories lie behind the fictional outcomes. Javier Marías is one example whose father's story could make a novel in itself.

BACK TO THE 1930S

In the summer of 1933, three extremely bright students at the University of Madrid were in an almost 180-strong group that, along with their tutors, spent six weeks traveling around the Mediterranean, stopping off at various points in North Africa and the Middle East, Greece and southern Italy. Each of the three wrote a vivid diary of the journey, and their narratives were published together the following year in a single volume under the title *Juventud en el mundo antiguo* ("Young People in the Ancient World").[1] Like many of their contemporaries,

the trio had come under the influence of one of the most prominent liberal Spanish thinkers of the day, José Ortega y Gasset. All three were themselves to become powerful in the Hispanic intellectual world: Manuel Granell and Julián Marías as philosophers, Carlos del Real as an expert on what used to be called prehistory. There are glimpses of these futures in the diaries, particularly in the prodigious self-confidence of del Real's art-historical judgments. However similar their trajectories were in 1933, though, their lives took them far apart, in ways that epitomized much of what happened throughout Spain at the time.

The eldest of them, Granell, had grown up in Oviedo.[2] It is one of Spain's founding cities; the ancient Romans settled there early in their occupation of the peninsula, and later a Christian presence was reinforced by the town's position on one of the pilgrimage routes to Santiago de Compostela. From the point of view of the 1930s, though, and especially of people then who were thinking about the links between ancient civilizations and the contemporary world, Oviedo was important because much of its architecture, especially its ninth-century buildings, uniquely brought together Roman, Visigothic, and Nordic traditions. The Visigoths were a Germanic people who increasingly challenged the Roman Empire and, as it lost its hold, moved into its territory. They were tenacious in northern Spain, where their rule was characterized by a version of Christianity especially hostile to Judaism, and by a respect for public order that the Visigoths believed to represent a continuum between themselves and the Romans. To some conservative European intellectuals, they were the ancestors of the pan-European Aryanism in which Nazism saw not only a great past but also the future.

All this was more important to Carlos del Real than to Manuel Granell, who was a poetically inclined young man and more concerned with the here and now than del Real—though, in Spain's capacious memory, the now is rarely unconnected with the then. Granell's first subject at university was law, and even here the Visigoths had left a mark: Spanish family law continued their custom of protecting the property rights of married women. By the 1930s, sexual equality had become established as a key element in Republican thinking, and having turned to philosophy, Granell was to contribute to it, if in what now seems an incongruously paternalistic way, in his *Cartas filosóficas a una mujer* ("Philosophical Notes to a Woman"). The book is an introduction

to the basics of classical and Enlightenment philosophy, inflected by Unamuno and culminating in a long exposition of the thinking of Ortega y Gasset, by way of an imaginary correspondence—at first, almost an intellectual love affair—with a girl called Helena. The model was evidently Descartes's famous correspondence with Princess Elizabeth of Bohemia, and the book, published in Madrid in 1946, was notable in its Francoist time and place for its confidence in Enlightenment thinking and its reticence about religion.[3]

Nineteen forty-six was a tough year for most people in Europe but especially so for Granell and his family, who were Republicans. He was by then making an intermittent career teaching philosophy at a school in the formerly Republican town of Elche. Back in 1939, when Nationalist victory had become inevitable, he had managed to escape into France. His parents, though, were in trouble. Their property in Oviedo had been confiscated, and they fled to Barcelona, another Republican stronghold but soon to fall into Nationalist hands. Manuel returned in the hope of helping them, was captured, and was held for a time in a Francoist prison camp near Bilbao. Once released, he managed to resume his work but couldn't reconcile himself to what was in effect a system of intellectual and political apartheid in which former Republicans could find themselves treated as belonging to an inferior race. In 1949 he published a book on logic that brought him an invitation to teach at Venezuela's leading university. He accepted and, once democracy had been established in the country, took Venezuelan nationality. In South America, like many other exiled writers, he found scope to bring philosophy and his literary interests into some kind of harmony.

The younger Carlos del Real, meanwhile, had different concerns, though poetry was important to him, too. At university in the early to mid-1930s, he was taught by a young ethno-archaeologist called Julio Martínez Santa Olalla, whose father, a general, was a friend of Franco's. Santa Olalla had been studying in Bonn when Nazism was first on the rise and was attracted by Nazi racial theories, including those about ancient bonds between Germany and Spain via the Visigoths. Returning to Spain to teach and pursue his research, he became active in the Falange, which his pupil Carlos del Real also joined. As soon as the civil war ended, Santa Olalla was rewarded by being put in charge of a new national body responsible for all archaeological excavations—

a *comisaría* that was his own idea, explicitly modeled on a German equivalent. Santa Olalla's role as director went hand in hand with the facilitation of more pragmatic earth-moving activities such as road-building and the construction of reservoirs. It also involved the development of wider ideological links between Spain and Germany. In the Second World War, Nationalist Spain was officially neutral, but this didn't stop it from cooperating with Germany, including in research.

Extremely close to the top of the Nazi hierarchy was a man to whom archaeology and prehistory were particular interests: Heinrich Himmler, whose youthful preparation for his role as the architect of Nazi Aryanism included a fascination with ancient Teutonic tribes. In 1940, Himmler made a tour of Spain, and Santa Olalla was assigned to his entourage. He impressed the Nazi leader, who invited him to return to Germany. There, Santa Olalla helped plan a range of academic links between the two countries, including a joint excavation of a major Visigothic cemetery in central Spain and a number of projects investigating the Visigoths' expansion into North Africa.

So, in Santa Olalla, Carlos del Real had a powerful patron—one whose support quickly bore fruit. Of the three student authors of "Young People in the Ancient World," del Real was alone in being in tune with the new regime, and he prospered under it. By 1942 he had held jobs at the celebrated Instituto Cardenal Cisneros (alma mater of many leading Spanish politicians since the nineteenth century) and at the University of Madrid. At the age of twenty-eight he was put in charge of the city's main museum of "primitive man." In the years that followed he continued upward and onward: a chair at Salamanca in 1956; then a still-more-senior role in his faculty; a steady flow of books; an award from the Royal Academy of History; various medals, and before long a triumphant return to Complutense University, Madrid, where he took the chair held earlier by Santa Ollala, his old mentor. Carlos del Real died in 1993 and was subsequently honored by a one-thousand-page Festschrift.

Of the three student diarists, only Julián Marías lived long enough to see this homage to del Real published, and he must have had mixed feelings about it. Marías's formation was very like del Real's, and they were almost exact contemporaries.[4] When the time for taking sides came, though, Marías, like Granell, chose republicanism. Neither of

these young men can have had any idea how momentous such a choice would be for them—that Granell would eventually be forced into exile; that a rebel Nationalist victory would take del Real to the summit of his profession; least of all that on his way up the ladder, he would stamp so firmly on the fingers of his classmate Julián Marías, close behind him, that Marías would be denied his doctorate, imprisoned, and subsequently harassed; and that his career, in Spain at least, would be set back by a couple of decades.

What happened to Marías was on the one hand typical and on the other highly specific. Too shortsighted to be of any use to the army, he spent the civil war working for the Republicans as a translator, journalist, and policy adviser. After Franco's victory, Carlos del Real, with the active support of his mentor Santa Olalla and of a popular but now-forgotten novelist, Darío Fernández Flórez, denounced Marías to the authorities. As a result, Marías spent some time in prison and might easily have been shot, though he was freed when various influential people, including the conservative but always independent novelist Cela and members of the family of Ortega y Gasset, took up his case. Still, Marías's 1942 thesis was "referred" (in effect, failed), and like everyone identified with republicanism, he found many doors slammed shut against him.[5] He scraped together a living teaching and translating. In these hungry years of the 1940s and the early '50s, he married and his five sons were born—among them, the future novelist Javier Marías, who in fiction and in interviews has often dwelt on his father's misfortunes.

The dramatically different directions taken by these men's lives are movingly emphasized by the strong resemblances between them only three years before the beginning of the civil war. What comes through their diaries most strongly is a shared passionate seriousness founded on a high level of cultural literacy and fluency.[6] Even in religion and politics, little separated them. History's simplifications of history often make it appear that all Republicans were anti-Catholic, yet to Granell and Marías, as much as to del Real, Christianity was their historical and moral benchmark, and they all referred as confidently to the writers of the early Church as to those of ancient Greece and Rome. Marías later wrote about how his faith was enlivened by the trip—and he was no less shocked than del Real by his encounter with the unfamiliar Protestantism of British-ruled Malta.[7] The future Falangist del Real, on the

other hand, deplored what he saw of Italian Fascism in Palermo, commenting on how a statue of Garibaldi in the city center represented a liberal progressivism unable to withstand the violent assault of a Fascist parade.[8] It was a view he came to regret so much that fifteen years later he published a revisionist article about his account of the cruise, saying that though his memories of the trip remained vivid, he now felt he had hardly anything to do with the person he then was.[9]

It's important to be reminded, as Javier Marías reminds us, about betrayals such as del Real's and about the hardships suffered by former Republicans. But it's necessary, too, especially at the kind of distance that can erode the boundaries between history and myth, not to exaggerate them. Granell, as we've seen, managed to publish a number of works in the 1940s. So, too, did Marías. While the latter's doctoral award was held up, the thesis appeared as a book in 1941, and in that same year, Marías anticipated Granell by bringing out the readable history of philosophy that became one of his most widely translated and frequently reprinted works.[10] Censorship notwithstanding, the regime did not prevent this brilliant and productive young Republican from disseminating his ideas: a study of Unamuno in 1943; of twentieth-century Spanish philosophers more generally in 1948; an account in 1955 of the influence of existentialism in Spain. Hardly a year passed during the long dictatorship without something by Marías being brought out by a well-established Madrid publisher, for the most part Revista de Occidente, but also Escorial, Biblioteca Nueva, Guadarrama. Meanwhile, he founded a humanities institute with Ortega, was elected to the Spanish Academy in 1964, and held a number of distinguished positions in the United States. Almost a century after he was born, a ten-volume collected edition of his works is readily available, along with many other books by and about him. His right-wing denouncers, by contrast, are forgotten.

Julián Marías's current reputation owes something, of course, not only to his own work but to his appearances in novels by his son, Javier. Recent Spanish fiction often dwells on the experiences of the novelists' parents and grandparents, and while the novels of Javier Marías are an obvious case in point, they are far from being an isolated one.

———

A policeman courts a woman whose Republican husband is on the run; her clever child watches the scenario develop, his tart observations blurring into heroic fantasies about his missing father. A dissident couple tries to escape across the Pyrenees; the woman dies giving birth, and her husband nurses the ailing baby. A journalist whose father has recently died finds himself writing an enigmatic story that, while seeming to crystallize his country's past divisions, also leads to more questions. A priggish law student studies for exams in his mother's house while the old doctor next door ponders some secrets about his young neighbor's civil war ancestry. A clever, independent woman achieves an ingenious revenge on an opportunistic Nationalist collaborator who exploited her father and brought financial ruin on the family. A man who was once denounced by a Nationalist friend and spent half his adult life suffering the consequences explains to his son why pursuing justice was pointless at the time and would be wrong now.

More than sixty years after the Republican defeat, more than twenty-five since the restoration of democracy, all these scenarios found their way into novels published in twenty-first-century Spain.[11] What is it about such themes that continues to have a hold on readers' imaginations? The doctor in Manuel de Lope's *La sangre ajena* (*The Wrong Blood*, 2000) believes that the grandchildren's generation has passed beyond the misfortunes of his own time, yet de Lope's novel, while illustrating this possibility, has contradicted it by its own success. Certainly it would be hard for Spanish readers of any age not to be aware of their country's painful inheritance. Other readers, too: all the books just alluded to have been translated into English, some of them achieving high sales. In addition to their historical settings, they have several preoccupations in common. All involve questions concerning the role of fathers, and parenthood more generally; all dramatize riddles that face the postwar generation, especially its curiosity about the past, inability to determine everything about it, and, in the latter respect, underlying disagreements about how important it is to be able to do so. Most also embody shifts in the relative power of men and women, and in many, too, there is an interest in the boundaries between fact and fiction, reason and belief, the latter often expressed in Christian terms. In terms of historical detail, how these issues are treated is peculiar to Spain, but they speak to the concerns of readers everywhere.

JAVIER MARÍAS: *EL SIGLO* AND THE TRILOGY

It's often the books that "don't translate" that tell us most about the ones that do. Javier Marías's *El siglo* ("The Century") is a case in point. Among the most productive and in some ways most dazzling of current Spanish novelists, the philosopher's son can also be the most exasperating: ostentatiously ventriloquial in his (to English readers, often overfamiliar) literary borrowings, long-winded and repetitive even by the voluble national standards on which he himself comments and that some of his characters defend,[12] yet both moving and original in his handling of themes that derive from, while going far beyond, mid-twentieth-century traumas. Stylistically, his work owes a great deal to Juan Benet and W. G. Sebald—though he has put these debts into a more grandiose perspective, invoking self-comparisons with authors ranging from Sir Thomas Browne and Molière via Goethe to Conrad, Faulkner, and Hermann Broch.[13] Perhaps such boasts aren't to be taken entirely seriously. Marías runs a kind of club of which he is the king: he chooses the members and bestows titles on them. The harmless fantasy, with its baroque elaboration, has equivalents in much of his work, yet even this most self-referential and playful of writers may be unaware just how much it tells about him. There's an element of insecurity in his writing, unlike the self-confident lightness of Borges, another of Marías's all-male heroes. This may help explain why, when he defends the first novel in which he came to grips with some of his and his country's most intimate concerns, he's apparently unwilling to see either that its failures are intrinsic to it (the novel simply doesn't work) or that, in later fictions, especially the trilogy *Your Face Tomorrow* (*Tu rostro mañana*, 2002–07), he has found ways of putting them to better use. It's partly because of this subsequent success that *El siglo* is worth attention; partly also, though, because the strange, off-putting earlier fiction expresses in the harshest terms dilemmas that were more common in civil war Spain than mythologists care to admit: on the one hand, indecision, nonpartisanship, and passivity, perverted into active collaboration by the logic of tyranny; on the other, ruthless opportunism.

El siglo (1983) is a lugubrious, complexly constructed narrative about an upper-class man who, having avoided the civil war, becomes an informer after it has ended. The book is hard to read, but through a

combination of symbols of inertia and a highly ornate style, it communicates something important about not only the Spanish ruling class in the 1930s but also a wider fault line in the century as a whole. In the literature of the Spanish civil war, the central character, Casaldáliga, is distinctive in several ways. He not only has no interest in or grasp of the politics of his country but is at first untouched by it, spending the entire conflict across the border, in the safety of Portugal. When the war ends and he returns, he finds himself cut off from his acquaintances by the nature of what they have been through—a situation that in some ways has always been his, but that he feels now for the first time. In the Kafkaesque new world of the (never explicitly identified) dictatorship, everyone is guilty unless he can prove himself innocent, and the accuser may be "a friend, an enemy, a subordinate, a relative, a neighbour, someone acting on a whim or out of revenge . . . or someone who in turn is afraid of being accused and decides to make a move so as not to leave room for doubt about his own loyalty."[14] How, after all, can anyone prove that he didn't write a particular article or make a radio broadcast if somebody else claims the opposite? "Plenty of people are in prison for reasons like this, and they're the lucky ones." This is the situation in which Casaldáliga becomes an informer—and to his astonishment finds that, in doing so, he also turns himself into a suspect.

El siglo, then, can be read as a novel about any kind of totalitarianism, any kind of apoliticality, any kind of cowardice or treason. In this respect it anticipates Marías's trilogy *Your Face Tomorrow*. The simplest way of expressing the difference is to say that it's as if in the seventeen years between the appearance of *El siglo* and the first volume of *Your Face Tomorrow*, Marías had learned something from not only Ian Fleming, to whose merits as a writer he pays exaggerated tribute,[15] but also E. M. Forster. "Yes—oh dear yes," Forster lamented, "the novel tells a story."

The trilogy takes the reader into a part-real, part-romanticized world familiar to English readers from John le Carré. An Oxford that has now almost disappeared, and which was the main setting of Marías's earlier *Todas las almas* (*All Souls*), melds into a secret-intelligence ambience of similar remoteness, the two acting as both an escape from and a metaphor for themes of love and sexual betrayal. The details are vivid; the action is often gripping. Relatively recent ac-

tions by spies and agents provocateurs in relation, for example, to Venezuela are placed in a genealogical line that includes the Spanish Civil War, just as the activities of today's lovers and losers are seen through a long literary lens. Again and again, Marías's narrator asks the kinds of question, makes the kinds of observation, almost any reader has reasons to want articulated: "What is this strange proclivity we have for trust? . . . perhaps it is pride that leads us to believe that what happens and has always happened to our peers will not happen to us, or that we will be respected by those who—before our very eyes—have already been disloyal to others, as if we were different . . ."[16]

He offers no answers and, like any good storyteller, leaves new anxieties, new riddles, in his trail. Whereas the reader's experience of *El siglo* is mainly a struggle to keep going, the trilogy makes one look forward to the next installment. Its central character, Jacobo Deza, is drawn into the intelligence world in part by his curiosity about the past of one of his Oxford mentors, Peter Wheeler, who did secret work in the 1930s and '40s. What follows for Deza is not only increasingly absorbing but also frightening. For a time, at least, it changes his life and his assumptions about it, his philosophy. It also puts his family at risk; a large part of the story as it develops concerns Deza's relationship with his ex-wife and his responsibility for their children, and this element provides much of the tension. At the heart of the trilogy, though, is what he learns about, and from, two older men: Wheeler and, above all, his own father.

Any reader of Spanish fiction has to decide at some point how to deal with its frequent garrulity, and this is a particular issue with Marías, in whose work self-repetition is clearly intentional and is treated in the same spirit as a decorative harpsichord improvisation. Spanish writers exist whose work is fastidious, economical, sharp: among Marías's contemporaries, Juan Marsé, Alberto Méndez, and Manuel de Lope are good examples. Marías's trilogy, though, is essentially a single novel of 1,260 pages serialized in three volumes over a period of five years. This isn't simply a matter of counting words. Here is a typical fragment from a much longer piece of semiautomatic writing by Marías:

And thus we reach a domain in which what matters least is whether things do or do not exist, because they can always be talked about,

just as all dreams, even the most involved and absurd of dreams, can be recounted after a fashion, in fits and starts, recounted to ourselves at least, and not always grammatically; and to that extent whatever has passed through our thoughts has existed; and whatever preceded it or came before, that too has existed. What is the use, then, of the faint, nebulous nature of what happens and what we do when abroad or far away, in another city, in another country, in that unexpected existence that seems not to belong to us, in the theoretical, paren-thetical life we seem to be leading and which, up to a point, encour-ages us, in subterranean fashion, to think, without actually thinking it, that nothing contained by that time is irreversible and that every-thing can be cancelled, reversed, cured; that it has only half-happened and without our full consent?[17]

This is part of a text that, to repeat, is, by the standards of Marías's early work, an action thriller. It's also in the narrator's voice, a point worth making given the undifferentiated talkativeness of all his main characters. There are various ways in which one might mount a de-fense of some of its qualifications and repetitions, but not of all. No possible purpose beyond spinning out words can be attributed to the second halves of some the phrases here: "whatever preceded it or came before," "abroad or far away, in another city, in another country," "nothing . . . is irreversible and . . . everything can be cancelled, re-versed." Marías's affectations matter because so much of what he has to say in *Your Face Tomorrow* is too important to be silly about.

The novel is, as one reviewer wrote,

an occult history—a partial, painful understanding of the emotional and psychological effects of war on an entire society and its descen-dants. Deza's current preoccupations, even at their most domestic, come to seem part of a continuum, of an endless human struggle to balance action against consequences, desire against the risks of its fulfillment, of the complexity of unpicking motive.[18]

Among the effects attributed to war is that it has made a sharper division between those who use violence and those who don't—those to whom, indeed, violence is so intrinsically shocking, regardless of its

context, that by closing their eyes to it they put themselves and those for whom they are responsible in danger from it. Here as elsewhere in Spanish fiction of the past three decades, courage—heroism—is a big part of the question. What Deza's frightening boss, Tupra, teaches him, both intellectually and by example, is that to be brave in any useful way, you may have to act ferociously, a Darwinian lesson Tupra himself learned from a notoriously violent pair of British gangsters, the Kray twins. By the end of the novel, Deza finds himself applying it in defense of his estranged family when it becomes clear that his wife is having an affair with a sadist. We're left with the stark moral question Tupra has put to him: "Why can't one . . . go around beating people up and killing them?" The implied answer is that, in practice, one can, and all the more so the less effectively people protect themselves, but is this a message the trilogy as a whole imparts?

If it isn't, the reason is Deza's aging father, who in the second volume recounts his own experiences of war and dictatorship. It's the story of a life of fear, of daily violence, of necessary forgetting, and, later, of dilemmas about what is recalled and what recounted—especially to the next generation when they are children. It comes at the literal center of the trilogy[19] and is told with a scrupulous plainness that almost justifies its filigree surroundings, as if they are there to give this short text its emphasis. And among other things it constitutes a moving defense of the *pacto de olvido*. Deza's father recounts two incidents: a woman on a tram who describes to her neighbor having beaten out a child's brains on a wall; a Falangist writer called Emilio Marés who boasted of taking part in baiting and killing a Republican with the tools, and according to the conventions, of the bullring. This writer later reconstructed himself as a man of the left, a myth indulged by lazy journalists and believed in by his younger wife and their daughters.

Why not unmask him, now that he is dead? Deza asks. His father's answer is long and full. Part of it is simply that the man's daughters are still alive and that he likes them. But he ends by adopting an almost religious position: in light of eternity, nothing matters enough to warrant an act of violence, even if the violence is merely an act of communication and is on the side of justice. This is his position, too, not only on the results of the civil war but on war in general:

I don't know, I remember it and I can't believe it. Sometimes, it seems unbelievable to me that I lived through all of that. I just can't see the reason for it, that's the worst of it, and with the passing of the years, it's even harder to see a reason. Nothing serious ever appears quite so serious with the passing of time. Certainly not serious enough to start a war over, wars always seem so out of proportion when viewed in retrospect.[20]

One way or another, second-generation war fiction is almost always the story of fathers and sons. The reasons are obvious and old: men fight wars, and their having done so makes their sons feel inadequate. Among the successes of Bernhard Schlink's novel of postwar Germany, *The Reader*, was that it escaped this formula. Most other war novels that avoid it are by women who lived through the events described: Simone de Beauvoir, Elizabeth Bowen, Natalia Ginzburg, Carmen Laforet. For the second and third generations, the topic remains overwhelmingly masculine. This is the case even in a novel by a Spanish woman, focused on a woman character. While the action of Almudena Grandes's bestselling *El corazón helado* (*The Frozen Heart*, 2007) is driven by a daughter's desire for revenge, it centers on a man and on the legacy, in every sense, of his father. Again, while Manuel de Lope's *The Wrong Blood* (*La sangre ajena*, 2000) is, as we'll see, vividly attentive to its two main woman characters, and while Juan Marsé and Alberto Méndez both tell stories that are about what war does to women as much as to men, even in these fictions, fathers, proxy fathers, sons, and grandsons, in different ways and to different degrees, hold the foreground. As with Javier Marías, this is sometimes a matter of authorial biography.

Juan Marsé was a child in the civil war and, having been orphaned, was adopted by the couple whose name he took. His books are numerous and varied, but several of them—including the first, the as-yet-untranslated *Encerrados con un solo juguete* ("Locked in a Room with Only One Toy to Play With," published during the dictatorship in 1960)—involve young people growing up fatherless in the aftermath of war. An issue here, once more, is a dream of, or at least a question about, heroism. Spanish men born between the 1930s and '60s, such as Alberto Méndez (born 1941), Javier Marías (1951), and Javier Cercas (1962),

have in common with the British generations born during or after either world war a feeling that they in some sense involuntarily failed an exam they never had a chance to take. Whether or not their fathers acquitted themselves heroically is somehow beside the point.

JUAN MARSÉ, *LIZARD TAILS*

Marsé's *Lizard Tails* (*Rabos de lagartija*, 2000) is a moving and imaginatively complex exploration of the theme. Set in Barcelona in the mid-1940s and narrated by an unborn boy, the novel concerns a Republican family destroyed by civil war. The father, Víctor Bartra, a former anesthetist who has been active in the Resistance helping to smuggle Allied airmen to safety, is now an alcoholic on the run from the police. His pregnant wife, Rosa, once a schoolteacher, can find only menial work and struggles to make ends meet in a rented house owned by someone who disappeared in the war. One of the couple's sons was killed in an air raid; the other, David, lives in a vengeful fantasy world, dreaming on the one hand of gallant Spitfire pilots, on the other of elaborate schemes to oust a widowed police inspector who frequently calls on Rosa with presents. Simply by virtue of his job, Inspector Galván has the power to cause almost any harm he chooses to this marginal family, and his willingness to remind Rosa of the fact is one of the things that complicate our response to his in other ways more sympathetic character. Marsé shows us real people living unhappy lives in impoverished surroundings. Nothing good has come of Republican ideals. Heroes exist only in the books David reads, the films he sees, the elaborate games he plays. In one of his fantasies, his father is away fighting for the British in the Sudan, and David himself is a wily African native outwitting the investigations of "bwana" Galván.

Near the end of the book, Rosa dies giving birth to the narrator. By this time, she has rejected Galván, who as a result follows Víctor into alcoholic self-destruction. Yet the story concludes positively. The flamboyantly imaginative David, who has shown every sign of heading for a career as a transvestite prostitute, is persuaded to settle into his photographic job and makes a still-more-momentous decision of his own when faced with a choice between artistic license and showing the

truth. Rosa's baby, too, grows up well: the sympathetic dexterity of his narrative is itself witness to that. What's still less predictable is the cause to which these outcomes are attributed.

When Rosa dies, David and the baby are taken on by her younger sister, Lola Ribas. She and her husband bring them up with their own daughter. Until now, Lola has not been involved in the story, but we have some sense of her both from Rosa, who describes her as having been "always like an old woman, prejudiced and a religious devotee," and from Galván, who interrogated her about Víctor and who

> has a vivid image of her, not so much because of her unattractive ap-
> pearance—a thin woman who seemed to be constantly opening and
> closing her black velvet bag whose clasp made a metallic noise like a
> gunshot—but more because of her barely disguised disgust at her sis-
> ter Rosa for marrying such a worthless rogue. She showed him her
> Congregation of the Legion of Mary card and told him she knew
> nothing . . . No sir, I've no idea where that Red might be, and have no
> wish to.[21]

Lizard Tails is a story in which we can never be sure that anyone is telling the whole truth. Far from all its characters are religious, or even pretend to be, but in this setting there are good reasons for people to make the most of such religious credentials as they have. And Aunt Lola and her husband, whatever other cards of allegiance they may carry, have a history they don't want the police to know about. We've been told that in this family there's a recurring image of "Fire burning papers":

> Granny Tecla burning documents and passports and banknotes in
> her house at Mataró by the seashore, Pa burning books and maga-
> zines in the gully, along with folders, identity papers and pamphlets,
> and Aunt Lola and Uncle Pau doing the same in their house in Vall-
> carca . . . bonfires in the night, bonfires and grim faces . . . [22]

The context is one in which Rosa is again getting rid of incriminating papers, some of them concerning an RAF pilot saved by Víctor's network. Were Lola and her husband part of all this? Is Rosa protecting Lola from Galván when she disavows any affection for her? And

how should we interpret the firm resourcefulness with which Lola takes over in the hospital where her sister lies dead and Galván sits incapacitated by loss and drink?

The scene is described with the book's characteristic unsentimentality:

> it is Aunt Lola who deals with all the sad details and takes all the necessary decisions, doleful and uningratiating as ever, but resolute and without shedding a single tear. She has been standing at the operating theater door since she arrived, in her old-fashioned, gray-lapeled coat . . . listening to the surgeon's explanations . . . and considering the suggestions a priest is making about the religious service in the chapel, and all the while observing at close hand the collapse of the distraught man sitting on a bench in the corridor, the same man who some time ago had questioned her about the whereabouts of her brother-in-law Victor. She had heard rumours of a policeman's strange obsession with her sister: rumours which only served to confirm her impression of what she called Rosa's libertarian nonsense and the unhappiness and misfortune she was letting herself in for as a result of her disastrous marriage, but now she prefers not to get involved, to avoid any kind of familiarity with this gentleman.[23]

What makes this so moving, so right, is partly what isn't said. We aren't reminded, but we remember, that Galván was recently widowed when he started to visit Rosa. And then there are the assumptions about Rosa that we feel we know enough about to disagree with: the idea that she's feckless and irresponsible, for example, when we've seen how carefully she has attended to David and juggled her duties and affections toward him and her husband, while responding to the attentions of Galván: a man who, apart from everything else, has been supplementing the family's diet, though also holding power over them all. And there's the mix of irony and quiet justice in that word *gentleman* (*señor*) with which the paragraph ends. Foreign readers may be less alert than Spanish ones to the ways in which at this point and in the remaining pages the narrative, so robust in its exposure of Nationalist abuses, pays its small tribute to conservative Catholic values at their best.

ALBERTO MÉNDEZ, *BLIND SUNFLOWERS*

It still bears repeating that good fiction, like good history, goes beyond the simplistic paradigms of party politics. One of those who understood this is Alberto Méndez, a writer worth attending to for many reasons, among them his minimalist output and extreme fastidiousness of style. Méndez lived for sixty-odd years and was a real writer. Yet he published only four stories: about 150 pages of limpid prose, or prose poetry. They have in common an elegiac poetic density prepared for in an epigraph taken from the Spanish poet Carlos Piera:

> mourning . . . [is] completely independent of whether or not there is reconciliation or forgiveness . . . In Spain, we have not carried out this mourning, which implies amongst other things a public recognition that something is tragic and above all, that it is irreparable . . . It is accepting the existence of a void as part of us.[24]

The interconnections, however, can distract from what's more interesting: the way in which each story is an experiment in form, tone, and subject matter.

The first of them, "If the Heart Could Think, It Would Cease to Beat," rehearses some supposedly established facts about a Nationalist officer who, when victory became certain, crossed to the Republican side, gave himself up, was immediately recaptured by his own army, survived a firing squad, was nursed in the countryside by Republican sympathizers, gave himself up once again, and committed suicide. "More than anything," we're told, he wanted "to be on both sides,"[25] a paradoxical common sense that characterizes all he does and says.

In the second piece, "Manuscript Found in Oblivion," we're presented with a fragmentary sequence of diary entries, sketches, and scraps of poetry left by a Republican poet who died in the Pyrenees trying to nurse his baby after the mother died. Once again the achievement is partly a matter of a narrative mode that half-persuades the reader that the story is true. Some of the voice's statements are awkwardly but suggestively ambiguous: Eulalio, we're told, went to join not just the loyalist army but "the army that lost the war." He wanted to join the losing side? If so, the tragedy is once again, as in the first story,

to some extent voluntary, and this adds to an understanding that something beautiful—the events described, but also the story itself—has been made deliberately out of defeat. This, too, is surely the conclusion of the title story, "Fourth Defeat: 1942, or Blind Sunflowers." Some readers have been misled into judging the whole piece according to the familiarity of its scenario. Certainly, there's nothing new either in fiction or in history about the situation of a woman under siege from her enemy while her husband is in hiding. But *Lizard Tails* shows that old stories can be handled in new ways, and in "Blind Sunflowers" the approach is both structural and moral.

A cleric, Brother Salvador, who fought in the Nationalist army, now works in a school. One of the less tractable of his pupils, Lorenzo, is brought to and collected from school by his young mother, Elena. The father, Ricardo, is said to have died but is in fact hiding out in the family apartment. Salvador is increasingly drawn to Elena and takes to visiting her at home. Ricardo is shut in a well-concealed cupboard, but when Salvador's attentions to his wife become physical, he bursts out. Salvador calls for the police, and Ricardo throws himself out the window. The story is told by three people: the son, Lorenzo, looking back on it all in later life; an external narrator; and Brother Salvador, in a confessional letter to his superior. Salvador's voice is the one we hear first and last. What Méndez does with all this is extraordinary in its subtlety and richness. While the claustrophobia of Ricardo's existence isn't spelled out for us—the narrative never goes inside his cupboard, for example—we learn of it in oblique ways. One of these is the attention paid retrospectively by Lorenzo to the external spaces of his childhood: the streets of the Madrid district in which they lived, Salamanca, with its cinema, its improvised playgrounds, its sharp delineations of relative poverty; how the sun falls, and doesn't, on these streets; which ways the windows face.

But it's the intense depiction of Salvador's spiritual confusion that gives the story much of its depth and originality. He sees the origin of his doubts in the essential lesson of war, that human life doesn't matter, but is baffled by the contradictions between this and other aspects of Christian teaching and also between the Nationalist ideal of a Christian crusade against secular communism and the human fact of a Republican writer, a father and husband, driven to throw himself

ignominiously to his death out of a third-floor window. In his painful bewilderment, and in what he knows of the life of his pupil Lorenzo, Salvador suspects that his own sheltered religious upbringing and childhood vocation, which previously seemed entirely good, in fact failed him by leaving him ignorant not only of "how terrible the world was,"[26] but also how complicated.

ALMUDENA GRANDES, *THE FROZEN HEART*

Among other things, Méndez's final story holds up the idea of father-hood to scrutiny. Ricardo scarcely exists as a father to Lorenzo; it is Elena who is the important parent. And Salvador's confession is made to a spiritual father who is even more decisively absent from the narra-tive. In its belated shift from conservative nationalism to democracy, Spain has been forced into a rethinking of assumptions about gender—socially and politically, but also metaphorically—that surface again and again in the arts. Almudena Grandes is one of the writers who have been dealing with it in relation to the civil war. *The Frozen Heart* (*El corazón helado*, 2007) is a deceptively traditional-seeming family saga with a sharp contemporary edge.

The novel works together many crucial episodes in Spanish history during and since the civil war and has a strong, almost self-parodic plotline in the sexual relationship between Álvaro, married son of a rich man who has just died, and the manipulative Raquel, who was the father's solicitor and seems to have been his mistress. The complexities and perversities of all this are Almodóvar-like—Raquel herself thinks she may have seen some of it in a film—but at the center are the deal-ings between the families the protagonists come from and particularly between the male heads of those families: Republican on Raquel's side, coat-turning and profiteering on Álvaro's. It transpires that the latter's solid-seeming father, Julio Carrión, made much of his fortune from a mixture of political betrayal (Julio's Republican mother died in a Fran-coist prison) and commercial opportunism (he used Nationalist expro-priations of Republican property as a way of building his own portfolio). One of those on whom he preyed was the grandfather of Raquel, who exacts an elaborate multiple revenge in which a key part is played by

the new climate in which Nationalist crimes are being uncovered. In command of all the documentary evidence, Raquel blackmails Julio to repay the money he took from her family, with interest. Her trump card is the memory campaign:

"You see, in 1977, people were still scared to death to talk about these things. Not today . . . It's not just books, there are films too, they're making documentaries about the war, about the post-war period, about the Spanish camps, the French camps, the children that were taken away from republican prisoners, the disappearances . . ." She feigned surprise. "Back in 1977, nobody ever mentioned these things, did they?" She allowed a hard edge to creep into her voice. "Judges these days are happy to issue an exhumation order for anyone the fascists summarily executed during the war, or after the war. They've been digging them up from ditches on the roadside, finding them in wells and canyons . . . Have you seen it in the papers? They even mention it on TV sometimes. Imagine what the killers must feel like, because most of them are still alive, the Falangists, the members of the Guardia Civil . . . They'd be about your age now, though some of them would be younger. Imagine them, retired, happily watching TV and suddenly a judge makes an order and *bam!* It all comes out . . .

"... I understand why you feel you should be allowed to get away with it. But I think you're mistaken, Señor Carrion, I have to tell you, in all honesty. You're mistaken, like all those other men, and for them it's too late to stop their grandchildren finding out who they really were, the crimes they committed, the people they tortured or kidnapped . . . On the other hand, I've given this a great deal of thought . . . and I think one million euros is a fair price."[27]

The scene is melodramatic, the handling formulaic: so are many things in this big novel. But if any European country's history still lends itself to being depicted through a family saga, that country is Spain, and Grandes adroitly controls her human material, and a range of narrative modes. In basing the outcome of an entire novel on someone's threat to write a book that will exploit the memory campaign, she memorably turns her fiction against itself.

JAVIER CERCAS, *SOLDIERS OF SALAMIS*

The Frozen Heart is among a number of twenty-first-century Spanish works that reclaim their themes for women. Neither generational change nor the problematic nature of both memory and history is a masculine preserve, Grandes reminds us—a point made also in films such as *Los paraísos perdidos* and David Trueba's 2002 film version of Javier Cercas's *Soldiers of Salamis*. The Trueba film, though, does this at some cost.

Cercas's central character is called Javier Cercas. Like Semprún and Marías, the novelist uses his work to tease out autobiographical conundra. His father, José, born in 1929, was a Falangist. "They were Catholics worried about their families and jobs," Cercas has said. "Are they guilty for that? It's easy to say 'fucking bastards, fascists.' But they weren't political in character."[28] In his teens he condemned his father and others on both sides of his family who passively supported Franco. As an adult he has devoted part of his imaginative life to reaching a fuller understanding of them. Much of that understanding, in Cercas's case, is expressed in his historical study of the failed 1981 antidemocratic coup, *The Anatomy of a Moment*, discussed on pp. 145–47. It also lies behind his first big success, *Soldados de Salamina* (2001).

A failed novelist working as a reporter in Girona and going through a midlife crisis is given the job of writing an anniversary piece about the poet Antonio Machado, who died in France in February 1939 just after escaping the Nationalist victory. Researching the article in the hope of finding a new angle, the journalist is reminded that at almost the same time as Machado died, the Falangist poet and leader Rafael Sánchez Mazas faced a Republican firing squad near the sanctuary of Santa María del Collell, on the Catalan side of the border with France. Sánchez Mazas managed to escape. Although he was almost immediately spotted in his hiding place by a Republican soldier, the man let him go. Increasingly absorbed by this story, the journalist tries to find the benevolent soldier, a quest that leads him to an old people's home in Dijon and to an eighty-two-year-old inmate called Miralles. Whether or not Miralles is the man who spared Sánchez Mazas is never resolved, though Miralles denies it. What seems certain is that he fought in the Republican army, was at Collell at the right time, sub-

sequently joined the French Foreign Legion, saw serious action on the Allied side in North Africa, managed to hold together a band of several thousand demoralized men and march them across the desert, and eventually took part in the liberation of France. This story is pieced together from more than one source, and in considerable detail. In the process, it becomes clear that what "Cercas" is actually looking for is not so much the man who freed Sánchez Mazas as a hero.

The novel's search for heroism and its meaning is tied to two otherwise undeveloped elements. On the first page, we learn that "Cercas's" father died just before the outset of his investigation. And then there's what might seem a minor detail that comes to be significant. Early in his narrative, the journalist interviews one of Sánchez Mazas's sons, who is giving a lecture series in Girona. It's from him that he first hears about the Falangist. The story comes after a series of digressions by the garrulous interviewee: "The problem was that if I asked him, say, about his division of literary personae into those of fate and those of character, he would contrive to answer me with a discourse on, say, the causes of the rout of the Persian fleet at the battle of Salamis . . ." Later, the journalist confesses that the Spanish Civil War is something he had until then "known not much more about than I did the battle of Salamis," an admission the real-life Cercas has repeated about himself: "People of my generation liked Tarantino and Almodóvar—they weren't interested in the civil war."[29] The link between the Spanish Civil War and Salamis, though, is not as arbitrary as it looks.

One thing people who know next to nothing about the battle of Salamis do know about it is that Greece narrowly defeated the invading Persians and, in doing so, ensured that the vulnerable new democracy of Athens was left free to develop. In the 1930s it didn't take a big leap of imagination to link Athens with the Spanish Second Republic, the country's first democratically elected government. Anyone who made that connection might have been in a position to say something, too, about the links between history and fiction. Our main source of information about the battle of Salamis is the Greek historian Herodotus, who believed in research and impartiality but also in a strong narrative. Modern scholarship has defended Herodotus against some of his early critics, but he will always be known for having made up some things. Cercas doesn't mention Herodotus, but his story is what he

calls a "true tale," mingling fact and fiction and alert to the perils of both. At bottom, what's at stake comes back to heroism. How the Corinthians behaved matters to readers because what they want to know about a battle is not only who won and why, but who was bravest. And as Spanish Republicans had discovered, you can be brave and idealistic without winning.

Cercas's book explores twentieth-century versions of these matters through the confusions of a middle-aged man sixty years after the Spanish Civil War ended. In dealing with moments when partisanship breaks down, the novel is more interesting than when it plays the kinds of games with fictionality that have somewhat overburdened European and Latin American fiction in the past half century. We don't really need a narrator called "Javier Cercas" to remind us that novels often draw on autobiography and that people telling their own stories often make up parts of them.[30] The essential point is the sudden need of a grown human being at a transitional stage in life to understand what happened to grown human beings of previous generations. Trueba's film is true to all this, both in bringing to the fore the fact that the massacre at Collell was committed by Republicans and in including real people playing themselves; but it also radically changes it. The central character is a woman, Lola Cercas, memorably played by Ariadna Gil, and her crisis is in part sexual: the death of her father and the breakup of a relationship leave her open to new kinds of experience not present in the novel: a potential affair with a lesbian, another with a male student. These new elements distract us from what is treated by the novel as a specifically masculine dilemma: how a man positions himself vis-à-vis men of an earlier generation and masculine experiences he hasn't had.

MANUEL DE LOPE, *THE WRONG BLOOD*

One more example helps show the particular forms these concerns take in Spain. Brought up in Madrid, Manuel de Lope was a dissident in his student days. Arrested in 1969 for political activities, he realized that career opportunities would be closed to him in Spain, so he moved to the safety of Paris. From then until he was in his mid-forties

he spent most of his career as an art dealer in France, Switzerland, and the United Kingdom, but his exile, though long, was always temporary. Having returned to Spain in 1993, he made a series of journeys across the peninsula about which he wrote a book in two volumes: *Iberia: La puerta iluminada* ("The Lighted Doorway," 2004) and *La imagen múltiple* ("The Multiple Picture," 2005). It's conventional to say that de Lope sees his country from the perspective of both an insider and a foreigner, but this is true, if only metaphorically, of most writers. What defines his work, rather, is its sense of what changed between the last decade of the insular dictatorship and the establishment of Spain as part of modern Europe.

The Wrong Blood (*La sangre ajena*, 2000) deals with this through a distinctive approach not only to memory but to curiosity in general. The least interesting character in the novel is also the most important. Miguel Goitia, a young law student, arrives at a family house on the Bay of Biscay, where he spends a few months studying for his exams. Both house and family have a strange history, one we are given glimpses of before Goitia turns up and the details of which gradually become clear, but not to Goitia, whose mental world is occupied mainly by the present and by how it may, through the results of his studies, affect his future. Meanwhile, the house is to him a house; María Antonia, the woman who lives in it and looks after it, is a servant; the elderly, reminiscential doctor next door a bit of a nuisance; and Goitia's mother, though absent, is a mother nonetheless. *The Wrong Blood* is the opposite of a bildungsroman. At the end, when the young man leaves for Madrid with, under his arm, half a *bacalao*, dried salted cod, wrapped up for him by María Antonia, he has learned nothing apart from what he may have gleaned from his law books.

The reader, on the other hand, has learned a lot. The servant María Antonia is his grandmother. She was raped by a Carlist sergeant early in the civil war—not forcibly, but the act was not exactly consensual, either—and became pregnant. Goitia's "official" grandmother Isabel, meanwhile, was widowed when her husband, a Nationalist officer, was shot by a firing squad. She was pregnant, but the child died at birth. María Antonia, who successfully bore a girl, Verónica, was persuaded to give the baby up to her employer, and in return inherited the house. The doctor was party to these secret transactions. In old age, he's keen

to transmit his memories, though he recognizes that the impulse "responds to a pernicious notion that doing so guarantees some form of immortality" and that Goitia and he not only are members of different generations but also live "within distinct frames of reference."[31] This is confirmed when, at his insistence, he and Goitia have lunch together and the young man proves impervious to his hints about the past. The doctor's efforts and his frustration throw into relief both María Antonia's less obtrusive but more intense feelings about the boy who doesn't realize he is her grandson, and the apprehensions the two old people share about the future. Each of them, though, has learned what the doctor articulates to himself:

> This was the third generation, which former misfortunes could not reach, and in which were dissolved the vicissitudes of the past and the mysteries of bad luck . . . One could imagine that Verónica knew who her real mother was and didn't want to spend a summer vacation under the eyes of that mother, who was also a servant. Someone, perhaps Isabel herself, could have revealed the truth to her. Perhaps it had happened that way, and the doctor suspected it had, but in any case he hadn't spent any time trying to unravel *that* mystery. It wasn't important to investigate the most trivial details, or to be more rigorous, or to assume that all this represented an obscure grief . . . [32]

It's a different version of what Deza senior concludes, but the point is essentially the same. Memory has its uses but demands the same kind of discretion as any other faculty.

None of which means that *The Wrong Blood* encourages readers to ignore the past. On the contrary, the book begins with a plain, unromanticized evocation of the history of María Antonia and her family, and the war enters in all its arbitrary bloodiness. De Lope has, too, a strongly visual sense of the worlds he describes: one in which memory is as much to do with landscapes, buildings, vehicles, and implements as with humans themselves. He presents change as a series of facts, relatively free of emotional association; or perhaps it's better to say that the reader is left free to invest them with feeling, rather than being directed to do so. Etxarri's bar, where María Antonia grows up and some of whose contents she still possesses when her grandson comes to stay,

is vividly described (the roses on its façade, the metallic-tasting water piped from its cistern), but the changes that it undergoes, some violent, some evolutionary, and the human losses and sufferings and comedies that take place there, are presented mutedly. Tragedy is always available to the narrative: a mother runs away, a husband dies, the doctor mentions insouciantly to Goitia, "I know a marvellous place to commit suicide around here."[33] De Lope understands, though, with Méndez and Marsé, how much can be achieved in fiction, as in life, by what isn't done and isn't said.

Postscript

Nineteen sixty-eight: Prague Spring; the sinking of Israeli, French, and U.S. submarines; the Tet Offensive and the My Lai Massacre; Martin Luther King Jr. and Robert F. Kennedy assassinated. Students demonstrate all over the world, Saddam Hussein gains power in Iraq, Pope Paul VI condemns the new contraceptive pill. Whatever you personally associate with those times, it's unlikely to be Spain's victory in the Eurovision Song Contest with a number called "La la la." Unless, that is, you're a Cliff Richard fan: his song "Congratulations" was the favorite that year, when Great Britain hosted the event at the Albert Hall, but at the last minute the Spanish entry came through. It has been claimed since then that the result was bought by a campaign of cash handouts and contract deals offered to European TV companies by the national broadcasting company Radio Televisión Española, but this rumor is less interesting than a story that is certainly true. "La la la" was originally composed in Catalan and was intended to be sung by a Catalan, Joan Manuel Serrat. On orders from above, Serrat was replaced by the twenty-one-year-old Massiel (María de los Ángeles Felisa Santamaría Espinoza), who sang it in Castilian.

It might be thought that the language of "La la la" doesn't matter much. The song does contain real words, but they're of the all-purpose kind parodied in *¡Bienvenido, Mister Marshall!*: "I sing to my mother

who gave me life / I sing to the earth which has seen me growing / And I sing to the day when I felt love." Certainly, apart from being a bad loser, Bill Martin, the lyricist of "Congratulations" (". . . and celebrations / When I tell everyone you're in love with me / Congratulations and jubilations . . .") was in no position to declare that the surprise winner was "a piece of rubbish."[1] Yet the outcome meant a lot to ordinary people in Spain who felt that their country was not only cut off from but underrated by the rest of Europe, and whose long history of feelings of this sort had been rekindled by a sense that, for all the disasters being experienced by the rest of the world, more fun was being had there, too. This Mediterranean version of what Australians used to call cultural cringe was sharpened by the sight of glamorous-seeming foreign tourists on Spanish beaches, and by the music on the radio. Massiel was a good singer and now she was famous, but she wasn't Diana Ross.

Nineteen sixty-eight saw the breakthrough, too, of the Madrid group Fórmula V, which was taken on by the Philips label with "Tengo tu amor" ("I Have Your Love") and almost immediately produced another hit, "Cuéntame cómo pasó" ("Tell Me How It Was"), a lover's song to someone who has gone away and has now returned—returned in the singer's mind at least, and perhaps physically, too, but not emotionally. The last line, "Volverá, en un nuevo día" ("Some new day she'll come back") took on an additional meaning when the song itself came back, a generation later. In 2001 "Cuéntame cómo pasó" gave the title and theme tune to what's now one of the longest-running drama series in the history of Spanish television, with a regular audience of more than five million. Almost 250 episodes have been broadcast.[2]

Launched to coincide with the twenty-fifth anniversary of democracy and produced by the public service channel Televisión Española (TVE), *Cuéntame* tells the story of a family in a suburb of Madrid from 1968 on, as narrated by the youngest of three children, Carlos. It's a human saga about ordinary family occurrences, from the opening episode, in which the then-eight-year-old Carlos is given one of his sister's contraceptive pills (illicitly imported from Paris), mistaken for an aspirin; to his by-now-middle-aged mother's being treated for breast cancer. All this is set against political and social changes in Spain as they

impact the Alcántara family, whether directly or through the media. In the first episode, they buy a television set specifically so they can watch the Eurovision Song Contest: Massiel's triumph provides the climax. In the second, Carlos's restless elder sister, Inés, wants to go on a trip to Paris, and although she eventually decides instead to join in the family's celebrations of Carlos's Primera Comunión (first Holy Communion), her independence and cosmopolitanism are a continuing source of tension both with her elders and with her cautious, conventional boyfriend. Before long, Inés will meet a rock singer in London, have an affair with a divorced Spanish actor, and move to a commune in Ibiza. The other sibling, Toni, becomes politicized at university, where he has fallen in love with the radical daughter of a Francoist official. She becomes pregnant by Toni and has an abortion. These and other adventures of the children add to the pressures imposed on their parents by a combination of economic instability and social and political change. The mother, Mercedes, works in a fashion business that folds. The father, Antonio, like many middle-class Spanish men of the time, has to hold down two jobs to make enough money for everyone to live on. Antonio's own father died in the civil war, an event that, together with the subsequent repression and his native caution, has made him timid and politically conservative.

As in other narratives set in the Franco era, the child's-eye view lets in humor and, usefully, irrelevancy, and offers a vividly fresh perspective on otherwise highly charged situations. Reminiscing about his military service in Morocco in the 1940s, the paterfamilias talks about Islamic practices and beliefs. When he and Mercedes subsequently have a quarrel about the cost of the first Communion, young Carlos very believably retreats into a fantasy about becoming a Muslim, which he thinks will exempt him from school and promise a more interesting afterlife. Antonio's prosaic efforts to secure a raise to help pay for the family party, while themselves offering insight into the hierarchical relationships of his workplace, are offset by the next turn in Carlos's story, in which he imagines himself as Lawrence of Arabia and startles the parish priest with his brief but vivid conversion.

The social good intentions of the series—its resolute liberalism about sexuality, gender politics, and multiculturalism—become a little predictable, especially when episodes set in the 1960s and early '70s

and first broadcast in the early 2000s are watched again a decade later. Too many boxes are ticked, and there's what can seem, especially from today's perspective, an overoptimistic confidence that despite the occasional setback, things will go on getting better. But its stories remain compelling, as does the surrounding historical narrative. *Cuéntame cómo pasó* does tell us something about how it was in Spain: about families divided by exile; about the censorship of news; about compulsory military service, and the suppression of opposition; about how easily patriotic nationalism can become racism; about changes in the relationship between church and state; about reactions to Franco's death, the subsequent political referendum, and general elections, and the huge adjustments encompassed by ordinary people in dealing with rapid social shifts that had been happening more gradually in other countries. The historian Julián Casanova has described the series as a model of how to relate history to members of a younger generation.[3]

History remains as much a living element in every other area of Spanish culture, even while the past recedes and is turned into myth. "Nationalists or Republicans? You decide the course of history!" proclaims the publicity for *Shadows of War*, "the first real-time strategic video game of the Spanish Civil War"; "Remember: Spain's destiny is in your hands." The game involves twenty-five "missions" and can be played by either one person or, in the online version, any number up to fourteen. You choose which side you want to be on, and also the level of difficulty at which you want to play: for beginners, "the enemy units have 15% less capacity in defense and attack," while at the "expert" fourth stage they have 30% more. There are also choices to be made between versions of play in which the aim is to destroy all the enemy's buildings, or to kill a general, or ("Total Victory") to eliminate not only every enemy building and vehicle but also every soldier. The capacities of most of the figures involved are limited, but there are key characters whose abilities change as a result of their virtual experiences of combat. They include generals—Republican, Nationalist, German, Italian, and Soviet—and also five "heroes" whose life stories are told in an accompanying printed document marked "Confidential." These are, first, Ghanin Shabah, the adopted name of a dark-skinned Spanish

marksman previously called Manuel, who has joined a Moroccan mercenary group; and Marion Barrena, a huge-breasted Republican volunteer ("Women in the rear guard? Never!") who was Manuel's girlfriend and is the daughter of his hated former boss. (Under the influence of "revisionist texts from the East," she has learned to oppose his conservative values.) Then there is a hatchet-faced German called Alfred von Richthofen, determined to prove himself in combat but secretly at odds with his Nazi superiors; the reckless motorcyclist Matteo Ferrero, whose great-grandfather founded the Italian light infantry corps known as the Bersaglieri; and Félix Brezhnev, a Soviet pilot "the red of whose blood makes [his] heart pump with pride" and who "knows how to take care of himself without his aircraft when circumstances require it." Beyond these principals, a number of other characters can be deployed, each of whom has a unique skill: among them an explosives expert, an infantryman with skills in close combat, and a Canadian doctor who can restore life to any soldier within a limited area. These qualities are counterbalanced by particular vulnerabilities, as are those of the various armed vehicles at the player's disposal.

So much, at any rate, for what's claimed. In practice, fighting this version of the Spanish Civil War is complicated and unpredictable. Many players have expressed their frustrations in ways that real-life participants in the conflict might have recognized and been unsurprised by: "You order your troops to a position and they get lost there or get stuck on a rock or something. Mainly the weapons are useless: seven or eight shots from a tank to kill one soldier"; "since when have you been able to machine-gun somebody at two meters without killing them?"; "the Republicans had four farm laborers against tanks and airplanes," and so on.[4]

Measuring *Sombras de Guerra* against other electronic war games, most players' online criticisms are technical, to do with the quality of the graphics and the relative ease and speed of play. "Zalin87," it's true, regards the poor standard of the troops and armor in this Spanish-made software as a national own-goal, particularly insulting to older Spaniards who took part in the war. And while there are complaints about lack of verisimilitude—for example, in the relative size of human figures and buildings when the game is compared with similar

Japanese products—no one has publicly challenged the claim to historical realism. This is cartoon history of the kind in which warriors launch themselves headfirst through glass windows while fortresses disappear in puffs of smoke. Just as the minibiographies of the central characters raise psychological expectations that simply aren't and perhaps can't be met, so the introduction of each "campaign" with a brief passage of documentary footage accompanied by historical text is at odds with what's ultimately a test of dexterity and speed of response, rewarding various skills or knacks but resistant to thought and interpretation and unrewarding of knowledge. Interestingly, while players can take either side in the conflict, the game sets out by contradicting the assumption that it's the losers whose story prevails in modern Spain. In the busy title sequence, three images are dwelt on: first, the yoke-and-arrows symbol of the Falange, in brightly lit gold; then a solitary Moroccan on a camel, gazing across sand dunes; then a Communist five-pointed star blown into shards across the whole screen.

Even in the time it takes to write a book, nothing stays quite the same.

The Museum of the Civil War in Salamanca has been given a new look. More of the exhibits—most, in fact—are now from the Republican side, and the Masonic lodge is contextualized in a ten-minute video. The postcard of the green pig-faced enemy has gone. One wall is dominated by Picasso's *Guernica*—not a reproduction but a new work that remakes the original out of a collage of miniature photographs from the war. Castilian, though, remains the only language used, and the guards still carry truncheons.

The Association for the Recovery of Historical Memory continues its work, but funds are less easy to come by and its organizers are having to be more imaginative: in the summer of 2012, the association wrote to Angela Merkel requesting German reparations for bomb damage done in Spain seventy-five years ago by the Condor Legion.[5] Historians and novelists persist with their own excavations. Javier Cercas has described the "real war" of the Transition generation as that of heroin against the unemployed and opportunity-less who are the sadly timely subjects of his 2012 novel, *Las leyes de la frontera* ("Frontier Law").

The PP's successes in the 2011 elections have found expression at local level in a new flurry of street renamings, an activity that now comes close to being Spain's national sport. In central Seville, one street has had three different names in not many more years. It was believed that calle General Merry commemorated one of the leaders of the División Azul. Pedro Merry Gordon took part in the division's last big engagement in Russia, at Krasny Bor in February 1943, when, at heavy cost, Spanish troops held up a Soviet attempt to lift the German siege of Leningrad. Sixty-six years later, the then-leftist administration of Seville invoked the Law of Historical Memory and decided to rename the road after Pilar Bardem, a TV actress born in the city. In the ensuing row, some protested that the General Merry for whom the street was earlier named was not the hero of Krasny Bor but his father, Francisco Merry Ponce de León; others, that Pilar Bardem's main claim to fame was that she was the mother of Javier Bardem and that she didn't deserve to have a street named after her. In due course, Seville elected a conservative mayor whose campaign had included a promise to reopen the case. In January 2012 he announced that the street would henceforth be called Nuestra Señora de las Mercedes ("Our Lady of Mercy," one of the ways of referring to the Virgin Mary). The idea had come from a petition organized by the parish in which the street stands, signed by more than two thousand local people. Ah, but the parish church in question was once supported by the notorious Nationalist propagandist Queipo de Llano, who had his headquarters in Seville and whose wife was baptized there with the very name Mercedes: Was Javier Bardem's mother being ousted in honor of Queipo's wife? The debate continues—one waggish blogger has suggested that, as a compromise, the street be named "Pilar Bardem and All Saints"[6]—but what's clear is that where money is involved, the PP has been using its unarguable financial predicament to roll back overindulgent commemorative spending by the other side. In Elche, in the southeast, the PSOE had promised for his archive a bonanza of 3 million euros (150,000 euros a year for twenty years) to descendants of Miguel Hernández, a local working-class Republican writer who died in a Francoist prison in 1942, an undertaking withdrawn by the new PP mayor. The reawakening of such feuds is happening at every level, in a way

that makes many people nostalgic for what's increasingly referred to as the Transition Spirit.[7]

Few tourists these days visit Franco's crypt in Cuelgamuros, a fact that potentially adds to its allure as a right-wing theme park—albeit one that, so far, comes to life for only a couple of days each year. The basilica and abbey can safely be left in the Church's hands, but the big plaza with its scarcely used college-cum-conference-center and the magnificent surrounding park and natural landscape offer opportunities that Spain must now take. It's too easy to say that the country's bitter divisions will never be sufficiently surmounted to make possible the all-party-and-none kind of place it could be. Challenged to come up with ideas, most Spanish intellectuals tend to shrug and say, "Who would run it?" An exception is the quietly forceful current director of the Centro Documental de la Memoria Histórica in Salamanca, María-José Turrión. When I put the difficulty to her, she, too, shrugged, but in the way that meant not "It's hopeless" but "It's really not that much of a problem."[8] "All that's needed," she said, "is management," gestión.

The exhumations in San Rafael cemetery have come to an end. Twenty-eight hundred boxed sets of remains are now stored in Málaga's new municipal graveyard, outside the ring road; the whereabouts of a further 1,900 people known from documentary records to have been executed remain undiscovered. Here, too, Spain's economic difficulties have brought some adjustment of the project's early ambitions: DNA testing of what has been found will have to wait, as will the 6-million-euro park planned for San Rafael, but the town's popular, long-serving conservative mayor says that the promise of a pyramid-style mausoleum will be kept. Diego Ruiz Schacht's skeleton is among those to have been provisionally identified—in his case, by its size; he was more than six feet tall—and as far as his grandson Ignacio is concerned, that chapter has ended: "In my heart it is closed," he told me three years after we first met. "Now it is time to work."

Soon after the aborted dig for Waldo Ruiz's remains on the hill above Valdecaballeros, his daughter Benilde died unexpectedly. She was eighty-seven. In what proved to be their last conversation, Marina Gómez asked her grandmother if she had a picture of Waldo. Benilde explained that when she was a girl, people like them couldn't

afford photographs. For a time, Marina remained hopeful that there might be another attempt to find where her great-grandfather is buried, and we stayed in touch. I last contacted her in the summer of 2012, but she had just a baby, her first, and no longer wanted to talk about the past.

Notes

1. Bad Memory

1. We first met in December 2008.
2. Partido Socialista Obrero Español (Spanish Socialist Workers' Party).
3. See Arthur Koestler, *Spanish Testament*, 1937, and Franz Borkenau, *El reñidero español* (*The Spanish Cockpit*, 1977).
4. *New Statesman*, September 5, 1980. "I have tried to explain to myself the poverty" of the contents, Schmidt wrote. "In the first place, there were not, relatively speaking, *that* many notable British poets involved. Secondly, much of the verse was written not out of experience but out of unlived commitment: it lacks particular *voice*. Then there is the horrible influence of Marxist theoretical prose with its infuriating penchant for the passive voice, as though History were inexorable and process had absolute authority over the conscious will."
5. Dedication to Camilo José Cela, *San Camilo, 1936*, tr. John H. R. Polt (Raleigh, NC: Duke University Press, 1991).
6. Introduction to Carmen Laforet, *Nada*, tr. Edith Grossman (London: Harvill, 2007), p. ix, orig. pub. under the same title (Barcelona: Destino, 1945). A *sacristía* is a church vestry.
7. For example, *El Mundo* found in 2005 that 37 percent of those polled thought that there had been an improvement in the quality of life under the *dictadura*; the proportion of those polled whose impression of Franco was "bad" or "very bad" was 51 percent (in 2000 it had been 38 percent); 24 percent either claimed there had been no significant damage to human rights under the regime or said they didn't know or didn't care. The more negative findings were among younger

respondents and those who voted for the PSOE. See www.elmundo.es/elmundo
/2005/11/19/espana/1132371627.html (accessed December 8, 2012).

8. "War of Ideas," *The Guardian*, February 17, 2007.

9. Carlos Jerez-Farrán and Samuel Amago, eds., *Unearthing Franco's Legacy: Mass Graves and the Recovery of Historical Memory in Spain* (South Bend, IN: University of Notre Dame Press, 2010), p. 6.

2. Whose Graves?

1. An overview of all this is given by Paul Preston in *The Spanish Holocaust: Inquisition and Extermination in Twentieth-Century Spain* (New York: W. W. Norton, 2012).

2. *La represión nacionalista de Granada en 1936 y la muerte de Federico García Lorca* (Paris: Ruedo ibérico, 1971). In what follows I have also drawn on Gibson's full biography of the poet, *Federico García Lorca* (New York: Pantheon, 1989).

3. *ABC*, October 7, 2009.

4. Javier Marías, "Figuraciones sólo nuestras," *El País Semanal*, October 12, 2008, p. 106.

5. And, more recently, as a legal adviser of the Wikileaker Julian Assange.

6. In his *"Auto,"* or deposition, of November 18, 2008 (Sumario Proc. Ordinario 53/2008 E) Garzón gives as his sources Miguel Ángel Rodríguez Arias, *El caso de los niños perdidos del franquismo* (Valencia: Tirant Lo Blanch, 2008), and Ricard Vinyes, *Irredentas: Las presas políticas y sus hijos en las cárceles franquistas* (Madrid: Temas De Hoy, 2002).

7. Lorca's nephew Manuel Fernández-Montesinos, quoted in *El País*, October 18, 2008.

8. Zapatero's paternal grandfather, Juan Rodríguez Lozano, was shot in 1936 in León, his home town. His maternal grandfather, Faustino Zapatero Coronel, a pediatrician, lived and worked in the Nationalist zone in Valladolid. As a headline in the newsletter of the State Federation of Memory Groups put it in August 2009, "Who didn't have a Falangist grandfather?" See www.foroporlamemoria .info/noticia.php?id_noticia=7099 (accessed May 24, 2011).

9. Antonio Muñoz Molina, "Desmemorias," *El País*, September 6, 2008.

10. Tzvetan Todorov, for example, on a visit to Spain to collect the Prince of Asturias Prize for Social Sciences, said, "La memoria de Lorca no se va a transformar por coger sus huesos," *ABC*, October 22, 2008.

11. ETA stands for Euskadi Ta Askatasuna, "Basque Homeland and Freedom."

12. For example, the carnivorous Australian C. Bogue Luffmann (*Quiet Days in Spain* [New York: Dutton, 1910], p. 49).

13. Paul Preston, *Franco* (London: HarperCollins, 1993) p. 322.

14. Emilio Silva and Santiago Macías, *Las fosas de Franco* (Madrid: Ediciones Temas de Hoy, 2003), p. 47.

15. Ibid., p. 119.
16. www.memoriahistorica.org (accessed January 4, 2013).

3. The Alligator's Dams

1. Pío Moa, *Franco: Un balance histórico* (Barcelona: Grupo Planeta, 2005), p. 145. For more on Pío Moa, see pp. 139–42.
2. Here as elsewhere in this chapter I'm indebted to guidance from Christopher George, and to Gabriel Tortella's book *The Development of Modern Spain: An Economic History of the Nineteenth and Twentieth Centuries*, tr. Valerie J. Herr (Cambridge, MA: 2000; for these particular figures, see the table on p. 260). I have also drawn on a paper on "Dams in Spain" contributed by Enrique García to the World Commission on Dams, 2000, and on Dirección General de Obras Hidráulicas, *Inventario de presas españolas, 1986* (Madrid: Mopu, 1986).
3. Raymond Carr and Juan Pablo Fusi, *Spain, Dictatorship to Democracy*, rev. ed. (1979; repr. New York: HarperCollins, 1981) p. 65.
4. See note 2.
5. Conversation with Ignacio Ruiz, whose father was as an electrical engineer during the dictatorship.
6. Julio Llamazares, *En Babia* (Barcelona: Seix Barral, 1991), pp. 86–88, 123–26.
7. Julio Llamazares, *The Yellow Rain*, trans. Margaret Jull Costa (London: Harvill, 2003); originally published as *La lluvia amarilla* (Barcelona: Seix Barral, 1988).
8. Ibid., p. 115.
9. In the 2005 *Guía Campsa: España*, for example, Jánovas is marked in the same typeface as Broto, a flourishing village up the valley, and shown as connected to Planillo and Lacort by a main road that in fact no longer exists.
10. My account of the history of the never-completed Jánovas dam draws on Marisancho Menjón's book, *Jánovas: Víctimas de un pantano de papel* (Jaca: Pirineum, 2006), to which Julio Llamazares contributed the foreword.
11. Llamazares, *En Babia*, pp. 19–21.
12. Milagros Palacio, quoted by Menjón, *Jánovas*, p. 51.
13. The Spanish Act of 1986 and its Regulation of 1988: see García, "Dams in Spain," note 2, section 5.
14. February 12, 2001, quoted by Menjón, "Dams in Spain," p. 141.
15. As explained by Christopher George (who was not himself expressing this view).
16. It is now known as Ribadelago Nuevo. Was the regime to blame? In terms of the long history of dam construction, the country's safety record is good: as one engineer has put it, "only" two disasters since the reign of Philip II (García, "Dams in Spain," section 6). Both, though, involved dams built or begun under Franco. Ribadelago, and the later Tous dam in the Júcar River, completed in 1978, which collapsed in 1982 with the loss of nine lives and hundreds of buildings. Spain's poverty in the 1940s and '50s, and the resulting shortage of good

construction materials, was certainly due in part to the civil war. Under Franco, too, the haste with which public works were carried out was a matter of policy.

17. Ediciones Destino (Barcelona) is one of Spain's most discriminating and cosmopolitan houses, publishing—to name only writers touched on in this book—Camilo José Cela, Miguel Delibes, Carmen Laforet, and Rafael Sánchez Ferlosio.

18. *Central eléctrica*, rev. ed. (1958; repr. Barcelona: Ediciones Destino, 1970), pp. 250, 180.

19. Ibid., p. 335.

20. Ibid., p. 298.

4. Franco's Crypts

1. Rafael Torres, *Víctimas de la victoria* (Madrid: Oberon, 2002), p. 12.

2. I'm grateful to Manuel de Lope for this comparison.

3. Quoted by Ángel Llorente in *Arte e ideología en el franquismo (1936–1951)* (Madrid: Visor, 1995), p. 287.

4. Ibid., p. 288.

5. Some of these changes have been reversed since the conservative electoral victories of 2011: see pp. 276–79.

6. The evidence is rehearsed by Sheelagh Ellwood in *Prietas las filas: Historia de la Falange Española, 1933–1983* (Barcelona: Editorial Crítica, 2001), pp. 90–91.

7. E-mail from Manuel de Lope to the author, June 13, 2011.

8. Their story is told in José María Calleja's book *El Valle de los Caídos* (Madrid: Espasa Libros, 2009) and in Manuel Lamana's autobiographical novel *Otros hombres*, published by Losada in Argentina in 1956 (filmed by Fernando Colomo in 1998 as an over-jaunty period piece, *Los años bárbaros*).

9. There are three other annual Francoist commemorations at the basilica, as the result of a state agreement made with the abbey during the *dictadura*. They are: July 17, the eve of the military coup, or "Crusade"; April 1, the anniversary of the Nationalist victory; and October 1, Franco's birthday. See Katherine Hite, *Politics and the Art of Commemoration: Memorials to Struggle in Latin America and Spain* (Abingdon, UK: Routledge, 2012), ch. 2, "Memorializing Spain's Narrative of Empire," p. 29. This chapter gives valuable descriptions and historically contextualized analyses of the artwork in the crypt.

10. See www.fnff.es.datos.htm (accessed June 23, 2006).

11. According to a *Financial Times*/Harris poll of five European countries, 84 percent of respondents in Spain believe that church and state should be kept separate—after France, the second-highest percentage. Only 40 percent believe religion should be taught in schools; once again, the smallest percentage except for France.

12. José Luis Sancho, *Santa Cruz del Valle de los Caídos* (Madrid: Patrimonio Nacional, 2004), p. 15.

13. This idea, proposed as a kind of Parthian shot by Zapatero in the postelectoral weeks before he left office in 2011, had been floated earlier by, among others, the

historian Antonio Cazorla Sánchez, "¿Qué hacer con nuestra guerra?" *El País*, April 3, 2005, p. 23.

14. Information supplied by the director of the archive, María José Turrión García.

15. Is Salamanca unique among world cities in having a prominent monument to its language, Castilian? It stands directly outside the cathedral.

16. *Tribuna de Salamanca*, April 10, 2005; *El Norte de Castilla*, June 20, 2008; www.mcu.es/archivos/MC/CDMH (accessed March 16, 2007).

17. DidPatri is short for "Didáctica i Patrimoni." The project was reported in the *Heraldo de Aragón*, March 22, 2009, and set out more fully by Joan Santacana Mestre in "¿Un memorial para la paz en Teruel?" *Ebre* 38 (2010): 257–65.

18. *El País*, October 31, 2008.

19. *Oikos: Cuadernos Monógráficos del Ecomuseo del Río Caicena* 1 (2009): 53.

20. Private communication, June 7, 2012.

21. *Emilia Pardo Bazán: Su época, su vida, su obra* (A Coruña: Fundación Pedro Barrié de la Maza, 2003), vol. 2, p. 511, note 83.

22. Fuerzas Eléctricas del Noroeste, Sociedad Anónima—see p. 36.

5. Art's Abstractions

1. See, for example, Paul Julian Smith's claim in *Contemporary Spanish Culture, TV, Fashion, Art and Film* (Cambridge, UK: Blackwell, 2003), p. 66, that it wasn't until the Socialist victory of 1982 that Spanish artists "for the first time" enjoyed "both state sponsorship and access to the outside world."

2. Juan Manuel Bonet et al., *Celebración del arte: Medio siglo de la Fundación Juan March* (Madrid: Fundación Juan March, 2005), p. 19.

3. Partly because of shortages in food supplies, the number of agricultural workers in Spain rose from 45 percent to 50 percent of all workers in the years after 1939. Javier Tusell, *Spain: From Dictatorship to Democracy, 1939 to the Present*, tr. Rosemary Clark (Oxford: Blackwell, 2007), p. 86, orig. pub. as *Dictadura franquista y democracia* (Barcelona: Crítica, 2005).

4. Today part of MNAC, the Museo Nacional d'Art de Catalunya.

5. As a young man he was a friend of Lorca's and a member of the same *tertulia*, where he proposed the famous toast "To Federico, who will die one starry night hearing Chopin in his soul and a soft hand on his heart." He was now the state director general of fine arts.

6. Franco's home province of Galicia seems to have contributed nothing at all, though its capital, La Coruña, put up 5,000 pesetas.

7. See María Dolores Jiménez-Blanco Carrillo de Albornoz, *Arte y estado en la España del siglo XX* (Madrid: Alianza Editorial, 1989), p. 89.

8. José Gutiérrez Solana, *Exposición Nacional de Bellas Artes*, Barcelona, 1960, no. 205.

9. Ibid., no. 503.

10. Ibid., no. 581. The annotator of this copy, now in the British Library, is unknown. Work by Tharrats was already in the collection of the new Spanish Museum of Contemporary Art; see pp. 91–95.

11. Ibid., no. 550.

12. For example, Román Vallés and Juan Vila Casas, ibid., nos. 594, 595, 604, and 605.

13. Ibid., no. 359.

14. The previous year, however, Menchu Gal had become the first woman to win the Premio Nacional de Pintura. Born in 1919 to a cultivated Basque family, Gal studied in Paris and went back there at the beginning of the civil war. She returned to Spain in 1943 and became part of the "Young Madrid School," which included Zabaleta (see pp. 94–95) and Benjamín Palencia.

15. *Hotel en Torre-Valentina* (no. 4).

16. For example, Jaume Mercadé (born 1887), Joaquín Vaquero (born 1900), Godofredo Ortega Muñoz (born 1905), and the Basque Antonio Santafe Lagarcha (born 1911).

17. Javier Tusell, "El ambiente cultural, político y artístico en el Madrid de la posguerra," in *Arte para después de una guerra* (Madrid: Dirección General de Patrimonio Cultural, 1993), p. 15.

18. Another was Rafael Zabaleta; see pp. 94–95.

19. Quoted by Francisco Calvo Serraller in "¿Aislamiento internacional o vacío social?," in Jiménez, *Arte y estado*, pp. 72–73.

20. Quoted by Tusell, "El ambiente cultural," pp. 72–73.

21. Quoted by Jiménez, *Arte y estado*, p. 94, n. 87.

22. Francisco Pompey, *Museo de Arte Moderno: Guía grafica y espiritual*, 1943.

23. Quoted by Jiménez, *Arte y estado*, p. 59.

24. See, for example, Michelle Vergniolle Delalle, *La palabra en silencio: Pintura y oposición bajo el franquismo*, tr. María Sirera Conca (Valencia: Universidad de Valencia, 2008), p. 32, orig. pub. as *Peinture et opposition sous le franquisme: La parole en silence* (Paris: L'Harmattan, 2004).

25. See Francisco Javier Álvaro Oña, "La 'I Bienal Hispanoamericana' de 1951: Paradigma y contradicción de la política artística franquista," www.ahistcon.org/docs/Santiago/pdfs/s1b.pdf (accessed December 8, 2011).

26. Quoted by Jiménez, *Arte y estado*, p. 72.

27. Tusell, "El ambiente cultural," p. 13.

28. *Museo Español de Arte Contemporáneo* (Madrid: Ministerio de Educación y Ciencia, 1975).

29. See the interesting if mainly unfavorable account of the museum's acquisitions by Delalle, *La palabra en silencio*, p. 179, n. 22.

30. Ibid., pp. 182–83, is satirical about the fact that the gallery paid only 100,000 pesetas for Miró's *Mujer, pájaros, estrellas,* at a time when his work was selling on the open market for tens of millions. But this could equally be regarded as a mark of curatorial acumen, the collection's growing reputation, or the artist's generosity, rather than of the museum's stinginess.

31. Luis Miguel Sánchez Tostado, "Mortalidad penitencia en la represión franquista: Izquierdistas muertos en prisión (1939–50)," www.laguerracivilenjaen.com/listado10.pdf (accessed January 12, 2012).

32. A photograph discovered by Luis Miguel Sánchez Tostado may record one of these: see "¿Una obra inédita de Zabaleta en la cárcel de Jaén?," www.sancheztostado.com/prensa_6.php (accessed January 12, 2012).

33. Delalle, *La palabra en silencio*, p. 50.

34. Peter Selz, *Chillida* (New York: Harry N. Abrams, 1986), p. 89.

35. *El País*, July 24, 2008. Another sign of change was the fact that debate over whether the piece should be erected was finally resolved after intervention by Jesús Aguirre, second husband of the city's de facto monarch, the Duchess of Alba.

36. Roland Penrose, *Tàpies* (London: Thames and Hudson, 1978), p. 39.

37. Ibid., p. 179.

38. Catalogue of the Museo Español de Arte Contemporáneo, 1975, pp. 121 and 741. One of González's *Montserrat* bronzes was, like *Guernica*, shown at the 1937 Paris International Exhibition; his *Montserrat gritando* was among the large holdings of his work at the Museo Español de Arte Contemporáneo by 1975 (pp. 146–49).

39. Catalogue of the Museo Español de Arte Contemporáneo, p. 21.

40. For all its doglike features, *El grito no. 7* is clearly related to the *Dama* series as well as the *Bardot* picture. Some possible meanings behind the generic title are discussed by Francisco Calvo Serraller in "Entre damas anda el juego," Catalogue of the Museo Español de Arte Contemporáneo, pp. 7–14. *El grito no. 7* and the *Bailaora* are in the Reina Sofia, *Brigitte Bardot* in the Museum of Spanish Abstract Art in Cuenca.

41. I owe much of this account to Eduardo Westerdahl's essay on his friend, published as a pamphlet titled *Manolo Millares* in Gran Canaria in 1980.

42. Millares quoted by Westerdahl, p. 19.

43. See also *Homúnculo* (1960) in the Collection Central Hispano.

44. Manolo Millares, "El homúnculo en la pintura actual," in *Papeles de Son Armadans* 13, no. 37 (1959): 79–86.

45. Delalle, *La palabra en silencio*, p. 23.

46. See, for example, Juan Álvarez de Estrada, *La extravagancia en la pintura moderna* (Madrid: Estades, 1951). Gabriel Ureña Portero writes about this kind of hysteria in Antonio Bonet Correa, ed., *Arte del franquismo* (Madrid: Ediciones Cátedra, 1981), p. 162.

47. Delalle, *La palabra en silencio*, p. 96, n16.

48. Antoni Tàpies, *Mémoire: Autobiographie* (Paris: Editions Galilée, 1981), p. 397.

49. Ibid., p. 244.

50. Antonino González, *Eugenio d'Ors: El arte y la vida* (Madrid: Fondo de Cultura Económica de España, 2010), p. 13.

51. The title refers to the famous opening of Unamuno's *Sentimiento trágico de la vida*, about the human being who "plays and sleeps and thinks."

52. Quoted by González, *Eugenio d'Ors*, p. 36.

53. A vivid personal account of what this work involved on the Nationalist side, architecturally as well as in terms of transportable works, can be found in Luis Monreal y Tejada's *Arte y Guerra Civil* (Huesca: La Val d'Onsera, 1999).

54. Tusell, *Spain*, p. 28.

55. TVE interview, 1979, quoted by Ángeles Villalba Salvador in "Enseñar a 'ver,' aprender a 'ver': Fernando Zóbel antes y después de 1966," an essay in *La ciudad abstracta 1966: El nacimiento del Museo de Arte Abstracto Español*, 2006, p. 56.

56. Zóbel, Diaries, October 1963, quoted by Villalba Salvador, "Enseñar a 'ver,'" p. 59. The black-and-white "Sarcophagus" is indeed "para Felipe II."

57. Zóbel, Diaries, March 1964, quoted by Villalba Salvador, "Enseñar a 'ver,'" p. 62.

58. María Bolaños, "'El futuro empieza hoy': Los comienzos de un pequeño museo moderno," in *La Ciudad Abstracta 1966*, p. 47.

59. The rags-to-riches banker Juan March (1880–1962) had been among the backers of the 1936 military rebellion.

60. Zóbel, Diaries, September 1964, quoted by Villalba Salvador, "Enseñar a 'ver,'" p. 70.

61. In their seventh show, in 1949.

62. This was in 1959. Interest in the Basque landscapist was revived by an exhibition at the Instituto Valenciano de Arte Moderno (IVAM) in 2012.

63. Bolaños, "El futuro empieza hoy," pp. 31–52.

64. *Colección de Arte Abstracto Español*, catalogue of the Casas Colgadas museum, Cuenca, 1966 (unpaginated).

65. John Richardson, *A Life of Picasso*, vol. 3: *The Triumphant Years, 1917–1932* (New York: Alfred A. Knopf, 2007), p. 491f. Richardson quotes Picasso's dealer Daniel-Henry Kahnweiler as saying that Picasso was "the most apolitical man I ever met."

66. W. G. Sebald, *On the Natural History of Destruction*, tr. Anthea Bell (New York: Modern Library, 2003), pp. 24–26.

67. The quotations are from Robin Adèle Greeley's *Surrealism and the Spanish Civil War* (New Haven, CT: Yale University Press, 2006), pp. 23, 88.

6. History's Wars

1. The official date was 2009, but actual publication did not occur until later.

2. http://publicaciones.rah.es.

3. For example, that of the early twentieth-century writer and politician Juan Armada y Losada, Marquis of Figueroa.

4. See Antony Beevor, *The Battle for Spain: The Spanish Civil War, 1936–1939* (London: Weidenfeld and Nicolson, 2006), p. 415.

5. *El País*, March 31, 2011.

6. He is followed closely by the formidable historian of ideas Carmen Iglesias, who was on four: economic, political and social sciences; literature and humanities; political and administrative history; and the one-woman "history (various)."

7. For example, the Dominican headmaster Antonio Abad Bernal, whose biogra-

pher is Maximiliano Rebollo, himself a Dominican priest. Clearly the word *martyr* is being used in its official ecclesiastical sense, but that reinforces the point.

8. In his article on Carlos Asensio Cabanillas. I have not been able to find any information about the author.

9. The author of the entry is Carlos Seco Serrano (born 1923), a fellow of the Academy of History since 1977, author of works on Spanish conservatism, and biographer of King Alfonso XIII. For Juliá's critique see www.santosjulia.com /Santos_Julia/Notas_files/Azan%CC%83a%20en%20el%20Diccionario%20de %20la%20Real%20Academia%20de%20la%20Historia.pdf (accessed August 3, 2012). Juliá's *Vida y tiempo de Manuel Azaña, 1880–1940,* published in 2008, is listed in Seco's bibliography, which, at more than three and a half columns, is only one column shorter than the article itself.

10. *El País,* June 1, 2011.

11. Joan Saura, quoted in *El País,* March 1, 2011.

12. It was noted that fellowships had not been awarded to Santos Juliá or Juan Pablo Fusi, among other distinguished contemporary historians.

13. Unlike the Academy of History, for example, the Spanish Royal Academy has done away with life-tenured posts.

14. *La Razón,* June 3, 2011.

15. Iñaki Urdangarin.

16. *ABC,* June 1, 2011.

17. *La Gazeta,* January 24, 2012.

18. Pérez de Tudela died in 2004.

19. Still unpublished in 2012.

20. *ABC,* February 14, 2012.

21. He was a leading contributor to an influential report on conditions in Las Hurdes, in Extremadura, the outcomes of which included Buñuel's 1933 film about the region.

22. Marañón's books on *la vida sexual* include a critique of the Don Juan legend and the kinds of behavior it encouraged.

23. Antonio López Vega, *Gregorio Marañón: Radiografía de un liberal* (Madrid: Taurus, 2010), prologue by Juan Pablo Fusi.

24. *Españoles fuera de España* (Buenos Aires: Espasa-Calpe, 1947).

25. J. H. Elliott, *History in the Making* (New Haven, CT: Yale University Press, 2012), ch. 2.

26. "Con Santos Juliá por Sevilla," in José Álvarez Junco and Mercedes Cabrera, eds., *La mirada del historiador: Un viaje por la obra de Santos Juliá* (Madrid: Taurus, 2011).

27. Félix Sardá y Salvany, *El liberalismo es pecado* (Barcelona: Libería y Tip, 1884). Santos Juliá says he has more favorable memories of the staff (private communication).

28. *Madrid, 1931–1934: De la fiesta popular a la lucha de clases* (Madrid: Siglo Veintiuno, 1984); *Historia económica y social moderna y contemporánea de España*

(Madrid: UNED, 1988). In this section I am indebted to Álvarez Junco and Cabrera, eds., *La mirada del historiador,* and in particular to the essays in that book by Javier Moreno, Pedro Carlos González Cuevas, and Francisco Sánchez-Blanco.

29. *Manuel Azaña, una biografía política: Del Ateneo al Palacio Nacional* (Madrid: Alianza Editorial, 1999). Juliá was, nonetheless, not commissioned to write on Azaña for the *DBE* and has published a long list of errors in the eventual article by Carlos Seco. It was excessive of Juliá, all the same, to call for the *DBE* to be destroyed (*ABC,* June 21, 2011).

30. Mercedes Cabrera, "Algo más que 'Un tiempo digno de ser descifrado': La Segunda República," in Álvarez Junco and Cabrera, *La mirada del historiador.*

31. The example is taken from *Así quiero ser (el niño del nuevo estado): Lecturas cívicas* (Burgos: Casa Editorial Burgos, 1944).

32. www.geohistoria.net/paginas/4eso.htm (accessed February 14, 2012).

33. Carmen Cortés Salinas and Juan Fernández-Mayoralas Palomeque, *Ciencias sociales: Historia—4° ciclo de la ESO (Navarra)* (Boadilla del Monte: Ediciones SM, 2008), pp. 178ff.

34. Boxed quotation attributed to M. Tuñon de Lara, ed., *Historia de España,* 9 "Labor (Adaptación)."

35. http://socialesparaeso.wordpress.com/2011/03/08/el-voto-femenino (accessed March 29, 2012).

36. www.geohistoria.net/paginas/2bhis13.htm (accessed March 29, 2012).

37. http://historia.libertaddigital.com/la-constitucion-de-la-segunda-republica -1276237011.html (accessed March 29, 2012).

38. See, for example, http://blogs.libertaddigital.com/presente-y-pasado (accessed May 23, 2011).

39. *Franco: Un balance histórico* (Barcelona: Planeta, 2005), p. 10.

40. Ibid., p. 60.

41. Ibid., p. 59.

42. Ibid., p. 81.

43. Ibid., p. 120.

44. Ibid., pp. 197–99.

45. Among the most famous of those involved was the Jesuit worker-priest José María de Llanos.

46. Pío Moa, *"De un tiempo y de un país": La izquierda violenta (1968–1978)* (Madrid: Ediciones Encuentro, 2002).

47. Moa, *"De un tiempo,"* p. 210.

48. Ibid., pp. 265, 302.

49. Santos Juliá, *Elogio de historia en tiempo de memoria* (Madrid: Marcial Pons, 2012), especially ch. 10, "Y los políticos recuperan la memoria."

50. Javier Cercas, *The Anatomy of a Moment,* tr. Anne McLean (London: Bloomsbury, 2011), p. 160.

51. Ibid., p. 13.
52. Ibid., p. 92.

7. Fiction's Memories [i]

1. Luis Romero, *Tres días de julio* (Barcelona: Ariel, 1967), pp. 301, 387, 587.
2. Ibid., prologue, p. xxii.
3. Ibid., pp. xxiii–iv.
4. Ibid., p. xxxiv.
5. Ibid., p. xxxvi.
6. Ibid., pp. xxv–vii.
7. Ibid., p. xxvii.
8. Ibid., p. xxv.
9. Ángel María de Lera, *Las últimas banderas* (Barcelona: Planeta, 1967), p. 34.
10. Ibid., p. 83.
11. Ibid., p. 143.
12. Ibid., p. 258. The title of de Lera's first novel is *Los olvidados*.
13. The novel was published in Italian translation in 1944 and in English (tr. John Marks) in 1946.
14. Chris Perriam, Michael Thompson, Susan Frenk, and Vanessa Knights, *A New History of Spanish Writing, 1939 to the 1990s* (Oxford: Oxford University Press, 2000), p. 75.
15. The book appeared in Buenos Aires in 1951 and later the same year in both Madrid and Barcelona. The first English translation, by J. M. Cohen with help from Arturo Barea, came out in 1953.
16. *San Camilo, 1936*, translated by John H. R. Polt, was published by Duke University Press in 1991.
17. *San Camilo, 1936*, p. 206. It is relevant that the word Polt translates as "men" here is *nombres*, "names."
18. Cited in Gareth Thomas, *The Novel of the Spanish Civil War (1936–1975)* (Cambridge, UK: Cambridge University Press, 1990), p. 213.
19. *Papeles de Son Armadans.* De Lara's "La circunstancia histórica de la novela *San Camilo 1936*" appeared in the journal in 1970 (207 [1970]: 229–52).
20. *San Camilo*, p. 87.
21. In 1969—oddly, the year when Cela's novel was published—it was changed to July 14 and upgraded to what Catholics call "an obligatory memorial."
22. *Vísperas*, p. 67.
23. *San Camilo*, p. 86.
24. Ibid., p. 108.
25. *San Camilo*, p. 273. "Form of knowledge" and "craft" are my own translations of, respectively, *ciencia* and *maña*, which John H. R. Polt renders as "science" and "cunning."

26. The hastily prepared 1937 English version is by Peter Chalmers Mitchell.

27. Fernández Flórez, *Una isla en el mar rojo* (Madrid: Ediciones Españolas, 1940), p. 137: ". . . peones de albañil, horteras, comicastros, poceros, ladrones y locos . . ."

28. It also appeared in editions of the author's collected works published during the Franco dictatorship: *Obras completas* (Madrid: M. Aguilar, 1945), reprinted 1947 and 1950, vol. 4.

29. As *Un'isola nel mare rosso.*

30. La Banda de la República, 1935. Américo Castro and José Ortega y Gasset were similarly decorated at the same time.

31. Presumably the 1935 MGM production directed by Jack Conway, with Ronald Colman as Sydney Carton.

32. *Una isla en el mar rojo*, p. 14.

33. "ese populacho típico de todas las revoluciones . . . infra-hombres sucios, de ceño asesino; mujeres hienas, vociferadoras y desgreñadas," ibid., p. 39.

34. *Una isla en el mar rojo*, p. 31.

35. Ibid., p. 61.

36. Ibid., p. 215. The Spanish rendered as "pushing and shoving" here is *las apreturas*, which could equally well mean "poverty."

37. See Perriam, Thompson, Frenk, and Knights, *A New History of Spanish Writing*, p. 43. In the general election of June 1993, Prime Minister Felipe González's PSOE lost 16 of its seats (about 10 percent) while the PP under José María Aznar's gained 34, an increase of almost one third.

38. Agustín de Foxá, *Madrid de corte a checa* (1938; repr. Barcelona: Planeta, 1993), p. 79.

39. Ibid., p. 129.

40. Ibid., p. 97.

41. Ibid., p. 225.

42. Ibid., pp. 72–78.

43. Ibid., p. 74.

44. Ibid., p. 149.

45. Juan Iturralde, *Días de llamas* (1979; repr. Barcelona: Random House Mondadori, 2006), p. 69.

46. Max Aub and Antonio Muñoz Molina, *Destierro y destiempo: Dos discursos de ingreso en la academia* (Valencia: Pre-Textos, 2004).

47. Max Aub, *Campo de sangre* (1945; repr. Bogotá: Ediciones Santillana, 1998), p. 27.

48. Ibid., p. 44.

49. Ibid., pp. 51–53.

50. Ibid., p. 85.

51. Aub and Muñoz Molina, *Destierro y destiempo*, pp. 18, 58.

52. Max Aub, *Field of Honour*, tr. Gerald Martin (London and New York: Verso, 2009), p. 52, orig. pub. as *Campo cerrado* (Mexico: Ediciones Tezontle, 1943).

53. *La verdadera historia de la muerte de Francisco Franco y otros cuentos* (Mexico City: Libro Mex, 1960). Aub's story enacts the fulfillment of a widespread fantasy. In 1964 a Scottish teenager was tried and imprisoned in Madrid for his part in a plot to assassinate Franco. Ian Christie had carried five packs of plastic explosives along with a range of detonators under his clothes in high summer from Paris to Madrid. He spent three years in Spanish prisons—"the only places in Spain where there was genuinely free and frank discussion on politics, history and contemporary literature"—and by his own account was well treated (Stuart Christie, *Granny Made Me an Anarchist* [London: Scribner, 2004]). Christie remains a cheerfully vociferous propagandist for anarchism: see www.christiebooks.com.

54. *La verdadera historia*, p. 32.

55. Very unsuccessfully. He was Independent candidate for the Combined Scottish Universities constituency but took less than 14 percent of the vote.

56. Ramon J. Sender, *The War in Spain: A Personal Narrative*, tr. Peter Chalmers Mitchell (London: Faber and Faber, 1937), "Translator's Introductory Note."

57. Ibid., p. 305.

58. A detailed analysis of these aspects of Sender's career is provided by Donatella Pini Moro in *Ramón José Sender tra la guerra e l'esilio* (Alessandria: Edizioni dell'Orso, 1994).

59. The translator was Florence Hall.

60. Originally titled *Mosén Millán*, the book first appeared as *Réquiem por un campesino español* in 1960, and in English in the same year.

61. "el deslumbramiento que produce la aparición de la novela, leída clandestinamente, comparada subrepticiamente en librerías recónditas . . ."; "un estilo arrebatado, bronco, duro" see http://beta.lacronicabadajoz.com/noticias/badajoz/mario -camus-arturo-barea-vio-venir-guerra-civil-predijo-_26262.html (accessed November 30, 2010).

62. See Michael Eaude, *Triumph at the Midnight of the Century: A Critical Biography of Arturo Barea* (Brighton: Sussex Academic, 2009).

63. Ibid., appendix 1, "Publishing History."

64. Arturo Barea, *The Clash* (*The Forging of a Rebel*, vol. 3) (London: Fontana, 1984), pp. 242–43.

65. Ibid., p. 378.

66. Ibid., p. 337.

67. These crosscurrents in Gironella's reputation are summarized by Thomas, *Novel of the Spanish Civil War*, pp. 163–82. Thomas himself tends to accept that while the Republican exile Ramón Sender is to be admired as a pioneer of *littérature engagée*, Gironella is compromised by his different form of engagement.

68. "Prose Statement on the Poetry of War," in *Parts of a World* (New York: Alfred A. Knopf, 1942).

69. "An Essay on Cultural Criticism and Society," *Prisms*, 1967.

70. The phrase is George Eliot's, in *Middlemarch*, at the end of chapter 21.

71. José María Gironella, *The Cypresses Believe in God*, tr. Harriet de Onís (1955; repr. San Francisco: Ignatius, 2005), p. 9.

72. Carmen Laforet, *Nada*, tr. Edith Grossman (London: Harvill Secker, 2007), p. 5.

73. Mario Vargas Llosa, introduction to ibid., pp. ix–xi.

74. See Cristina Cerezales's fictionalized biography of her mother, *Música blanca* (Barcelona: Destino, 2009).

75. The phrase "moral misery" is Iganicio Sanz's: http://latormentaenunvaso.blogspot .com/2009/02/musica-blanca-cristina-cerezales.html (accessed August 11, 2008).

76. Edith Grossman's translation, which keeps the original title, appeared in 2007.

77. Rafael Sánchez Ferlosio, *The River*, tr. Margaret Jull Costa (Sawtry, UK: Dedalus, 2004), p. 13.

78. The best brief account of the battle in English is Antony Beevor's in *The Battle for Spain*. Beevor is also as reliable as one can be about casualty figures.

79. Ferlosio, *The River*, p. 20.

80. Ibid., p. 23.

81. Ibid., p. 35.

82. Ibid., pp. 54–55.

83. Ibid., p. 177.

84. Ibid., p. 263.

85. "Waiting for 'Waiting for Godot,'" *Areté* 14 (Spring/Summer 2004): 88–90.

8. Franco's Films

1. In *El País*, June 27, 2009.

2. "Tengo miedo del encuentro / con el pasado que vuelve / a enfrentarse con mi vida . . . / Pero el viajero que huye, / tarde o temprano detiene su anda. / Y aunque el olvido que todo lo destruye / haya matado mi vieja ilusión / guarda escondida una esperanza humilde, / que es toda la fortuna de mi corazón."

3. "The Women of Pedro Almodóvar," *New York Review of Books*, March 1, 2007.

4. The film historian Josep María Caparrós Llena made this discovery in the archives of El Pardo. See "Sesión de tarde con Franco," www.elpais.com/articulo /revista/agosto/Sesion/tarde/Franco/elpten/20110821elpepirdv_1/Tes (accessed June 9, 2012).

5. There have been many studies of this topic. Among the best for English-speaking readers is Virginia Higginbotham's *Spanish Film under Franco* (Austin: University of Texas Press, 1988).

6. See Preston, *Franco*, p. 418.

7. Román Gubern, *"Raza": Un ensueño del general Franco* (Madrid: Ediciones 99, 1977), p. 114.

8. Preston, *Franco*, p. 418.

9. Gubern, "*Raza*," p. 11.

10. Ibid., pp. 31, 42.

11. Ibid., p. 26.

12. For example, *El pisito*, 1959, and *El cochecito*, 1960, both made in collaboration with the writer Rafael Azcona.

13. Higginbotham, *Spanish Film*, p. 28.

14. Ironically, Saénz de Heredia was indebted to Buñuel, who had arranged for him to be freed from a Republican prison early in the civil war. John Baxter, *Buñuel* (London: Fourth Estate, 1994), pp. 159–60.

15. The most vivid account of the whole story is John Baxter's in *Buñuel*, pp. 4–8.

16. To take just one example, the British Board of Film Classification was, until 1983, known as the British Board of Film Censors.

17. Caparrós Llena, "Sesión de tarde con Franco."

18. Its original title was the Instituto de Investigaciones y Experiencias Cinematográficas (Institute of Cinema Research and Practice).

19. See note 4.

20. See Peter Besas, *Behind the Spanish Lens: Spanish Cinema under Fascism and Democracy* (Denver: Arden, 1985), p. 36.

21. Marvin D'Lugo, *Guide to the Cinema of Spain* (London: Greenwood, 1997), p. 75.

22. Quoted in Preston, *Franco*, p. 691.

23. D'Lugo, *Guide to the Cinema of Spain*, p. 57.

24. *New York Times*, May 13, 1977.

25. www.basiliomartinpatino.com/critica04.htm (accessed March 12, 2012).

9. Fiction's Memories (ii)

1. I don't exclude his first book, the collection *Nunca llegarás a nada* (1961), which Iberia published in 1986 as *You'll Never Get Anywhere*. This pidgin version, full of words such as *insatisfaction* and *cementery* and phrases rendered with automatist literalism ("something . . . made all the insufficient banality of an afternoon acidulated with passion leap in my insides"; "an unknown, voracious moment that, spreading itself, had to procreate the terrible shadow of revenge"), seems to have been designed to make Benet incomprehensible, though it is almost redeemed by the comedy of lines such as "'Let's flee,' he said, draining his glass."

2. Luis Martín-Santos, *Time of Silence*, tr. George Leeson (London: John Calder, 1965), p. 11.

3. Ibid., p. 13. My words "that prevent him from becoming himself" are instead of Leeson's "that destroy his manhood," an exaggerated way of rendering "*le impiden llegar a ser.*"

4. Martín-Santos, *Time of Silence*, p. 42.

5. Luis Martín-Santos, *Tiempo de silencio*, 1st ed. (Barcelona: Seix Barral, 1962), pp. 42–43.

6. Martín-Santos, *Time of Silence*, p. 184.

7. Antonio A. Gómez Yebra, introduction to *El príncipe destronado* (Barcelona: Ediciones Destino, 2011), p. 30.

8. The bird is a *milana*, a female kite. Ivan dismisses it as a *pájaro*, any old bird but particularly a sparrow, and both here and in the title, with its evocation of Herod's massacre of innocent children, the novel invokes Christian values. According to Matthew 10:29, Jesus told the Apostles that although sparrows— *pájaros* in the traditional Spanish version—are two a farthing, not one falls to the ground unseen by God. Ivan's undervaluing the species of Azarías's fledgling, which will grow into a predator, meanwhile hints at his fatal mistake in underrating her owner (*Los santos inocentes*, p. 23).

9. Miguel Delibes, *Los santos inocentes* (Barcelona: Planeta, 1981), p. 67.

10. Ibid., p. 75.

11. Premio Nadal, 1947; Premio Nacional de Literatura, 1955; Premio de la Fundación Juan March, 1959; Premio de la Crítica, 1962.

12. Rafael Conte in *Información de las Artes y las Letras*, September 5, 1968; Pere Gimferrer in *Ínsula*, January 1969, reprinted as appendices to Ignacio Echevarría, ed., *Volverás a Región* (Barcelona: Random House Mondadori, 2009), pp. 321–30.

13. *Volverás*, p. 167.

14. Ibid., p. 19.

15. Ibid., p. 42.

16. Ibid., pp. 214–15.

17. "¿Qué fue la guerra civil?," 1976, reissued with other essays in Juan Benet, *La sombra de la guerra: Escritos sobre la Guerra Civil española* (Buenos Aires: Taurus, 1999).

18. Ibid., p. 27.

19. Jorge Semprún, *Autobiografía de Federico Sánchez: Novela* (Barcelona: Planeta, 1977), tr. Helen R. Lane as *Communism in Spain in the Franco Era: The Autobiography of Federico Sánchez* (Brighton: Harvester, 1980).

20. Especially *Eurocomunismo y estado* (Barcelona: Crítica, 1977).

21. Semprún, *Autobiography of Federico Sánchez*, p. 7.

22. Jorge Semprún, *El largo viaje*, tr. Estéban Sánchez (Lima: Huáscar, 1969); tr. Jacqueline and Rafael Conte (Barcelona: Seix Barral, 1976).

23. See Semprún, *Autobiography of Federico Sánchez*, p. 181. One of those captured was Julián Grimau, shot by the regime in 1963. Semprún implies that Grimau had been deliberately left exposed by Carrillo.

24. Semprún, *The Long Journey*, tr. Richard Seaver (New York: Grove Press, 1964), pp. 99–100, orig. pub. as *Le grand voyage* (Paris: Gallimard, 1963).

25. Ibid., p. 74.

26. Ibid., p. 190.

27. Epigraph to *L'écriture ou la vie*, 1994, tr. by Linda Coverdale as *Literature or Life?* (New York: Viking, 1997). Blanchot's main exposition of the idea is found

in *L'écriture du désastre* (Paris: Gallimard, 1980; Semprún echoes the title), tr. by Ann Smock as *The Writing of the Disaster* (Lincoln: University of Nebraska Press, 1986).

28. Semprún, *Literature or Life?*, p. 31.
29. Ibid., p. 180.
30. Ibid., p. 123.
31. The song was by Hoagy Carmichael. Louis Armstrong was among those who recorded it.
32. Semprún, *The Long Journey*, p. 104.
33. Ibid.
34. Translated into English by Margaret Sayers Peden as *Sepharad* (Orlando: Harcourt, 2003).
35. Ibid., p. 93.
36. Ibid., p. 108.

10. Fiction's Memories (iii)

1. Carlos A. del Real, Julián Marías, and Manuel Granell, *Juventud en el mundo antiguo: Crucero universitario por el Mediterráneo* (Madrid: Espasa Calpe, 1934).
2. Carlos del Real was born on May 2, 1914, Julian Marías on June 17, the same year. Manuel Granell was eight years older but had made a couple of false starts at university: he tried the sciences, then architecture, and having failed the exams in the latter, spent some time in Paris, where he met Unamuno. He resumed his studies in the Faculty of Philosophy and Literature at Madrid in 1930, so was only one year ahead of the others.
3. There are many echoes of Unamuno, stylistic as much as substantive, most obviously in such sentences as "El hombre, querida Helena, es una unidad viviente de gran complejidad. Quiere y siente, ama y padece, recuerda e imagina, calcula y razona . . .": *Cartas filosóficas a una mujer* (Madrid: Revista de Occidente, 1946), p. 121.
4. See note 2.
5. Marías describes his viva voce examination and its outcome in his memoirs, *Un vida presente* (Madrid: Páginas de Espuma, 2008), pp. 237–40.
6. There are other resemblances, common to the work of many diarists, particularly the solipsism of the narratives. There's nothing in them that indicates—as we learn from Marías's much later memoirs (*Una vida presente*)—that the young men traveled with one another, let alone in so large a party.
7. Marías's later reflections on the expedition can be found in *Una vida presente*, pp. 100–103.
8. "Esa estatua de Garibaldi . . . acaba de imprimir a la calle un aire liberal y progresista que injuria violentamente el paso soreliano y marcial de los balillas." Del Real, Marías, and Granell, *Juventud*, p. 156.
9. "Revisión de un viaje," *Alférez* 12 (1948): 8.

10. The book, based on the Ph.D. thesis, is a study of a French Catholic thinker, *La filosofía del Padre Gratry*. This was published in Madrid in 1941, as was *Historia de la filosofía*. By the time of Franco's death, the latter had gone into twenty-eight editions, and had also been translated into English and German.

11. They are: Juan Marsé, *Rabos de lagartija*, 2000; Alberto Méndez, *Los girasoles ciegos*, 2004; Javier Cercas, *Soldados de Salamina*, 2001; Manuel de Lope, *La sangre ajena*, 2000; Almudena Grandes, *El corazón helado*, 2007; Javier Marías, *Tu rostro mañana*, 2002–07.

12. For example, Peter Wheeler toward the end of *Fever and Spear*, vol. 1 of *Your Face Tomorrow* (London: Chatto and Windus, 2005), pp. 351–54.

13. Afterword to *El siglo* (1983; repr. Barcelona: Mondadori, 2007), pp. 228, 244, 246.

14. *El siglo*, pp. 207–8.

15. For example, in *Fever and Spear*, p. 147.

16. Ibid., p. 148.

17. Javier Marías, *Dance and Dream*, vol. 2 of *Your Face Tomorrow*, p. 95.

18. Alex Clark, "Enigma Variations," *New Statesman*, December 30, 2009.

19. In the English version, from page 244 of the second volume—that's to say, 618 pages into the 1,240-page whole.

20. *Dance and Dream*, pp. 277–78.

21. Juan Marsé, *Rabos de lagartija* (Madrid: Once, 2000), tr. Nick Caistor as *Lizard Tails* (London: Harvill, 2003), p. 131.

22. Ibid., p. 69.

23. Ibid., p. 223; 343 in original.

24. Epigraph to Alberto Méndez, *Los girasoles ciegos* (Barcelona: Anagrama, 2004), tr. Nick Caistor as *Blind Sunflowers* (London: Arcadia, 2008).

25. Méndez, *Blind Sunflowers*, p. 18.

26. Ibid., p. 79.

27. Almudena Grandes, *El corazón helado* (Barcelona: Tusquets, 2007), pp. 822–24.

28. Interview with Maya Jaggi, *Guardian Review*, April 2, 2011, pp. 10–11.

29. Ibid.

30. Cercas disagrees: "I think that, for a number of reasons, it is absolutely necessary that the narrator of *Soldiers* is called Javier Cercas (among others: the book is a false chronicle and all the characters have real names)" (private communication). Either way, David Trueba's film confuses the issue.

31. Manuel de Lope, *The Wrong Blood*, tr. John Cullen (London: Chatto and Windus, 2010), p. 118, orig. pub. as *La sangre ajena* (Barcelona: Círculo de Lectores, 2000), p. 118.

32. Ibid., p. 276.

33. Ibid., p. 185.

Postscript

1. See www.m-magazine.co.uk/features/congratulations-the-best-song-never-to-win -eurovision (accessed August 15, 2012).
2. All the episodes can be seen at the series website, www.rtve.es/television /cuentame (accessed January 14, 2012), which also carries information about the history of the program.
3. Isabel Gallo, "Ajustar cuentas con el pasado," *El País*, January 12, 2012.
4. Comments on YouTube at www.youtube.com/watch?v=gHewZxwZBPY, www .youtube.com/watch?v=valud407Ypw, and www.3djuegos.com/juegos/analisis /lectores/1556/0/sombras-de-guerra-la-guerra-civil-espanola (accessed July 16, 2012).
5. www.europapress.es/nacional/noticia-armh-pide-merkel-salde-deuda-victimas -dictadura-franquista-20120727124543.html (accessed September 1, 2012).
6. http://blogs.elconfidencialdigital.com/javierfumero/2012/01/30/pilar-bardem -de-todos-los-santos (accessed September 6, 2012).
7. On May 13, 2012, in an article titled "De la angustia cívica al pacto político," the columnist Gregorio Marañón wrote in *El País* that "it's crucial that . . . we get back to a consensus, as if this were a second transition. Otherwise our political system, our civic life and economic stability will all be at risk."
8. On July 27, 2012.

Acknowledgments

I owe my interest in Spain in part to the work of V. S. Pritchett and my first visits there to the hospitality of Bobs and the late Bruce Urquhart. In terms of writing about it, some early results appeared in *Granta, The Times Literary Supplement*, and the *Dublin Review*, and I'm grateful to the editors concerned. By good luck, one of these articles was read in 2005 by William Chislett, a former British foreign correspondent in Spain who still lives in Madrid and who, along with his wife, Sonia, has ever since been a source of help and encouragement, introductions, suggestions, and quiet nagging.

I've enjoyed and learned from conversations with many other friends and acquaintances, old and new, among them José Miguel Carillo de Albornoz, Rose Cobbe, Manuel Fontán del Junco, Roy Foster, Paul Freedman, Maureen Freely, Christopher George, Ian Gibson, Javier Gomá, Manuel de Lope, Diego de Mora Figueroa, the late Sandy Pratt, Paul Preston, Eric Southworth, Benito Vázquez, and above all María Álvarez and her *familia numerosa de honor.*

I'm grateful to the Liguria Center for the Arts and Humanities, Bogliasco; and the Rockefeller Foundation, Bellagio; which gave me research fellowships. The Santander program at the University of Warwick provided support, as, and in many ways, did the Department of English and Comparative Literary Studies there. I also thank the staff of the archives, libraries, museums, and foundations mentioned in the text, especially the Hispanic Society of America, the Centro Documental de Memoria Histórica in Salamanca, the British Film Institute, the British Library, the Instituto Cervantes in London, the London Library, and the Taylor Institution Library, Oxford.

Helpful suggestions about individual sections were made at various stages by the late Holly Eley, Santos Juliá, Ángel Llorente, and Karen Sanders, and entire drafts

were read by Javier Cercas, Juanan Delgado, Sir John Elliott, and Antonio Muñoz Molina. It was a privilege to receive their comments. I'm indebted, too, to my British agents, the late Kate Jones and her successor, Karolina Sutton, and, as always, to the redoubtable Amanda Urban in New York. I also thank the book's U.S. publisher, Jonathan Galassi; his assistant, Miranda Popkey; the copy editor, Jenna Dolan; and my sympathetic and constructive UK editor and old friend, Jenny Uglow.

Index

dictatorship. Almost all were in *fosas comunes*, "mass graves." Now their bones were being dug up, put into separate boxes, and prepared for DNA testing. No one knew how long the job would take, or even how many *fosas*—let alone how many bodies—were still to be found. It was organized very systematically, under the direction of a senior archaeologist, Sebastián Fernández. The project, locally based but loosely connected to a national program, was being paid for jointly by the town, the region of Andalucía, and the University of Málaga, where Fernández heads the humanities faculty. "Once all the exhumations are finished," Ignacio told me, "the whole area will be turned into a park. In the middle will be a memorial carrying the names of everyone who can possibly be named."[1]

For several years, all Spain has been searching for its disappeared. They are everywhere—in every region, in every kind of terrain. Families who stayed silent for decades have been urged, often by the victims' grandchildren or great-grandchildren, to say what they suspect, or know, or saw. Politics has played its part. Under a law passed in 2007, when the socialist party PSOE[2] was in power, anyone who can produce reasonable evidence of the existence of a mass grave is entitled to help in excavating it. The dotted map of likely sites, between the Basque country and Andalucía, Castilla-León and Valencia, makes the peninsula look like the face of a child with chicken pox.

One of the skeletons in Málaga belongs to Ignacio's paternal grandfather, Diego Ruiz Schacht. Ignacio isn't superstitious; he doesn't imagine, he said, that Diego's spirit haunts the cemetery, or is anywhere, in fact, but he is proud of his grandfather and showed me a picture of him that he carries in his wallet. Diego was a prodemocracy lieutenant in the Guardia Civil, well known for his resistance to corruption. Within the force, he had set up a multiparty group to police the police, and this may have been why he was picked for elimination.

The family had already seen a lot of changes before Diego was eliminated. Miguel Primo de Rivera's military dictatorship, which had taken over Spain in 1923, collapsed after seven years. The king abdicated, and in 1931 a democratically elected government was installed—Spain's first. It commanded the loyalty of working people and liberal intellectuals but was weakened by internal divisions, by questions about the legitimacy of the electoral process, by the apparent impossibility of

1

Bad Memory

Ignacio Ruiz Vara is a security guard in Málaga, on the southern coast of Spain. He grew up there, as did his father and grandfather. There's plenty of work these days for people in his business, especially looking after second homes and holiday developments, augmented now by building projects abandoned "until the economy picks up." His own duties changed for a time, though, in 2007, when he volunteered to help take charge of San Rafael cemetery, a sixteen-acre sprawl on the west side of the town. This was once the place where Málaga's poor, *los humildes*, were buried—originally well outside the old town, in the middle of farmland mainly given over to sweet potatoes. Now the area, on the way to the huge tourist airport, is part industrial, part social housing and blocks of flats. A small chapel with a lamp hanging off its corner was demolished to make way for a wider road. Much of the original cemetery wall has fallen down, and been replaced with high temporary fencing. A single-story gatehouse still stands, and here Ignacio had his base. The cemetery gates are kept locked.

The reason Ignacio volunteered, and the reason the cemetery needed a security guard in the first place, is that among its dead were more than four thousand people—mostly men but also women and children—executed without trial between 1936 and 1955: the period of Spain's civil war and of the long, grim first phase of Francisco Franco's

FRANCO'S CRYPT

A Note on Translations

Many of the novels and works of history discussed in these pages have not been translated into English, and surprisingly few of the films are available with subtitles. Perhaps the book will prompt Anglophone publishers and film distributors to do more. In saying this, however, I'd like to put in a word for learning Spanish. The language is spoken by more people in the world today than English, or Hindi-Urdu, or Arabic. These include a lot of wonderful writers and filmmakers.

Poetry, in Robert Frost's famous definition, is what's lost in translation, so to try to communicate the effects of Spanish poetry in a book written primarily for people with little or no Spanish would be self-defeating. But my main reason for having left the genre out, along with live drama (which presents the related problem that so much depends on having been at a particular production at a particular time), is that the most powerful creative energies have been going elsewhere.

In what follows, titles of works are always given in both Spanish and English. Where the English title is printed in italics, it's that of a published translation or bilingual DVD. Where it's in ordinary roman type, between quotation marks, the title is my version of what a so-far-untranslated work is called.

Quotations are always given in English. Again, if they are attributed to an italicized English-language title (i.e., a published translation), that's where the quotation comes from; otherwise the versions are my own.